# AI Tools for Protecting and Preventing Sophisticated Cyber Attacks

Eduard Babulak
*National Science Foundation, USA*

A volume in the Advances in
Information Security, Privacy, and
Ethics (AISPE) Book Series

Published in the United States of America by
IGI Global
Information Science Reference (an imprint of IGI Global)
701 E. Chocolate Avenue
Hershey PA, USA 17033
Tel: 717-533-8845
Fax: 717-533-8661
E-mail: cust@igi-global.com
Web site: http://www.igi-global.com

Library of Congress Cataloging-in-Publication Data

Names: Babulak, Eduard, 1957- editor.
Title: AI tools for protecting and preventing sophisticated cyber attacks /
   edited by Eduard Babulak.
Description: Hershey, PA : Information Science Reference, an imprint of IGI
   Global, 2023. | Includes bibliographical references and index. |
   Summary: "AI Tools for Protecting and Preventing Sophisticated Cyber
   Attacks illuminates the most effective and practical applications of
   artificial intelligence (AI) in securing critical cyber infrastructure
   and internet communities worldwide. The book presents a collection of
   selected peer-reviewed chapters addressing the most important issues,
   technical solutions, and future research directions in cyber security.
   Covering topics such as assessment metrics, information security, and
   toolkits, this premier reference source is an essential resource for
   cyber security experts, cyber systems administrators, IT experts,
   internet and computer network professionals, organizational leaders,
   students and educators of higher education, researchers, and
   academicians"-- Provided by publisher.
Identifiers: LCCN 2023004834 (print) | LCCN 2023004835 (ebook) | ISBN
   9781668471104 (h/c) | ISBN 9781668471111 (s/c) | ISBN 9781668471128
   (ebook)
Subjects: LCSH: Computer security. | Artificial intelligence. | Computer
   networks--Security measures. | Computer crimes--Prevention.
Classification: LCC QA76.9.A25 A4155 2023 (print) | LCC QA76.9.A25
   (ebook) | DDC 005.8--dc23/eng/20230207
LC record available at https://lccn.loc.gov/2023004834
LC ebook record available at https://lccn.loc.gov/2023004835

This book is published in the IGI Global book series Advances in Information Security, Privacy, and Ethics (AISPE) (ISSN: 1948-9730; eISSN: 1948-9749)

British Cataloguing in Publication Data
A Cataloguing in Publication record for this book is available from the British Library.

All work contributed to this book is new, previously-unpublished material.
The views expressed in this book are those of the authors, but not necessarily of the publisher.

For electronic access to this publication, please contact: eresources@igi-global.com.

# Advances in Information Security, Privacy, and Ethics (AISPE) Book Series

Manish Gupta
State University of New York, USA

ISSN:1948-9730
EISSN:1948-9749

## MISSION

As digital technologies become more pervasive in everyday life and the Internet is utilized in ever increasing ways by both private and public entities, concern over digital threats becomes more prevalent.

The **Advances in Information Security, Privacy, & Ethics (AISPE) Book Series** provides cutting-edge research on the protection and misuse of information and technology across various industries and settings. Comprised of scholarly research on topics such as identity management, cryptography, system security, authentication, and data protection, this book series is ideal for reference by IT professionals, academicians, and upper-level students.

## COVERAGE

- Security Information Management
- Electronic Mail Security
- IT Risk
- Risk Management
- Cyberethics
- Computer ethics
- Device Fingerprinting
- Security Classifications
- Privacy-Enhancing Technologies
- Tracking Cookies

IGI Global is currently accepting manuscripts for publication within this series. To submit a proposal for a volume in this series, please contact our Acquisition Editors at Acquisitions@igi-global.com or visit: http://www.igi-global.com/publish/.

# Titles in this Series

*For a list of additional titles in this series, please visit:* http://www.igi-global.com/book-series/

*Emerging Perspectives in Systems Security Engineering, Data Science, and Artificial Intelligence*
Maurice Dawson (Illinois Institute of Technology, USA)
Information Science Reference • © 2023 • 315pp • H/C (ISBN: 9781668463253) • US $250.00

*Global Perspectives on the Applications of Computer Vision in Cybersecurity*
Franklin Tchakounte (University of Ngaoundere, Cameroon) and Marcellin Atemkeng (University of Rhodes, South Africa)
Engineering Science Reference • © 2023 • 300pp • H/C (ISBN: 9781668481271) • US $250.00

*Handbook of Research on Data Science and Cybersecurity Innovations in Industry 4.0 Technologies*
Thangavel Murugan (United Arab Emirates University, Al Ain, UAE) and Nirmala E. (VIT Bhopal University, India)
Information Science Reference • © 2023 • 600pp • H/C (ISBN: 9781668481455) • US $325.00

*Perspectives on Ethical Hacking and Penetration Testing*
Keshav Kaushik (University of Petroleum and Energy Studies, India) and Akashdeep Bhardwaj (University of Petroleum and Energy Studies, India)
Information Science Reference • © 2023 • 300pp • H/C (ISBN: 9781668482186) • US $225.00

*Malware Analysis and Intrusion Detection in Cyber-Physical Systems*
S.L. Shiva Darshan (Department of Information and Communication Technology, Manipal Institute of Technology, India) M.V. Manoj Kumar (Department of Information Science and Engineering, Nitte Meenakshi Institute of Technology, India) B.S. Prashanth (Department of Information Science and Engineering, Nitte Meenakshi Institute of Technology, India) and Y. Vishnu Srinivasa Murthy (Department of Computational Intelligence, Vellore Institute of Technology, India)
Information Science Reference • © 2023 • 310pp • H/C (ISBN: 9781668486665) • US $225.00

IGI Global
PUBLISHER of TIMELY KNOWLEDGE

701 East Chocolate Avenue, Hershey, PA 17033, USA
Tel: 717-533-8845 x100 • Fax: 717-533-8661
E-Mail: cust@igi-global.com • www.igi-global.com

*I dedicate this book to people I love most, including my family and to my best friend Pierrette with the family.*

# Table of Contents

**Preface** ..................................................................................................... xiv

**Acknowledgment** ...................................................................................... xvi

**Chapter 1**
The Role of Artificial Intelligence in Cyber Security ............................................1
    *Karmel Arockiasamy, Vellore Institute of Technology, Chennai, India*

**Chapter 2**
The AI Application in Cybersecurity ...................................................................25
    *Kiranbhai Dodiya, Gujarat University, India*
    *Dipak Kumar Mahida, Gujarat University, India*
    *Ankita Patel, Gujarat University, India*
    *Kapil Kumar, Gujarat University, India*

**Chapter 3**
AI Applications in Cybersecurity: Worldwide and Saudi Arabia Focus .............50
    *Ahmad Fahad Aljuryyed, Robert Morris University, USA*
    *Nawaf Ahmed Almufarriji, University of Jeddah, Saudi Arabia*
    *Sulaiman Sami Refaee, University of Jeddah, Saudi Arabia*
    *Naif Ayub Hussain, University of Jeddah, Saudi Arabia*
    *Rayan Saadullah Aziz, King Abdulaziz University, Saudi Arabia*

**Chapter 4**
Artificial Intelligence for Information Security ...................................................85
    *Lubana Isaoglu, Istanbul University-Cerrahpaşa, Turkey*
    *Derya Yiltas-Kaplan, Istanbul University-Cerrahpaşa, Turkey*

**Chapter 5**

Hardware and Software Cyber Security Tools..................................................109

    *Tamalika Das, Pailan College of Management and Technology, India*

    *Nabonita Nath, Pailan College of Management and Technology, India*

    *Kshounish Acharyya, Pailan College of Management and Technology, India*

    *Shirsa Chakraborty, Pailan College of Management and Technology, India*

    *Parag Chatterjee, Pailan College of Management and Technology, India*

**Chapter 6**

Zero Day Vulnerabilities Assessments, Exploits Detection, and Various Design Patterns in Cyber Software ..................................................................132

    *Vidhanth Maan Thapa, University of Petroleum and Energy Studies, India*

    *Sudhanshu Srivastava, University of Petroleum and Energy Studies, India*

    *Shelly Garg, University of Petroleum and Energy Studies, India*

**Chapter 7**

Detection of Phishing Websites ......................................................................148

    *Lakshmipathi Gejjala, Kalasalingam Academy of Research and Education, India*

    *Muthukumar Arunachalam, Kalasalingam Academy of Research and Education, India*

    *Bala Manikanta Eswar Duggisetty, Kalasalingam Academy of Research and Education, India*

    *Jaswanth Kumar Reddy Vardireddy, Kalasalingam Academy of Research and Education, India*

**Chapter 8**
Real-Time Object Detection in Video for Traffic Monitoring ..........................166
>  *Sai Deepak Alapati, Kalasalingam Academy of Research and Education,*
>     *India*
>  *Muthukumar Arunachalam, Kalasalingam Academy of Research and*
>     *Education, India*
>  *Chandana Chennamsetty, Kalasalingam Academy of Research and*
>     *Education, India*
>  *Pujitha Dantam, Kalasalingam Academy of Research and Education,*
>     *India*
>  *Anusha Dabbara, Kalasalingam Academy of Research and Education,*
>     *India*

**Conclusion** ....................................................................................... 180

**Compilation of References** ............................................................ 181

**Related References** ........................................................................ 205

**About the Contributors** ................................................................ 230

**Index** ................................................................................................ 232

# Detailed Table of Contents

**Preface**................................................................................................ xiv

**Acknowledgment** ............................................................................. xvi

**Chapter 1**

The Role of Artificial Intelligence in Cyber Security...........................................1
*Karmel Arockiasamy, Vellore Institute of Technology, Chennai, India*

Security experts coalesced the strength of artificial intelligence (AI) with cybersecurity to defend vulnerable networks and data from cyber attackers. The propagation of artificial intelligence (AI) systems in conjunction with the cyber-attacks are transforming the way the online social media systems are used, automating threat detection, and solving hundreds of attack vectors and attack surfaces. Resources, data sets, and neural fuzzing are the few hindrances that intercept AI from becoming a prevailing security tool. The challenge is to break through the divisional line between the black hat and white hat hackers to regularize technological deployment. Hence, in the current scenario, it is essential to explore how AI can be made use of for basic human needs and for cybersecurity control development. This chapter presents the methods and issues that are still an open challenge for the researchers, engineering managers, and leaders, educators, and students while incorporating artificial intelligence for developing cybersecurity controls.

**Chapter 2**

The AI Application in Cybersecurity..................................................................25
*Kiranbhai Dodiya, Gujarat University, India*
*Dipak Kumar Mahida, Gujarat University, India*
*Ankita Patel, Gujarat University, India*
*Kapil Kumar, Gujarat University, India*

The 21st century is a century of technology. With the increase of new technology, life becomes easy, but as no technology is 100% safe and secure, every technology has some drawbacks. Information technology and cyber security are frequently used interchangeably. Nowadays, national and global security is at risk due to the world's growing reliance on a robust but vulnerable internet and the disruptive powers of cyber attackers. Various security agencies and cyber security researchers prepare the patch and prevention methods for detecting cybercrime, but it's not the proper solution for all types of cybercrime. The existential values of artificial intelligence led to a solution to many problems of cyber security. The main objective of the use of artificial intelligence in cyber security is to enhance the detection of the rate of cybercrime. Another application of artificial intelligence in cybersecurity is to improve the resistance and response to cyber-attacks.

## Chapter 3

AI Applications in Cybersecurity: Worldwide and Saudi Arabia Focus ..............50

*Ahmad Fahad Aljuryyed, Robert Morris University, USA*
*Nawaf Ahmed Almufarriji, University of Jeddah, Saudi Arabia*
*Sulaiman Sami Refaee, University of Jeddah, Saudi Arabia*
*Naif Ayub Hussain, University of Jeddah, Saudi Arabia*
*Rayan Saadullah Aziz, King Abdulaziz University, Saudi Arabia*

Since the creation of the internet, technology has evolved and continues to mass produce systems that humans can rely on and make their lives more productive. Artificial intelligence (AI) is one of those software as it is a tool that mimics human intelligence to perform tasks that we sometimes find repetitive and time-consuming. Another important use of this technology is the introduction of cybersecurity, which ensures the protection of a user's sensitive data online to prevent unauthorized use. When cybersecurity and AI interlay, an increment of protection shows a tangible result; it assures greater protection against cybercriminals. First, this chapter discusses and introduces terms related to cybersecurity and AI; then it goes on to widely explore multiple methods of how AI tools are being integrated within the cybersecurity space, as well as what characteristics of AI pose a threat to the protection that cybersecurity offers. The main idea explored in this chapter is how AI tools are being used to improve and revolutionize the way cybersecurity works worldwide.

## Chapter 4

Artificial Intelligence for Information Security ....................................................85

*Lubana Isaoglu, Istanbul University-Cerrahpaşa, Turkey*
*Derya Yiltas-Kaplan, Istanbul University-Cerrahpaşa, Turkey*

The internet is becoming a widely used source of both online services and information. The primary function of the internet is to move data between nodes. It is a vast collection of interconnected devices and computers, and it has become the target of different cybercrimes. Due to the rapid development of the internet and the increasing number of cyber-attacks, the detection of these attacks has become more important. The traditional security methods are not enough to face these threats;

thus, researchers have been developing smarter techniques such as deep learning and machine learning to address these problems. This chapter explores the various aspects of deep learning and machine learning on information security. It also focuses on the challenges and motivations of this new technology. This chapter reviewed previously conducted surveys and papers in the last two years in the field; thus, it can be used by researchers who are interested in learning more about the various aspects and trends of deep learning and machine learning in information security.

**Chapter 5**

Hardware and Software Cyber Security Tools.....................................................109
*Tamalika Das, Pailan College of Management and Technology, India*
*Nabonita Nath, Pailan College of Management and Technology, India*
*Kshounish Acharyya, Pailan College of Management and Technology, India*
*Shirsa Chakraborty, Pailan College of Management and Technology, India*
*Parag Chatterjee, Pailan College of Management and Technology, India*

The issue of cybercrime is becoming crucial in society. This is partly a result of the widespread adoption of technology in both essential government infrastructure and our daily lives. Due to an overreliance on technology, hackers and other people with bad intentions now have more ways to exploit systems and access databases containing sensitive data, including records relating to people's personal, financial, educational, and medical records. The importance of cybersecurity can be understood through research. Cyber security follows real-time information on the latest IT data. So far, various methods have been proposed by researchers around the world to prevent cyber-attacks or reduce the damage caused by them.

**Chapter 6**

Zero Day Vulnerabilities Assessments, Exploits Detection, and Various Design Patterns in Cyber Software ...................................................................132
*Vidhanth Maan Thapa, University of Petroleum and Energy Studies, India*
*Sudhanshu Srivastava, University of Petroleum and Energy Studies, India*
*Shelly Garg, University of Petroleum and Energy Studies, India*

In this technology-driven era, software development and maintenance is a rapidly growing domain and is predestined to thrive over the coming decade. But the growing demand for software solutions also brings its own implications. Software vulnerabilities are the most crucial of these. Software Vulnerabilities can be referred to as weaknesses or shortcomings of the software solutions which increase the risks of exploitation of resources and information. In the past few years, the number of exploits has been increasing rapidly, reaching an all-time high in 2021 affecting more than 100 million people worldwide. Although, even with the presence of existing vulnerability management models and highly secure tools and frameworks, software vulnerabilities are harder to identify and resolve as they may not be independent, and resolving them may cause other vulnerabilities. Moreover, a majority of the exploit are caused due to known vulnerabilities and zero-day vulnerabilities..

**Chapter 7**

Detection of Phishing Websites ........................................................................148
*Lakshmipathi Gejjala, Kalasalingam Academy of Research and Education, India*
*Muthukumar Arunachalam, Kalasalingam Academy of Research and Education, India*
*Bala Manikanta Eswar Duggisetty, Kalasalingam Academy of Research and Education, India*
*Jaswanth Kumar Reddy Vardireddy, Kalasalingam Academy of Research and Education, India*

Phishing attacks are one of the biggest security threats to personal and financial information on the internet. They are a type of cyber-attack where attackers pretend to be a trusted entity in order to trick people into revealing sensitive information, such as passwords and credit card numbers. To address this issue, a web application has been developed for detecting phishing websites. This application utilizes the Beautiful Soup library in Python to extract HTML and XML content and machine learning algorithms for detection. The application was created using the Streamlit software, making it user-friendly and easy to access through a web interface.

**Chapter 8**

Real-Time Object Detection in Video for Traffic Monitoring ...........................166
*Sai Deepak Alapati, Kalasalingam Academy of Research and Education, India*
*Muthukumar Arunachalam, Kalasalingam Academy of Research and Education, India*
*Chandana Chennamsetty, Kalasalingam Academy of Research and Education, India*
*Pujitha Dantam, Kalasalingam Academy of Research and Education, India*
*Anusha Dabbara, Kalasalingam Academy of Research and Education, India*

This chapter presents the application of YOLO, a deep learning-based object detection algorithm, for traffic monitoring. The algorithm was applied to real-time video streams from roadway cameras to detect and track vehicles. The results were compared with traditional computer vision methods and showed superior accuracy and processing speed. This study highlights the potential of YOLO for traffic monitoring and the significance of incorporating deep learning into intelligent transportation systems. YOLO V7 outperforms all other real-time object detectors on the GPU V100 in terms of speed and accuracy in the range of 5 to 160 frames per second and has the highest accuracy of 56.8% AP. YOLO V7 also introduces a new training methodology that improves the convergence rate and the generalization capabilities of the model. Experimental results show that YOLO V7 outperforms existing methods in terms of accuracy, speed, and efficiency, making it an attractive solution for real-world applications.

**Conclusion** ................................................................................................ 180

**Compilation of References** ........................................................................ 181

**Related References** ..................................................................................... 205

**About the Contributors** ............................................................................. 230

**Index** .......................................................................................................... 232

# Preface

Welcome to *AI Tools for Protecting and Preventing Sophisticated Cyber Attacks*, a comprehensive reference book that delves into the realm of artificial intelligence (AI) and its pivotal role in ensuring the integrity, availability, and confidentiality of the Internet. In today's interconnected world, where access to global resources is ubiquitous and continuous, the need for robust and effective cyber security measures cannot be overstated.

This book aims to shed light on the most effective and practical applications of AI in safeguarding critical cyber infrastructures and internet communities worldwide. The escalating complexity and dynamic nature of sophisticated cyber-attacks have made cyber security a formidable challenge, both in terms of technological advancements and financial implications. In this regard, the utilization of AI has proven to be a powerful tool in proactively defending against cyber threats.

Within the pages of this book, you will find a collection of carefully selected peer-reviewed chapters that address crucial issues, propose technical solutions, and outline future research directions in the field of cyber security. We have assembled a team of renowned experts, researchers, and practitioners who have contributed their invaluable insights and expertise to provide a comprehensive overview of the subject matter.

*AI Tools for Protecting and Preventing Sophisticated Cyber Attacks* is intended to be a valuable resource for cyber security experts, cyber systems administrators, IT professionals, internet and computer network specialists, as well as faculty members and students in universities and research institutions. However, we have also made an effort to ensure that the book remains accessible to decision-makers, non-professionals, and non-technical personnel in government, military, business, and industry sectors worldwide.

The book is organized into several sections, each addressing a distinct aspect of AI in cyber security. Topics covered include the current state-of-the-art and greatest challenges in cyber security, the diverse applications of AI in this field, the AI toolkit for securing critical cyber infrastructures, hardware and software cyber security tools, cyber security provision assessment metrics, application case scenarios, and an exploration of current and future research directions.

I extend my heartfelt gratitude to all the contributors for their dedication and commitment in sharing their knowledge and expertise. We hope that the insights and practical solutions presented in this book will serve as a catalyst for further advancements in AI-driven cyber security, enabling us to effectively protect and preserve the digital ecosystems we rely on.

*Eduard Babulak*
*National Science Foundation, USA*

# Acknowledgment

I would like to use this opportunity to express my sincere gratitude to contributors, reviewers, to Ms Barrantes, Ms Wagner, Ms Travers, Ms McLouglin, Ms Wertman and the IGI Global Colleagues and Friends for their excellent support, kind guidance and good counsel during the course of the project. I would like to say great thank you to my family and friends for their kind support and encouragement during the Book project.

## Editorial Advisory Board

David Al-Dabass, *School of Computing and Informatics, Nottingham Trent University, UK*
Jorge E. López de Vergara Méndez, *Department of Technology Information and Communications, Escuela Politécnica Superior, Universidad Autónoma de Madrid, Spain*
Gaurav Sharma, *Computer Science Department, Université libre de Bruxelles, Belgium*
A. K. Verma, *Thapar Institute of Engineering and Technology, Patiala, India*

Chapter 1

# The Role of Artificial Intelligence in Cyber Security

**Karmel Arockiasamy**
*Vellore Institute of Technology, Chennai, India*

## ABSTRACT

*Security experts coalesced the strength of artificial intelligence (AI) with cybersecurity to defend vulnerable networks and data from cyber attackers. The propagation of artificial intelligence (AI) systems in conjunction with the cyber-attacks are transforming the way the online social media systems are used, automating threat detection, and solving hundreds of attack vectors and attack surfaces. Resources, data sets, and neural fuzzing are the few hindrances that intercept AI from becoming a prevailing security tool. The challenge is to break through the divisional line between the black hat and white hat hackers to regularize technological deployment. Hence, in the current scenario, it is essential to explore how AI can be made use of for basic human needs and for cybersecurity control development. This chapter presents the methods and issues that are still an open challenge for the researchers, engineering managers, and leaders, educators, and students while incorporating artificial intelligence for developing cybersecurity controls.*

DOI: 10.4018/978-1-6684-7110-4.ch001

# INTRODUCTION

Cybersecurity is defined as "the organization and collection of processes, resources, and structures used to defend cyberspace and cyberspace-enabled systems" (Craigen et al., 2014). Cisco, a worldwide pioneer in data innovation, cybersecurity networking and appraises that more than 8.7 billion gadgets were associated with the internet before the finish of 2012, which is a number that will probably ascend to more than 40 billion of every 2020 (Singer & Friedman, 2014). In the public circle, the government network safety divisions like the US Cyber Command, provides security to basic public security resources (Singer & Friedman, 2014). In the private circle, organizations are battling to stay aware of the necessary requirement for security notwithstanding progressively advanced assaults from an assortment of sources. Figure 1 shows the number of reported data breaches. The main impulse of the attack can range from intelligence gathering, state security, to financial incentives etc. The peril of false positives and negatives still exists in identifying an attack. Any attack recognition missed by smart Information system then it may be considered as false negative alarm. In contrast in SIS may also produces false positives and the action may not permitted to proceed further (Tucker, 2018).

## Protection From Harm

Cybersecurity can possibly make hurt its clients, in any event, when that damage isn't expected. Concerns exist with respect to the exposure of weaknesses. In the event that not, at that point the vulnerability involves that an individual might be in risk of attack, which is especially concerning if the gadget in danger is clinical in nature (Nichols, 2016; Spring, 2016). Nonetheless, exposure could carry the weakness to the consciousness of potential assailants who had not considered it beforehand.

## Privacy and Control of Data

Privacy, a key problem in cybersecurity, increases as the quantity of personalized data that are highly sensitive are collected and stored in the cloud (Manjikian, 2017). The on-going exploitation of user"s personal profile, in turn concerns monitoring user behaviour online. Data control a critical factor, may be a facet of privacy (Moore, 2015) or in addition to privacy concern (Macnish, 2018). If data control is lost, then it may results in privacy violations and other political advertisements (Cadwalladr & Graham-Harrison, 2018; Ienca & Vayena, 2018).

# Vulnerabilities, Disclosure, Trust, Risk, and Responsibilities

An awareness to exploit vulnerabilities in a network can help cybersecurity professionals interpret the importance of a each attack. Disclosure of vulnerabilities to a particular individual, may lead to the leakage of that vulnerability from the liable individual to hackers community (Scientific American, n.d.). Trust plays a vital role in associating the cybersecurity experts to the protected individuals.

# Fathoming Artificial Intelligence

Artificial intelligence (AI) is a quickly developing part of software engineering that investigates and creates hypotheses, strategies, procedures, and application frameworks to reenact, broaden, and extend human knowledge. Computer based intelligence innovation has gained extraordinary ground lately. Artificial intelligence has a wide scope of utilizations, for example, facial acknowledgment, discourse acknowledgment, and advanced mechanics, however its application scope goes a long ways past the three parts of picture, voice, and conduct. It likewise has numerous other extraordinary applications in the field of network protection, for example, malware checking and interruption location.

In the early improvement of AI innovation, AI (ML) innovation assumed a crucial part in managing the internet dangers. Despite the fact that ML is incredible, it depends a lot on include extraction. This defect is especially gross when it is applied to the field of network protection. For instance, to empower a ML answer for perceive malware, we need to physically assemble the different highlights related with malware, which without a doubt restricts the effectiveness and precision of danger recognition. This is on the grounds that ML calculations work as per the pre-characterized explicit highlights, which implies that highlights which are not pre-characterized will get away from location and can't be found. It very well may be presumed that the presentation of most ML calculations relies upon the precision of highlight acknowledgment and extraction (Macnish & van der Ham, 2019).

In the perspective on clear blemishes in customary ML, scientists started to concentrate profound neural organization (DNN), otherwise called DL, a sub-area of ML. A major distinction in idea between the conventional ML and DL is, DL can be utilized to legitimately prepare the first information without extricating its highlights. In the previous hardly any years, DL has accomplished 20%–30% execution improvement in the fields of PC vision, discourse acknowledgment, and text understanding, and accomplished a noteworthy jump in the advancement of AI (Golovko, 2017). DL can distinguish nonlinear connections covered up in the information, uphold any new document types, and recognize obscure assaults, which is an appealing favorable position in digital protection safeguard. As of late, DL has gained incredible ground in forestalling network protection dangers, particularly in forestalling APT assaults.

DNN can get familiar with the significant level theoretical attributes of APT assaults, regardless of whether they utilize the most exceptional avoidance procedures (Deng & Yu, 2014). Albeit tale AI advances, for example, DL, assume a significant part in the internet safeguard, AI framework itself may likewise be assaulted or bamboozled, bringing about erroneous characterization or forecast results. For instance, in antagonistic conditions, controlling preparing tests will bring about harmful assaults, and controlling test tests will bring about avoidance assaults. Assaults in antagonistic conditions are proposed to sabotage the honesty and convenience of different AI applications, and delude neural organizations by utilizing ill-disposed examples, making classifiers infer wrong order. Obviously, there are comparing safeguard measures against ill-disposed assaults. These safeguard estimates center fundamentally around three viewpoints (Yuan, 2017):

A.  Altering the preparation cycle or information tests;
B.  Adjusting the organization itself, for example, including more layers/ sub-organizations and changing the misfortune/initiation work;
C.  Utilizing some outside models as organization additional items when characterizing tests that have not showed up.

Conveyed learning modes, for example, unified learning dispatched by Google, have risen, empowering numerous clever terminals to become familiar with a common model in a cooperative manner. Notwithstanding, all preparation information is put away in terminal gadgets, which brings numerous security challenges. The most effective method to guarantee that the model isn't noxiously taken and that it can build a circulated ML framework with security assurance is a significant exploration hotspot.

Customary ML approaches expect that the dispersion of preparing information is nearly equivalent to that of testing information. In an ill-disposed climate, in any case, present day profound organizations are inclined to assaults by ill-disposed examples. These ill-disposed examples force just a slight aggravation on the first examples, and in this way a human virtual framework couldn't identify the unsettling influence. Such an assault can prompt wrong order of the profound neural organization. The profound centrality of such wonders has pulled in numerous specialists to contemplate antagonistic assaults and DL security. In proposal frameworks, infusing harming information may bring about inaccurate suggestions. In facial acknowledgment, including even few adjusted pictures can make the application make a totally off-base characterization. Forcing just a little ill-disposed irritation on a generative model may create absolutely mistakenly reproduced tests.

# MACHINE LEARNING AND DEEP LEARNING IN CYBER SECURITY

## Machine Learning for Anomaly Detection

The intense exchange of information has made the organization an appealing and vulnerable target to determine and examine the various types of attacks. Consequently, numerous IDS techniques have been advancing to secure cloud administrations by identifying the distinctive attacks types on the organization. AI procedures have been vigorously applied in intrusion detection techniques with various procedures. Intrusion detection systems arise to help in including a layer of assurance over the organizations by distinguishing unapproved Intrusion situations. Two primary methodologies are utilized for IDS to be specific, signature-based and anomaly-based location. Almost intrusion detection systems are known as signature-based that utilizations rules for the detecting the intrusion. A huge dispersed organization would require countless principles for IDS, which could be expensive and tedious. Besides, an IDS utilizes assault marks to identify malevolent practices. Thus, if the signatures are not adequately delineated, attackers may have the option to get to the organization. To beat these issues, anomaly-based systems that don't rely upon human intercession have been proposed dependent on AI and all around prepared models to improve the abnormality recognition execution essentially with a sensible expense and multifaceted nature (Akhtar & Mian, 2018).

## Neural Networks

Improved data representation to construct good model can be done by using Neural Networks in intrusion detection systems, implementing forward and back propagation. Tuning the neurons in each layer and the number of layers, increases the processing time in NN techniques. RNN applies the feedback of the last information to the current output. Binary classification and multi-class classification can be utilized to measure the performance of RNN. Multi-layer perception can be trained using (Bhamare et al., 2016) RBNN algorithm [Resilient Back propagation artificial Neural Network], which achieves 89% and 15.7% of detection rate and false positive rate. EDM [Euclidean Distance Map], sequential algorithms based anomaly detection, exploits second order statistics on new attribute generations to improve the accuracy detection. CADF [Collaborative Anomaly Detection framework] (Naoum et al., 2013) involves data capturing, data network logging and pre-processing the data. Gaussian Mixture Model (GMM) that that creates non-convex clusters is used for abnormal pattern identification.

## Support Vector Machines

The supervised learning approach [Support Vector Machine] SVM used to obtain optimal results by analyzing data classification (Moustafa et al., 2017) is not recommended for large dataset because of time consumption. MI [Mutual information], a feature selection based algorithm and LS-SVM [Least Square Support Vector Machine] be used to classify various classes and to measure the relation between the label and features (Jose et al., 2018). An SVM based anomaly traffic detection algorithm in combination with the Particle swarm optimization (PSO) algorithm calculates the normalized entropy, sets threshold value to identify abnormal behavior in the network (Ambusaidi et al., 2016).

## Unsupervised Machine Learning Algorithms

Labeled datasets are not necessary for Unsupervised machine learning algorithms to distinguish the different classes. But, it analyzes and discovers the structure of the given data. LSTM RNN [Long- Short Term Memory Recurrent Neural Network] is used to reveal the anomalies in a SWaT [Secure Water Treatment] plant. It is used for detection of abnormal behaviors based on the cumulative sum (Lei, 2017). In probabilistic based deep neural network approach, if the probability of a point is greater than a threshold value then it is advised as anomalies. The sliding window based OC-SVM method, each window is classified as either normal or abnormal (Goh et al., 2017). The K-means algorithm, excitable to the allotment of noise data points and initial centroids, is used for anomaly detection (Inoue et al., 2017). The Genetic clustering algorithm is used for anomaly-based detection (Li, 2010). Based on the similarity measures, the optimal partitioning clusters of the abnormal and normal examples are determined. A two-level fitness function is used to filter and refine the clusters based on co-variance matrix and confidence interval. Genetic operators can be used to reassign cluster instances.

## Machine Learning for Hybrid Detection

TANN [Triangle Area Based Nearest Neighbors] (Aissa & Guerroumi, 2015), a hybrid learning based on advantages of unsupervised and supervised learning techniques. The center of the attack class in the cluster can be obtained using k-means clustering to improve the attack classification. A hybrid IDS using weighted k-means algorithms and Random Forest, based on clustering and data mining techniques. The random forest algorithm is used to for misuse detection in online phase and weighted k-mean algorithm is used to classify random attacks in offline phase (Tsai & Lin, 2010). An improved Support Vector Machine (SVM) for bundle order is joined with Self-Organizing Feature Map (SOFM) and Genetic Algorithms (GA) for include choice (Elbasiony et al., 2013) to distinguish assaults in network traffic. Innocent Bayesian classifier and is joined with Iterative Dichotomiser 3 (ID3) choice tree for network dissects. Grouped form of Self Organized Map (SOM) neural organizations (Shon et al., 2005) is utilized in building an interruption discovery framework. The grouping of neurons with closer weight esteems were executed utilizing the k-implies bunching calculation. The NSL-KDD dataset was utilized in preparing, testing, and assessing the proposed arrangement later being pre-handled by changing over the scope of non- mathematical highlights to mathematical ones, normalizing and by eliminating steady component esteems the cleaning of dataset is finished.

## Machine Learning for Profiling Network Traffic

NTA is the way toward identifying, recording and investigating communication patterns so as to recognize and react to security hazard, in any event, when messages are scrambled. Traffic analysis is essentially performed to discover the information type, the traffic coursing through an organization just as information sources. NTA solutions permit network managers to gather information and screen download/transfer speeds on the traffic that moves through the organization. The NTA tools have been ordinarily used to break down and recognize network security and execution issues (Qiao et al., 2012). The traffic insights from network traffic investigation helps in comprehension and assessing networks usage, download/upload speeds and type, size, birthplace and objective and substance of information.

## Need for Traffic Pattern Analysis and Mechanisms

Traffic pattern analysis tool is required to detect unknown threats, malware communication with trusted sources and malware communications via HTTPS. The security administrators can identify external IP address and monitor the large network traffic. Traffic analysis mechanism includes Self-Similarity and TES for analysis communication system and to discover the attacks, Wireless Sensor Networks WSN for attack classification to explore the possible patterns, Flow Analysis for anonymity network identification and to determine the network traffic with profiling applications, User Intention-Based Traffic Dependence Analysis (Taylor et al., 2017) for detecting anomalies and to assess accuracy, efficiency and security, Traffic Anomalies Detection Algorithms (Zhang, 2012) to detect flow outliners and trajectory outliners and Intrusion Detection System to detect malicious actions in the network. Machine learning is applied in various arena"s of cybersecurity with the aim to detect and respond to an attack with enhanced safety operations. Network-based defense for reducing the risk of victim exposure (Djenouri et al., 2019) and Intrusion detection are the generic machine learning mechanisms in traffic analysis. Network-based defense method defends the network by attempting to reduce the attack risk with additional security layer. Each layer has constituted policies and controls to define the authorized users accessing the network. Network monitoring system that differentiates hackers and the normal user, can determine the identity. Characterizing network traffic requires occasional refreshing and preparing of the model, notwithstanding that it needs to characterize the assignment in the robotized model. This sets aside some effort to assess the information and its degree through cautious information the board Data respectability and information investigation until you get clear information. Accordingly, it tends to be hard for gadgets that identify oddities in an ideal way.

## AI AND CYBERSECURITY ROLE IN SOCIAL MEDIA

Social media systems are playing are assuming a significant part in the public arena associating over a billion people worldwide and empowering them to communicate and impart data to one another just as inside a gathering of people. These online media frameworks can immeasurably help humankind, for example, spread data about irresistible diseases and examine answers for issues looked by mankind including forestalling kid dealing and savagery against women. Artificial Intelligence (AI) systems together with cybersecurity on social media systems are transforming the way the social media systems are being utilized by humans (Thuraisingham, 2020). AI methods can likewise be utilized to decide the notable individuals in an online media system just as make forecasts about where the disease will spread straightaway. Various advantages have been accounted for to deal with crisis exercises during quakes, typhoons, cyclones, psychological warfare occasions and the spread of fatal sicknesses. These procedures have likewise been utilized to find the focal point of disasters and send help in convenient way (Thuraisingham et al., 2016).

Social media systems are liable to cyber-attacks.. For instance, malicious software could change/modify the messages posted. Such software could likewise make fake profiles that would then post bogus messages. The pictures and video materials posted via online media could likewise be liable to attacks. At last, the machines and cell phones utilized by the clients of the online media could be assaulted and could thus taint a huge aspect of the web-based media framework. The inquiry at that point is by what means can AI procedures recognize such malicious actions (Masood, 2011). Fake news can result because of malicious software. Be that as it may, regularly the fake news can result because of the people violently posting bogus gossipy tidbits, for example, a conspicuous individual being a pedophile, or another unmistakable individual stealing a huge number of dollars. Distinguishing such phony news is a gigantic challenge. Some of the strategies that have been created for examining advancing information streams could be utilized to recognize counterfeit news (Masud et al., 2011; O'Brien, 2018; Thuraisingham et al., 2017).

Another issue with social media systems is ensuring the protection of people. The people may move diverted and post unique data about themselves which on the whole could bring about their security being disregarded. A firmly related issue is the inference problem where data collected could be exceptionally ordered while singular pieces might be unclassified (Thuraisingham et al., 2014). The machine learning methods could be attacked. That is, the attacker could sort out the learning model and attempt and thwart the methods. The defender would then adjust the model. The attacker would find out about the new model and attempt and obstruct it. This at that point turns into a game played between the defender and the attackers (Zhou et al., 2012).

## AI and Arena of Postulation in Cybersecurity

Over 50 various algorithms were known from the diverse acquisition that was utilized. The ascendant algorithms were: DT, KNN, AdaBoost, QL, RF, RNN and the most commonly used SVM, CNN and ANN (Wiafe et al., 2017). It is clear that artificial intelligence have made momentous commitments to fighting cybercrimes with noteworthy improvement in interruption discovery frameworks. It is learnt that there is a decrease in computational intricacy, training times of each model and false alerts. Data and correspondence innovation scientists concur that data security (InfoSec) is of essential significance (Karjalainen et al., 2019). Thus, various investigations have endeavored to address this by embracing improved strategies and innovative antiquities; including the utilization of malware indicators, interruption discovery and avoidance frameworks (IDPS), modern firewall arrangements and data encryption procedures. There is the requirement for a proper balance between people, innovation and policy management in authoritative security actions. Customary CyberSec avoidance advances use fix calculations and physical gadgets, like detectors and sensors, accordingly they are incapable at containing new the threats of cyber space (Patil, 2016)

Despite of the fact, the assort of signatures is refreshed on an everyday basis, the modernity and customary arrival of immense malware make this approach inadequate. Be that as it may, the presentation of signature less methodologies that are equipped for distinguishing and relieving malware attacks utilizing more current strategies like behavioral detection and AIs have been contended to be more viable (Deng et al., 2003; Shabtai et al., 2012). In spite of the apparent multitude of advantages AI gives, the quick advancement of approaches makes it amazingly hard for analysts to distinguish the most productive procedure and its sway on the cyberspace security. There is unambiguous that the general observation among Info-Sec and CyberSec analysts and professionals propose that AI has improved hierarchical data security, yet supposedly, these claims are theoretical and have not been experimentally validated. Most existing investigations have either illustrated how their development beat a determination of existing strategies or over-viewed an example of frameworks and evaluate the execution in contrast with theirs. In all cases, the degree of choice predispositions is generally high. As needs be, there is the requirement for a collective literature that give synopses on issues, difficulties and future exploration headings inside the domain.

Cybersecurity application domains were grouped into six: (i) intrusion detection and prevention systems (IDPS), (ii) traffic classification systems, (iii) imaging and captcha, (iv) Encryption and certification, (v) Denial-of service attack, and (vi) malware, virus, phishing. The outcomes showed that IDPS and malware, virus, phishing, and so on generally embrace ensemble methods. It was additionally seen that reviews on Encryption and Certification, DoS, and Imaging and Captcha don't lean toward ensemble methods. The most critical commitment of AI in the area is the improvement in false alarm rates for IDPS. All examinations on IDPS revealed improvement in false alarm rates. Computational complexity was referred as a key challenging aspect in IDPS and also the most challenging point in various algorithms of machine learning (Jordan & Mitchell, 2015; Webb et al., 2001). Genetic algorithm-based feature selection is used for effectively minimizing computational complexities in IDPS. With respect to network intrusion, the ability to sight anomalies and new traffic patterns using ensembles was identified to be among the most effective methods (Ahmed et al., 2018).

In image privacy protection methods, deep CNN (Yu et al., 2017) and SVM (Squicciarini et al., 2017) are used for improving accuracy and computational efficiency. Improved malicious webpage detection is improved using spectral clustering (Ben Neria et al., 2017). Artificial intelligence techniques have given compelling methods of identifying malevolent clients. The utilization of clickstream models, which doesn't need earlier information or suspicions of client classes, was seen to be compelling for catching unforeseen or recently known practices (Wang et al., 2018).

## Artificial Intelligence in Cyber Threats Intelligence

In the draft Bulgarian National Cyber Security Strategy (Republic of Bulgaria, 2016), Cyber Threats Intelligence (Trifonov et al., 2018) has the accompanying definition: a. foundation of systems and specialized intends to keep up a cutting-edge image of potential dangers of various scale, sources and character, patterns in international setting advancement and pertinent public digital picture investigation; b. improvement of capacities to help recognize attribution sources and take suitable types of protection and nullification. The Cyber Threats Intelligence Cycle (Brian, 2015) is a precise, persistent cycle of breaking down possible dangers to recognize a dubious arrangement of exercises that may undermine the association's frameworks, organizations, data, representatives, or clients by giving a methods for envisioning and surveying various explicit interruption sensor sources of info and open source data to derive explicit danger game-plans.

The model backings are the association's danger the executives system and the data security group"s decision making. The Cyber Threats Intelligence is created at three levels: vital, operational, and strategic. For the motivations behind this examination, the subsequent one is thought of: INSA characterizes (Operational Cyber Intelligence, 2014) the operational level as: "The level at which missions and significant activities are arranged, led, and supported to accomplish vital destinations inside theaters or other operational zones.

At this level, entertainers manufacture the capacities expected to help the strategic tasks. They move in the internet to situate ability where they have to so as to be compelling in their strategic missions. At the operational level, an association's working climate can be portrayed as far as physical, sensible, data and social layers".

## Artificial Intelligence and Cybersecurity Solutions (O'Brien, 2018)

Artificial intelligence incorporates threats and threat factors, yet it can likewise go about as a difficult solver. Artificial intelligence and cognitive information preparing are utilized to identify, shield against and look at digital attacks. Present day data security arrangements are either man-or machine-made. Explanatory arrangements depend on the principles made by IT security specialists, which ignore attacks that don't coordinate the set up rules. Cyberlance Protect is a coordinated data security threat prevention tool, which consolidates the advantages of man-made consciousness with data security controls to forestall malware contamination. Data security controls are utilized to ensure against content based, memory focused on assaults or assaults misusing outside gadgets. Dissimilar to customary security apparatuses dependent on the investigation of marks and client conduct in recognizing security dangers in the climate, cyberlance Protect utilizes artificial intelligence to distinguish and forestall known and obscure malevolent programming run on terminal gadgets. It also prevents known and obscure zero-day assaults and protects gadgets without upsetting the end-client.

Darktrace, a data security method, helps distinguishing and perceive developing cyber threats that can bypass conventional data security assurances. It utilizes the Enterprise Immune System innovation (EIS), AI calculations and numerical standards so as to distinguish peculiarities inside an organization"s data network. EIS utilizes numerical methodologies, which infers it doesn't have to exploit signatures/ rules, and it can distinguish obscure cyber security attacks that have not been experienced previously. EIS has capacities to distinguish and react to the majority of the capably actualized cyber threats, including the insider's threats covered up in the data organizations. By using AI and science, the EIS can adjust and consequently figure out how every client, gadget and data network carry on, so as distinguishing practices that reflect genuine cyber threats.

Cyberlytic Profiler is an apparatus created to distinguish dangers to sites. The profiler utilizes computerized reasoning to distinguish and organize digital assaults dependent on the greatness of the danger to the information.

The profiler dissects all HTTP-based web traffic by investigating web worker solicitations and reactions and creating an extensive danger appraisal progressively. This evaluation can be inspected through dashboard UI. By profiling web applications, Profiler can decide if sent solicitations begin from the ordinary dissemination of an application in a particular web application region. Profiler utilizes a protected classifier way to deal with decide attributes of assaults for the accompanying sorts of assaults: SQL infusion, cross-site scripting (XSS) and Bash.

## APPLYING ARTIFICIAL INTELLIGENCE METHODS TO NETWORK ATTACK DETECTION

The key to build an intelligent and automated security system are security incident patterns and data driven models. Various security incidents such as unauthorized access (Li et al., 2015), Digitalization and Internet-of-Things (IoT) (Almi'Ani, Ghazleh, Al-Rahayfeh, & Razaque, 2018), zero day attack (McIntosh et al., 2019), data breach (Alazab et al., 2010), malware attack (Sun et al., 2018), social engineering or phishing (Shaw, 2009), Denial of Service (DoS) (Li et al., 2015), etc. have matures at an exponential order in modern age. Each year the number of breached records are around triple in the next 5 years, that leads to the necessity to accept and implement a powerful cybersecurity approach to rationalize the loss in each organization (Gupta et al., 2017). Confidentiality is a security property that prevents the access, information disclosure to unauthorized individuals/entities/systems and Integrity is a security property that prevents any modification or information destruction in an unauthorized manner; Availability is a security property that ensures timely and reliable access of information by an authorized entity. Threats, vulnerabilities and impacts are the risks of attacks (Juniper Research, n.d.).

A security incident threatens the confidentiality, integrity, or availability of information assets and systems. Unauthorized access is the accessing of information without authorization by violating the security policy. Malware (Malicious Software) are designed to cause damages to the devices. Ransom malware demands an anonymous online mercantilism to restore access. DoS attacks shut down a machine/network, by flooding the target with traffic that triggers a crash. In Phishing the fraudulent attempt takes part to obtain sensitive information from user by disguising as a trusted or entity. Zero- day attack happens when threat of an unknown security vulnerability for which the patch has not been released or the software developers is unaware.

In Intrusion recognition frameworks, Host-based Intrusion Detection System (HIDS), and Network Intrusion Detection System (NIDS) are the normal security the board strategies. In a HIDS, the framework screens fundamental records, In a NIDS; the framework investigates and screens network associations for suspect-capable traffic. In Signature-based IDS: A specific example is recognized as the location of relating assaults and it is otherwise called information based or abuse identification. Location of new/concealed assaults is significant difficulties looked by signature-based framework. In an oddity based interruption location framework, at first the organization conduct is inspected for deciding powerful examples, making information driven models and profiling the typical conduct. It recognizes obscure or zero-day assaults (Liao et al., 2013). In a half breed framework, the abuse discovery framework recognizes the known sorts of interruptions and irregularity identification framework has noteworthy function for novel assaults (Alazab et al., 2012). Managed learning is an assignment driven methodology. Arrangement and relapse strategies are the most known regulated learning methods (Dutt et al., 2018). Relapse methods are utilized to foresee the absolute phishing assaults in a specific period or the organization bundle boundaries and to watch the root source of cybercrime and different types of extortion (Sarker, Kayes, & Watters, 2019). Arbitrary Forest learning (Watters et al., 2012) is utilized to comprehend a specific security task.

In unsupervised learning the data-driven approach is suited (Breiman, 2001). Association rule learning is used to discover the rules/relationships among the available set of security features/attributes. Partitioning clustering algorithms like K-medoids (Sarker, 2019) is used in various application domains. Artificial Neural Network (ANN) is applied in deep learning and the Neural Network algorithm is most popularly used for back-propagation. Deep learning algorithms perform well on voluminous datas, whereas machine learning algorithms perform comparatively better on small datasets (Rokach, 2010). Deep learning approaches inspires the complete working mechanism of human brain to interpret voluminous of data or the complex data in the form of images, sounds and texts (Rokach, 2010; Xin et al., 2018).

Deep learning depends on high-performance computing machines (GPUs) rather than classical machine-learning algorithms (Sarker, Kayes, & Watters, 2019). In recent days, researcher"s working in the domain of cybersecurity using deep learning techniques (Coelho et al., 2017). Semi-supervised learning, a hybridization of supervised and unsupervised techniques works on both the labeled and unlabeled data. Reinforcement learning in combination with neural network classifier is used for detecting botnet traffic or malicious cyber activities (Berman et al., 2019). Deep reinforcement learning and genetic algorithms are used for detection to intrusions and similar kind of problems (Alauthman et al., 2020).

# TRENDS/EMERGING CHALLENGES IN CYBER SECURITY

Cybersecurity datasets:, Handling quality problems in cybersecurity datasets:, Security policy rule generation, Hybrid learning method, Protecting the valuable security information, Context-awareness in cybersecurity, Feature engineering in cybersecurity, Prioritizing and Remarkable security alert generation and Recency analysis in cybersecurity solutions: are the emerging challenges in cyber security. Source datasets play the major role to work in the areas/challenges of cybersecurity data science. The primary need is establishing a large quantity of recent datasets for a particular problem domain such as intrusion detection, cyber risk prediction is one of the major challenges and a tedious job in cybersecurity. The cyber datasets holding various information leads to performance degradation of machine learning-based models (Lopez-Martin et al., 2020).

Security strategy rules refers security zones and empower a client to permit, limit, and track traffic on the organization dependent on the relating client or client gathering, and administration, or the application. The strategy rules are analyzed against the approaching traffic in arrangement during execution, and the standard that coordinates the traffic is applied. The strategy rules utilized in a large portion of the network safety frameworks are static and produced by human ability or philosophy based (Sarker, 2019). A half breed procedure joining different learning strategies or a mix of profound learning and AI techniques can be utilized to separate the objective understanding for a specific issue space like interruption discovery, malware examination, access control, and so on and settle on the wise choice for comparing network safety arrangements. Digital experts can create calculations by examining the historical backdrop of cyber attacks to recognize the most every now and again focused on lumps of information. an ongoing noxious standard of conduct is bound to be fascinating and significant than more established ones for foreseeing obscure assaults. Along these lines, viably utilizing the idea of recency examination (Kayes et al., 2018) in network safety arrangements could be another issue in online protection information science. As a rule, the online protection framework may not be all around characterized and may cause a generous number of bogus alerts that are unforeseen in a wise framework. For example, an IDS conveyed in a certifiable organization creates around 9,000,000 alarms for each day (Sarker, Colman, & Han, 2019).

# REFERENCES

Ahmed, S., Lee, Y., Hyun, S., & Koo, I. (2018). Feature Selection – Based Detection of Covert Cyber Deception Assaults in Smart Grid Communications Networks Using Machine Learning. *IEEE Access : Practical Innovations, Open Solutions*, 6, 27518–27529. doi:10.1109/ACCESS.2018.2835527

Aissa, N. B., & Guerroumi, M. (2015). A genetic clustering technique for Anomaly-based Intrusion Detection Systems. *2015 IEEE/ACIS 16th International Conference on Software Engineering, Artificial Intelligence, Networking and Parallel/Distributed Computing, SNPD 2015 - Proceedings*, 1–6. 10.1109/SNPD.2015.7176182

Akhtar, N., & Mian, A. (2018). Threat of adversarial attacks on deep learning in computer vision: A survey. *IEEE Access : Practical Innovations, Open Solutions*, 6, 14410–14430. doi:10.1109/ACCESS.2018.2807385

Alauthman, M., Aslam, N., Al-kasassbeh, M., Khan, S., Al-Qerem, A., & Choo, K.-K. R. (2020). An efficient reinforcement learning based botnet detection approach. *Journal of Network and Computer Applications*, 150(102479). doi:10.1016/j.jnca.2019.102479

Alazab, A., Hobbs, M., Abawajy, J., & Alazab, M. (2012). Using feature selection for intrusion detection system. In *2012 International symposium on communications and information technologies (ISCIT)*. IEEE. 10.1109/ISCIT.2012.6380910

Alazab, M., Venkatraman, S., Watters, P., & Alazab, M. (2010). *Zero-day malware detection based on supervised learning algorithms of api call signatures*. Academic Press.

Almi'Ani, Ghazleh, Al-Rahayfeh, & Razaque. (2018). Intelligent intrusion detection system using clustered self organized map. *5th International Conference on Software Defined Systems, SDS 2018, 1*, 138–144.

Ambusaidi, M. A., He, X., Nanda, P., & Tan, Z. (2016). Building an intrusion detection system using a fifilter-based feature selection algorithm. *IEEE Transactions on Computers*, 65(10), 2986–2998. doi:10.1109/TC.2016.2519914

Ben Neria, M., Yacovzada, N.-S., & Ben-Gal, I. (2017). A Risk-Scoring Feedback Model for Webpages and Web Users Based on Browsing Behavior. *ACM Transactions on Intelligent Systems and Technology*, *8*(4), 1–21. doi:10.1145/2928274

Berman, D. S., Buczak, A. L., Chavis, J. S., & Corbett, C. L. (2019). A survey of deep learning methods for cyber security. *Information (Basel)*, *10*(4), 1–35. doi:10.3390/info10040122

Bhamare, D., Salman, T., Samaka, M., Erbad, A., & Jain, R. (2016). Feasibility of supervised machine learning for cloud security. *2016 International Conference on Information Science and Security (ICISS)*, 1–5. 10.1109/ICISSEC.2016.7885853

Breiman, L. (2001). Random forests. *Machine Learning*, *45*(1), 5–32. doi:10.1023/A:1010933404324

Brian, P. (2015). *Kime Threat Intelligence: Planning and Direction*. SANS Institute.

Buczak, A. L., & Guven, E. (2015). A survey of data mining and machine learning methods for cyber security intrusion detection. *IEEE Communications Surveys and Tutorials*, *18*(2), 1153–1176. doi:10.1109/COMST.2015.2494502

Cadwalladr, C., & Graham-Harrison, E. (2018). Revealed: 50 million Facebook profiles harvested for Cambridge Analytica in major data breach. *The Guardian*.

Chuan-long, Y., Yue-fei, Z., Jin-long, F., & Xin-zheng, H. (2017). A Deep Learning Approach for Intrusion Detection using Recurrent Neural Networks. *IEEE Access : Practical Innovations, Open Solutions*, *5*, 21954–21961. doi:10.1109/ACCESS.2017.2762418

Coelho, I. M., Coelho, V. N., Luz, E. J. S., Ochi, L. S., Guimarães, F. G., & Rios, E. (2017). A gpu deep learning metaheuristic based model for time series forecasting. *Applied Energy*, *201*, 412–418. doi:10.1016/j.apenergy.2017.01.003

Craigen, D., Diakun-Thibault, N., & Purse, R. (2014). Defining Cybersecurity. *Technology Innovation Management Review*, *4*(10), 13–21. doi:10.22215/timreview/835

Deng, L., & Yu, D. (2014). Deep learning: methods and applications. *Found Trend Sig Process, 7*(3-4), 197-387. doi:10.1561/2000000039

Deng, P. S., Wang, J.-H., Shieh, W.-G., Yen, C.-P., & Tung, C.-T. (2003). Intelligent automatic malicious code signatures extraction. *IEEE 37th Annual 2003 International Carnahan Conference on Security Technology*, 600–603. 10.1109/CCST.2003.1297626

Djenouri, Y., Belhadi, A., Lin, J. C.-W., Djenouri, D., & Cano, A. (2019). A survey on urban traffic anomalies detection algorithms. *IEEE Access : Practical Innovations, Open Solutions*, 7, 12192–12205. doi:10.1109/ACCESS.2019.2893124

Dutt, Borah, Maitra, Bhowmik, Maity, & Das. (2018). Real-time hybrid intrusion detection system using machine learning techniques. *Advances in Communication, Devices and Networking*, 885–94.

Elbasiony, R. M., Sallam, E. A., Eltobely, T. E., & Fahmy, M. M. (2013). A hybrid network intrusion detection framework based on random forests and weighted k-means. *Ain Shams Engineering Journal*, 4(4), 753–762. doi:10.1016/j.asej.2013.01.003

Farid, D. M., Harbi, N., & Rahman, M. Z. (2010). Combining naive bayes and decision tree for adaptive intrusion detection. *International Journal of Network Security & its Applications*, 2(2), 12–25. doi:10.5121/ijnsa.2010.2202

Fischer, E. A. (2014). *Cybersecurity issues and challenges: In brief.* Congressional Research Service.

Goh, J., Adepu, S., Tan, M., & Lee, Z. S. (2017). Anomaly detection in cyber physical systems using recurrent neural networks. *Proceedings of IEEE International Symposium on High Assurance Systems Engineering,* 140–145. 10.1109/HASE.2017.36

Golovko, V. A. (2017). Deep learning: An overview and main paradigms. *Optical Memory and Neural Networks (Information Optics)*, 26(1), 1–17. doi:10.3103/S1060992X16040081

Gupta, B. B., Tewari, A., Jain, A. K., & Agrawal, D. P. (2017). Fighting against phishing attacks: State of the art and future challenges. *Neural Computing & Applications*, 28(12), 3629–3654. doi:10.100700521-016-2275-y

Huang, C., Zheng, L., Wang, S., Leung, V. C. M., Lin, T., & Peng, K. (2018). Intrusion Detection System Based on Decision Tree over Big Data inFog Environment. *Wireless Communications and Mobile Computing, 2018*, 1–10.

Ienca, M., & Vayena, E. (2018). *Cambridge Analytica and Online Manipulation.* Scientific American Blog Network.

Inoue, J., Yamagata, Y., Chen, Y., Poskitt, C. M., & Sun, J. (2017). Anomaly detection for a water treatment system using unsupervised machine learning. *IEEE International Conference on Data Mining Workshops, ICDMW,* 1058–1065. 10.1109/ICDMW.2017.149

Jordan, M. I., & Mitchell, T. M. (2015). Machine learning: Trends, perspectives, and prospects. *Science, 349*(6245), 255–260. doi:10.1126cience.aaa8415 PMID:26185243

Jose, S., Malathi, D., Reddy, B., & Jayaseeli, D. (2018). A Survey on Anomaly Based Host Intrusion Detection System. *Journal of Physics: Conference Series, 1000*(1), 012049. doi:10.1088/1742-6596/1000/1/012049

Juniper Research. (n.d.). https://www.juniperresearch.com/

Karjalainen, M., Sarker, S., & Siponen, M. (2019). Toward a Theory of Information Systems Security Behaviors of Organizational Employees: A Dialectical Process Perspective. *Information Systems Research, 30*(2), 351–710. doi:10.1287/isre.2018.0827

Kayes, A. S. M., Rahayu, W., & Dillon, T. (2018). An ontology-based approach to dynamic contextual role for pervasive access control. In *AINA 2018.* IEEE Computer Society. doi:10.1109/AINA.2018.00093

Lei, Y. (2017). Network Anomaly Traffific Detection Algorithm Based on SVM. *Proceedings - 2017 International Conference on Robots and Intelligent System, ICRIS 2017,* 217–220.

Lei, Y. (2017). Network Anomaly Traffic Detection Algorithm Based on SVM. *Proceedings of International Conference on Robots and Intelligent System,* 217–220. 10.1109/ICRIS.2017.61

Li, H. (2010). Research and implementation of an anomaly detection model based on clustering analysis. *Proceedings - 2010 International Symposium on Intelligence Information Processing and Trusted Computing, IPTC 2010,* 458–462. 10.1109/IPTC.2010.94

Li, S., Da Xu, L., & Zhao, S. (2015). The internet of things: A survey. *Information Systems Frontiers, 17*(2), 243–259. doi:10.100710796-014-9492-7

Liao, H.-J., Lin, C.-H. R., Lin, Y.-C., & Tung, K.-Y. (2013). Intrusion detection system: A comprehensive review. *Journal of Network and Computer Applications, 36*(1), 16–24. doi:10.1016/j.jnca.2012.09.004

Lopez-Martin, Carro, & Sanchez-Esguevillas. (2020). Application of deep reinforcement learning to intrusion detection for supervised problems. *Exp Syst Appl, 141*(112963).

Macnish, K. (2018). Government Surveillance and Why Defining Privacy Matters in a Post- Snowden World. *Journal of Applied Philosophy, 35*(2), 417–432. doi:10.1111/japp.12219

Macnish, K., & van der Ham, J. (2019). Ethics and Cybersecurity Research. *Journal of Science and Engineering Ethics.*

Manjikian, M. (2017). *Cybersecurity Ethics* (1st ed.). Routledge. doi:10.4324/9781315196275

Masood, L. (2011). *Data Mining Applications in Malware Detection.* CRC Press.

Masud, M. M., Gao, J., Khan, L., Han, J., & Thuraisingham, B. M. (2011). Classification and Novel Class Detection in Concept-Drifting Data Streams under Time Constraints. *IEEE Transactions on Knowledge and Data Engineering, 23*(6), 859–874. doi:10.1109/TKDE.2010.61

McIntosh, T., Jang-Jaccard, J., Watters, P., & Susnjak, T. (2019). The inadequacy of entropy-based ransomware detection. In *International conference on neural information processing.* New York: Springer.

Moore. (2015). *Privacy, Security and Accountability: Ethics, Law and Policy.* Rowman & Littlefield.

Moustafa, N., Creech, G., Sitnikova, E., & Keshk, M. (2017). Collaborative anomaly detection framework for handling big data of cloud computing. https://arxiv.org/abs/1711.02829

Naoum, R. S., Abid, N. A., & Al-Sultani, Z. N. (2013). An Enhanced Resilient Backpropagation Artifificial Neural Network for Intrusion Detection System. *International Journal of Computer Science and Network Security, 13*(3), 98–104. Available: http://paper.ijcsns.org/07{\ }book/201203/20120302.pdf

Nichols, S. (2016). *St Jude sues short-selling MedSec over pacemaker "hack" report.* The Register. https://www.theregister.co.uk/2016/09/07/st_jude_sues_over_hacking_claim/

O'Brien, N. (2018). *Machine learning for detection of fake news* [MS Thesis]. MIT.

Operational Cyber Intelligence. (2014). INSA.

Patil, P. (2016). Artificial intelligence in cybersecurity. *Int. J. Res. Comput. Appl. Robot*, 4(5), 1–5.

Qiao, L.-B., Zhang, B.-F., Lai, Z.-Q., & Su, J.-S. (2012). Mining of attack models in ids alerts from network backbone by a two-stage clustering method. In *2012 IEEE 26th international parallel and distributed processing symposium workshops & PhD Forum*. IEEE. 10.1109/IPDPSW.2012.146

Republic of Bulgaria. (2016). *National Cyber Security Strategy "Cyber Resilient Bulgaria 2020", 2016- 03 NCSS Bulgaria final draft v 5 3*. Bulgarian Government.

Rokach, L. (2010). A survey of clustering algorithms. In *Data Mining and Knowledge Discovery Handbook* (pp. 269–298). Springer.

Sarker, I. H. (2019). Context-aware rule learning from smartphone data: Survey, challenges and future directions. *Journal of Big Data*, 6(95), 95. Advance online publication. doi:10.118640537-019-0258-4

Sarker, I. H. (2019). A machine learning based robust prediction model for real-life mobile phone data. *Internet of Things*, 5, 180–193. doi:10.1016/j.iot.2019.01.007

Sarker, I. H., Colman, A., & Han, J. (2019). Mining recency-based personalized behavior from contextual smartphone data. *Journal of Big Data*, 6(49), 49. doi:10.118640537-019-0211-6

Sarker, I. H., Kayes, A., & Watters, P. (2019). Effectiveness analysis of machine learning classification models for predicting personalized context-aware smartphone usage. *Journal of Big Data*, 6(1), 1–28. doi:10.118640537-019-0219-y

Sarker, I. H., Kayes, A., & Watters, P. (2019). Effectiveness analysis of machine learning classification models for predicting personalized context-aware smartphone usage. *Journal of Big Data*, 6(1), 1–28. doi:10.118640537-019-0219-y

Scientific American. (n.d.). https://blogs.scientificamerican.com/observations/cambridge-analytica-and-onlinemanipulation/

Shabtai, A., Kanonov, U., Elovici, Y., Glezer, C., & Weiss, Y. (2012). Andromaly: A behavioral malware detection framework for android devices. *Journal of Intelligent Information Systems*, *38*(1), 161–190. doi:10.100710844-010-0148-x

Shaw, A. (2009). Data breach: From notifcation to prevention using pci dss. *Colum Soc Probs.*, *43*, 517.

Shon, T., Kim, Y., Lee, C., & Moon, J. (2005). A machine learning framework for network anomaly detection using svm and ga. In *Proceedings from the sixth annual IEEE SMC information assurance workshop*. IEEE. 10.1109/IAW.2005.1495950

Singer & Friedman. (2014). *Review - Cybersecurity and Cyberwar*. https://www.e-ir.info/2014/01/06/review-cybersecurity-and-cyberwar/

Spring, T. (2016). *Researchers: MedSec, Muddy Waters Set Bad Precedent With St. Jude Medical Short*. https://threatpost.com/researchers- medsec-muddy-waters-set-bad-precedent-with-st-judemedical-short/120266/

Squicciarini, A., Caragea, C., & Balakavi, R. (2017). Toward Automated Online Photo Privacy. *ACM Transactions on the Web*, *11*(1), 1–29. doi:10.1145/2983644

Sun, N., Zhang, J., Rimba, P., Gao, S., Zhang, L. Y., & Xiang, Y. (2018). Data-driven cybersecurity incident prediction: A survey. *IEEE Communications Surveys and Tutorials*, *21*(2), 1744–1772. doi:10.1109/COMST.2018.2885561

Taylor, V. F., Spolaor, R., Conti, M., & Martinovic, I. (2017). Robust smartphone app identification via encrypted network traffic analysis. *IEEE Transactions on Information Forensics and Security*, *13*(1), 63–78. doi:10.1109/TIFS.2017.2737970

Thuraisingham. (2020). The Role of Artificial Intelligence and Cyber Security for Social Media. *IEEE International Parallel and Distributed Processing Symposium Workshops (IPDPSW)*, 1116-1118.

Thuraisingham, B., Pallabi, P., Masud, M., & Khan, L. (2017). *Big Data Analytics with Applications in Insider Threat Detection*. CRC Press. doi:10.1201/9781315119458

Thuraisingham, B. M., Cadenhead, T., & Kantarcioglu, M. (2014). *Access Control and Inference with Semantic Web*. CRC Press.

Thuraisingham, B. M., Kantarcioglu, M., Khan, L., Carminati, B., Ferrari, E., & Bahri, L. (2016). *Emergency-Driven Assured Information Sharing in Secure Online Social Networks: A Position Paper*. IPDPS Workshops. doi:10.1109/IPDPSW.2016.201

Trifonov, R., Nakov, O., & Mladenov, V. (2018). Artificial Intelligence in Cyber Threats Intelligence. IEEE European Union, 2018 International Conference on Intelligent and Innovative Computing Applications (ICONIC). doi:10.1109/ICONIC.2018.8601235

Tsai, C.-F., & Lin, C.-Y. (2010). A triangle area based nearest neighbors approach to intrusion detection. *Pattern Recognition*, *43*(1), 222–229. doi:10.1016/j.patcog.2009.05.017

Tucker, E. (2018). *Cyber security – why you're doing it all wrong*. https://www.computerweekly.com/opinion/Cyber-securitywhy-youre-doing-it-all-wrong

Wang, C., Zhao, Z., Gong, L., Zhu, L., Liu, Z., & Cheng, X. (2018). A Distributed Anomaly Detection System for In-Vehicle Network Using HTM. *IEEE Access : Practical Innovations, Open Solutions*, *6*, 9091–9098. doi:10.1109/ACCESS.2018.2799210

Watters, P. A., McCombie, S., Layton, R., & Pieprzyk, J. (2012). *Characterising and predicting cyber attacks using the cyber attacker model profile (camp)*. J Money Launder Control. doi:10.1108/13685201211266015

Webb, G. I., Pazzani, M. J., & Billsus, D. (2001). Machine learning for user modeling. *User Modeling and User-Adapted Interaction*, *11*(1/2), 19–29. doi:10.1023/A:1011117102175

Wiafe, Koranteng, Obeng, Assyne, Wiafe, & Gulliver. (2017). Artificial Intelligence for Cybersecurity: A Systematic Mapping of Literature. *IEEE Access*. doi:10.1109/ACCESS.2017

Xin, Y., Kong, L., Liu, Z., Chen, Y., Li, Y., Zhu, H., Gao, M., Hou, H., & Wang, C. (2018). Machine learning and deep learning methods for cybersecurity. *IEEE Access : Practical Innovations, Open Solutions*, *6*, 35365–35381. doi:10.1109/ACCESS.2018.2836950

Yu, J., Zhang, B., Kuang, Z., Lin, D., & Fan, J. (2017). iPrivacy : Image Privacy Protection by Identifying Sensitive Objects via Deep Multi-Task Learning. *IEEE Transactions on Information Forensics and Security*, *12*(5), 1005–1016. doi:10.1109/TIFS.2016.2636090

Yuan, X. Y. (2017). *PhD forum: Deep learning-based real-time malware detection with multi-stage analysis.* IEEE Int Conf on Smart Computing. doi:10.1109/SMARTCOMP.2017.7946997

Zhang, H. (2012). User intention-based traffic dependence analysis for anomaly detection. In *2012 IEEE Symposium on Security and Privacy Workshops.* IEEE. 10.1109/SPW.2012.15

Zhou, Y., Kantarcioglu, M., Thuraisingham, B. M., & Xi, B. (2012). Adversarial support vector machine learning. *KDD : Proceedings / International Conference on Knowledge Discovery & Data Mining. International Conference on Knowledge Discovery & Data Mining*, 1059–1067.

# Chapter 2
# The AI Application in Cybersecurity

**Kiranbhai Dodiya**
*Gujarat University, India*

**Dipak Kumar Mahida**
*Gujarat University, India*

**Ankita Patel**
*Gujarat University, India*

**Kapil Kumar**
*Gujarat University, India*

## ABSTRACT

*The 21st century is a century of technology. With the increase of new technology, life becomes easy, but as no technology is 100% safe and secure, every technology has some drawbacks. Information technology and cyber security are frequently used interchangeably. Nowadays, national and global security is at risk due to the world's growing reliance on a robust but vulnerable internet and the disruptive powers of cyber attackers. Various security agencies and cyber security researchers prepare the patch and prevention methods for detecting cybercrime, but it's not the proper solution for all types of cybercrime. The existential values of artificial intelligence led to a solution to many problems of cyber security. The main objective of the use of artificial intelligence in cyber security is to enhance the detection of the rate of cybercrime. Another application of artificial intelligence in cybersecurity is to improve the resistance and response to cyber-attacks.*

DOI: 10.4018/978-1-6684-7110-4.ch002

# 1. INTRODUCTION

Computer networks and information technology solutions are vital to all sectors of our society, from the government to the economy to crucial infrastructure. Cybersecurity is a technique, methodology, and practice that safeguards those networks, devices, processes, and data against attacks, damage, or unwanted access. Due to the rapid expansion of computer networks, cyberattacks have increased dramatically. Now cybersecurity has emerged as one of the most critical issues in cyberspace (Morovat & Panda, 2020).

Conventional security methods that are employed to safeguard networks and devices rely on static security system control and work in response to an attack. For example, in the case of a network intrusion attack, security systems scan nodes based on a predefined set of rules. These approaches take a long time to get notified of an attack. The traditional strategy, however, is no longer effective in light of the increasing number of cyberattacks. Additionally, attackers frequently carry out attacks before software developers are aware of the vulnerabilities by using emerging threat techniques like APTs (advanced persistent threats) and zero-day attacks; as a result, it takes some time to patch the vulnerable systems. The proliferation of personal data online undoubtedly contributes to several cybersecurity issues. The only way to secure data in the chaotic world of today, where cyberattacks occur often and are continuously changing, is by utilizing robust cyber tactics. AI-based methods are one solution to these problems. Artificial intelligence (AI) incorporates intelligence and can process massive volumes of data while performing real-time analysis and decision-making (Morovat & Panda, 2020).

## 1.1 Types of AI

AI can be classified into various type on the bases of their capability and functionality. On bases of capabilities there are three types of AI which are discussed in Figure 1.

### 1.1.1 Narrow AI or Weak AI

Narrow AI is the most prevalent and radially available AI which is intelligent enough to carry out certain task but it is only taught for a single job, it cannot accomplish tasks outside of its domain or set of constraints. As a result, it is often known as weak AI. If narrow AI exceeds its bounds, it may fail in unexpected ways. Apple Siri is a good example of narrow AI.

*Figure 1. Types of AI on the bases of their capabilities*

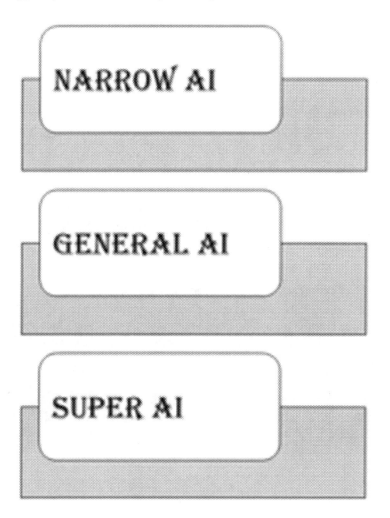

**Types of AI on the bases of their capabilities**

## 1.1.2 General AI

The goal of general AI is to create a system that is intelligent enough to think like a person on its own. Therefore, General AI is developed as capable of doing any intellectual job as effectively as a human. Since there is currently no system that falls under general AI that can carry out every work as well as a person. As generic AI systems are still being researched, it will take a long time and many resources to construct such systems.

### 1.1.3 Super AI

Super AI is a degree of system intelligence where computers are capable of outperforming people in any task due to their cognitive abilities. It results from general AI. Super AI includes ability to think, reason, solve puzzles, make decisions, plan, learn, and communicate on its own, among other vital traits. Super AI is currently only an ideal idea in the world of artificial intelligence. Real-world implementation of such systems is still a challenging endeavour.

On the bases of functionality, AI can be divided into four types which are shown in Figure 2.

*Figure 2. Types of AI on the bases of their functionalities*

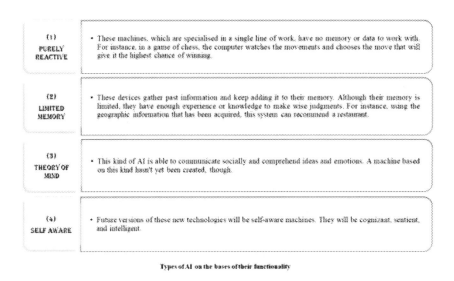

Types of AI on the bases of their functionality

## 1.2 AI and Cybersecurity

Artificial intelligence is a technique that enables machines and computer applications to replicate human intellect by learning from experience through iterative processing and algorithmic training. AI systems learn from patterns and attributes in the data they analyse by integrating a vast amount of data with sophisticated, iterative processing methods. AI system tests, evaluates and increases its performance with each cycle of data processing (*How Does Artificial Intelligence Work? | CSU Global*, n.d.). For instance, AI can be used to enhance security performance and overall protection against an expanding number of complex cyber-attacks. Computers must automatically perform everyday duties such as analysing network traffic, allowing access based on the set of rules, and identifying system anomalies. Automation and false positive detection may be obstacles that AI might help to overcome. The critical task of eliminating false positives now requires human assistance. To develop algorithms and investigate novel and emerging threats in cyberspace, cybersecurity experts started using AI (Chan et al., 2019).

## 1.3 Evolution of Artificial Intelligence

The origin of AI as we know it today dates back less than a century, yet its roots go deep and wide. Greek tales were the first to depict intelligent machines and artificial entities. The discovery of syllogism and its application of deductive reasoning by Aristotle was a major turning point in humanity's search to comprehend its intelligence (Mccarthy, 2007).

**1943:** The first mathematical framework for creating a neural network is presented in the paper "A Logical Calculus of Ideas Immanent in Nervous Activity" by Warren McCullough and Walter Pitts. To execute sophisticated computations using propositional logic, they developed a simplified computational model of how biological neurons may collaborate in animal brains. It was the first architecture for an artificial neural network (Mccarthy, 2007), (Nielsen, 2015).

**1949:** Donald Hebb contended in his book The Organization of Behaviour: A Neuropsychological Theory, that neural pathways are formed from experiences, and such connections between neurons become stronger the more frequently they are used. Hebbian learning is still an essential model in AI.

**1950:** In his article "Computing Machinery and Intelligence," Alan Turing introduced the concept, which is now known as the 'Turing Test' which determines if a machine is intelligent. Later in the same year, Marvin Minsky, and Dean Edmonds, two Harvard undergrads, created the first neural network computer, SNARC. The Stochastic Neural Analog Reinforcement Calculator (SNARC) was the first machine developed using an artificial neural network. Forty neurons were built and wired into a network utilizing analogue and electromechanical components, for each neuron created with a capacitor for short-term memory and a potentiometer (often found in volume controls) for long-term memory (Mccarthy, 2007; Toosi et al., 2021).

**1952:** To learn how to play checkers, Arthur Samuel created a self-learning program.

**1959:** While working at IBM, Arthur Samuel coined the term "machine learning."

**1974–80:** It was known as the "AI winter" period, during which state funding and investment in the area declined. Later, the field was revitalized in the 1980s only when the British government started sponsoring it, partly to counteract Japanese advances (Benko & Lányi, 2009; McCorduck et al., 1977).

**1980-90:** Another significant winter hit the field, along with the downfall of the market for a few of the early general-purpose computers and diminished government financing (Benko & Lányi, 2009; McCorduck et al., 1977).

**1997:** Deep Blue, developed by IBM, became the first computer to defeat a chess grandmaster when it defeated Russian maestro Garry Kasparov (Mccarthy, 2007).

**2008:** Google makes advances in speech recognition and incorporates it into its iPhone app (Mccarthy, 2007).

**2011:** The query-answering platform of the computer giant Watson defeated former winners Brad Rutter and Ken Jennings on the game program "Jeopardy!" (Mccarthy, 2007).

**2020:** Open AI has released the GPT-3 natural language processing model, which can generate text that is similar to how humans speak and write (Mccarthy, 2007).

**2022:** Gato, an artificial intelligence (AI) system unveiled by DeepMind, is capable of hundreds of activities, such as playing Atari, annotating photos, and stacking blocks with a robotic arm (Mccarthy, 2007).

## 2. TYPES OF CYBER THREATS

Cybersecurity experts are constantly defending computer systems from many forms of cyber threats. Cyber-attacks on organizations and private networks occur daily, and the variety of attacks has risen significantly. There are several motives for cyber-attacks. One of them is money. Cybercriminals may deactivate a system and then demand a ransom to reactivate it. Several high-profile cyber-attacks in recent years have resulted in the exposure of critical data. For example, the Equifax data breach in 2017 exposed the personal information of over 143 million people, including birth dates, addresses, and Social Security numbers (Jouini et al., 2014; Ullah et al., 2019). It is crucial to learn about the wide range of cyberattacks that exist today to understand the various technologies and applications related to AI in cybersecurity. There are numerous sorts of cybercrime, however, we will focus on the most typical attacks here.

i.   **Denial of Service attacks:** It is a kind of cyber-attack that overwhelms a computer or network, making it unable to respond to queries. It entails flooding a computer resource (such as memory or a web server) until the server overloads and crashes, leading the machine to slow down to the point where the user cannot use it. The same technique is implemented via a distributed DoS (DDoS), except the attack comes from a computer network.

ii.  **Remote to Local (R2L) attacks:** The goal of this attack is to get local network access by sending specific packets to a device over a network. Even though the attacker frequently lacks a user account on the actual machine, they can still transmit packets to the system across a specific network (Chan et al., 2019).

iii. **User to Root (U2R) attacks:** It is an attack in which the perpetrator manages to take control of the machine at the root level by attempting to obtain access privileges from the host. To accomplish this, the intruder must exploit the system by sniffing passwords or engaging in stereotypical hacking (Chan et al., 2019).

*Figure 3. Types of cyber threats*

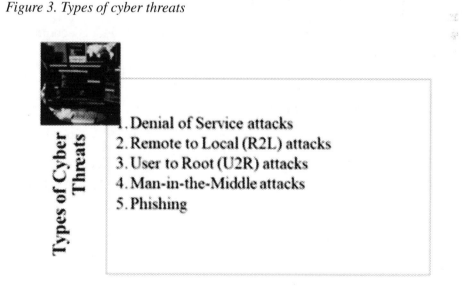

Types of Cyber Threats
1. Denial of Service attacks
2. Remote to Local (R2L) attacks
3. User to Root (U2R) attacks
4. Man-in-the-Middle attacks
5. Phishing

**Types of cyber threats**

iv. **Man-in-the-middle attacks:** It happens when hackers interject themselves into a two-party conversation. Hackers can monitor and steal data after disrupting communication. MITM attacks are typically carried out whenever a visitor connects to an unprotected Wi-Fi network. Attackers establish themselves between the network and the visitor to install malicious software and access data (Jouini et al., 2014; Ullah et al., 2019).

v. **Phishing:** It employs forged communication, such as fake emails, to dupe the recipient into reading it and following the instructions contained within, such as entering a credit card number. The primary purpose of this attack is to steal sensitive information such as credit card and login information or to install malware on the victim's PC (Jouini et al., 2014; Ullah et al., 2019).

# 3. WORKING MECHANISM OF AI IN CYBERSECURITY

AI technology can comprehend, learn, and act based on data obtained from events and consequences. Artificial intelligence (AI) aims to create a new class of automated intellect that reacts like human intelligence. To attain the above purpose, machines must be trained using learning algorithms. Even if methods are not significantly improved, AI can still learn via brute force using big data and massive computation. AI operates in three ways:

- **Assisted intelligence** is intelligence that helps individuals accomplish things better already.
- **Augmented intelligence** allows people to perform things they previously could not do.
- **Autonomous intelligence** refers to the characteristics of machines that act autonomously (Morovat & Panda, 2020).

In addition to these three areas, AI employs Learning algorithms to teach computers and improve performance via learning and experience-based training. Typically, there are three types of learning algorithms used to train machines:

i. **Supervised learning:** It uses a big, labelled data set to train. After training, the system must be evaluated using a test data set. Typically, these learning algorithms are used as classification or regression techniques. Based on the input, the regression algorithm produces outputs or prediction values that are one or more relatively constant numbers. Classification algorithms divide data into classes, and unlike regression algorithms, they generate discrete output.

ii.  **Unsupervised learning:** It makes use of unlabelled training data. Typically, unsupervised learning is employed to cluster data, decrease dimensionality, or predict density.

iii. **Reinforcement learning:** This learning algorithm learns the ideal actions based on incentives or punishments. Reinforcement is a blend of supervised and unsupervised learning. It is beneficial in instances where data is limited or unavailable.

AI encompasses various subfields, including machine learning, deep learning, neural networks, and expert systems, in addition to these learning algorithms.

- **Machine learning:** By utilizing statistical methods, machine learning enables computer systems to learn from data instead of being explicitly programmed and improves performance over time. It functions best when focused on a single goal (Truong et al., 2020; Wirkuttis & Klein, 2017). The most frequently employed algorithms in the field of cybersecurity are decision trees, support vector machines, Bayesian algorithms, k-nearest neighbour, random forests, association rule algorithms, ensemble learning, k-means clustering, and principal component analysis (Morovat & Panda, 2020).

- **Deep Learning:** It belongs to a broader class of machine-learning methods that rely on learning representations of data rather than task-specific algorithms. Deep learning is currently used to recognize images more accurately than humans, with a wide range of applications which includes driverless vehicles, scan analysis, and medical diagnosis (Truong et al., 2020; Wirkuttis & Klein, 2017). In the cybersecurity field, common deep learning (DL) methods include feed forward neural networks, convolutional neural networks, recurrent neural networks, deep belief networks, stacking autoencoders, generative adversarial networks, constrained Boltzmann machines, and ensembles of DL networks (Morovat & Panda, 2020).

- **Neural networks:** It uses a programming model that draws inspiration from biology to provide machines with the ability to learn from observational data. Each node in a neural network gives its input a weight that reflects how accurate or inaccurate it is for the operation being carried out. The sum of such weights determines the final output

(Truong et al., 2020; Wirkuttis & Klein, 2017). In the cybersecurity arena, the following techniques are most widely used: genetic algorithms, evolution strategies, ant colony optimization, particle swarm optimization, and artificial immune systems (Morovat & Panda, 2020).

- **Expert systems:** It is intended to tackle difficulties in specific domains. Expert systems solve issues and make judgments by emulating the thinking of human experts utilizing fuzzy rules-based reasoning and carefully curated libraries of knowledge (Truong et al., 2020; Wirkuttis & Klein, 2017). Expert systems can provide real-time monitoring in cybersecurity domains. In the event of a malicious intrusion, security expert systems produce a warning message and pertinent information, allowing security experts to choose appropriate security solutions (Morovat & Panda, 2020).

## 3.1 AI-Based Tool for the Cyber Security

### 3.1.1 Cyber Security Tool Kit (CyberSecTK)

CyberSecTK is a freely distributed python library for building the tools needed for processing and high-quality data extraction related to cyber-security. It aims to bridge between cyber security and technical divide. For cyber-security experts to create a technique from scratch, they need a collection of software modules, data sets, and tutorials that enable study and education in the field.

### 3.1.2 Sophos Intercept X Tool

A deep learning neural network is used by Intercept X to undertake deep analysis and assess, 20 milliseconds before a file is executed, whether it is safe or malicious. In order to produce highly accurate and zero-day malware and a lower false positive rate, the model is trained on real-world databases and bidirectional threat information sharing using access to millions of samples given by the data scientists.

### 3.1.3 Vectra's Cognito

An AI technology from Vectra called Cognito can analyze and stop attacks on business, IoT, cloud, and data center networks. It gathers network metadata and logs and it employs behavioral detection techniques. In order to reveal hidden attackers in workloads and IoT devices, it further analyzes the events and records them.

## 3.1.4 Targeted Attack Analytics (TAA) by Symantec

The Targeted attack analytics (TAA) tool developed by Symantec comes with cloud-based analytics that automatically adapts to new attack tactics by delivering continuous attack detections, plus the ongoing addition of new attack analytics. The business used the tool to safeguard against the Dragonfly 2.0 attack which targeted many energy firms in 2017 and aimed to get access to their networks.

## 3.1.5 BioHAIFCS

A framework termed "bio-inspired Hybrid Artificial Intelligence Framework for Cyber Security" (bioHAIFCS) combines timely and bio-inspired machine learning methodologies appropriate for the defense of vital network applications, such as military information systems. It includes a Hybrid Evolving Spiking Anomaly Detection Model (HESADM), which is used to successfully stop cyberattacks that passive firewalls cannot protect against. The Evolutionary Prevention System against SQL Injection (ePSSQLI) attacks, as well as the Evolving Computational Intelligence System for Malware Detection (ECISMD).

## 3.1.6 IBM QRadar Advisor

IBM's QRadar Advisor defends against online threats by utilizing IBM Watson technology. To continuously investigate signs of any compromise or exploitation, they are deploying AI. The cognitive reasoning of QRadar Advisor provides crucial insights and speeds up the reaction cycle. Security analysts can analyze threat situations and lower the likelihood of missing them with its assistance. It cuts down the number of times needed to examine incidents from days to weeks to just a few minutes or hours.

# 4. APPLICATIONS OF AI IN CYBER SECURITY

## 4.1 Detection of a New Threat

Cybersecurity is one of the fields in which the application of Artificial Intelligence has numerous benefits. When combined with machine learning, AI can help to automate threat identification and response more efficiently than traditional software-driven or manual operations. AI systems are trained to detect various malware, perform pattern recognition, and recognize even the tiniest characteristics of malware or ransomware attacks before they enter the system using complex algorithms. With natural language processing, AI enables higher predictive intelligence by scraping through articles, news, and cyber threat studies on its own. It can provide information on new intrusions, cyber-attacks, and preventative methods (Belani, 2021). Threats are identified using attack indications or signatures in conventional security tools. This approach is efficient for detecting previously identified threats. However, signature-based methods cannot detect newly found threats. With the use of behavior analysis, AI can enhance threat detection. For example, by evaluating the data from endpoints, you can create profiles for each application within your organization's network (Veiga, 2018).

## 4.2 Breach Risk Prediction

Data breaches may alter the overall trajectory of life rather than just being a momentary source of dread. Sensitive information exposure can impact people, businesses, and governments. Hackers can access you via the internet, Bluetooth, text messages, or the online services you use, whether you are online or offline. Without due care, a little flaw could result in a significant data breach. A data breach can affect everyone, including individuals to, high-level organizations, and governments. More significantly, if they are not protected, anyone can endanger others. There are more possibilities for data to be compromised as our computers and mobile devices gain more connected capabilities. Technology is developing faster than we can safeguard it (*What Is a Data Breach & How to Prevent One*, n.d.).

AI in data security can assist in forecasting the timing of a breach as well as a range of anticipated damage costs and the components of those expenses. It can provide individuals and groups within corporations with faster and more precise benchmarking forecasts and projected losses of cyber occurrences. Before an AI solution can effectively anticipate and quantify the possibility of a breach and how it would impact a business, it must first grasp what a company looks like.

AI can estimate the likelihood of a breach or hack using a random forest model. The random forest model' is built up of many decision trees, each with a branch — and questions that the program asks at each junction within the decision tree are based on the characteristics of previously breached companies (*AI in Cyber Security: Predicting and Quantifying the Threat*, n.d.).

## 4.3 Better Endpoint Solution

The shift to remote and hybrid work modes has altered business IT infrastructures, pushing corporate endpoints beyond the corporate network and perimeter-based security. Organizations require Endpoint security solutions to recognize and prevent the threats before they endanger the business because endpoints are now their first line of defense against cyberattacks. Endpoint security entails monitoring and safeguarding endpoints against cyberattacks. Desktops, laptops, smartphones, tablets, and other gadgets are examples of protected endpoints (*What Is Endpoint Protection? - Check Point Software*, n.d.). Organizations require more knowledge and understanding than traditional endpoint protection provides because the quantity, nature, and sophistication of attacks change. Threat actors are increasingly focusing on user-created vulnerabilities and poor cybersecurity awareness. The rapid proliferation of endpoint devices such as smartphones, tablets, wearable devices, and others has impacted first-generation endpoint protection. A security team that relies on conventional cybersecurity measures may run out of resources due to the growing number of potentially exposed endpoints. Next-generation endpoint security provides more comprehensive and adaptable protection than traditional endpoint security solutions by leveraging modern artificial intelligence (AI), machine learning, and tighter integration of network and device security. In order to examine executables, it combines real-time analysis of the user's and system's activity. Thus, it enables users to quickly identify fileless "zero-day" threats and core sophisticated technologies before and during execution.

Using artificial intelligence (AI) and machine learning, next-generation endpoint protection software can provide the following features that traditional endpoint protection cannot:

- Identifying unauthorized user, application, or network service activities
- Preventing suspicious actions from being carried out
- ML and AI-based data processing to detect harmful files or processes
- Preventing illegal data transfer

- Using isolated "sandboxes" to analyze dubious app data
- Restoring data and endpoints to a previous state after a ransomware attack
- Identifying and isolating suspicious endpoints and processes
- Providing endpoint detection and mitigation capabilities that can continually monitor networks and systems to reduce sophisticated threats (*What Is Next-Generation Endpoint Security? | Trellix*, n.d.)

## 4.4 Spam Filtration

Spam is the type of undesired, unsolicited digital information that delivers in vast numbers. In addition to SMS, phone calls, and social networking platforms, attackers can also send spam via emails. Since the attacker sends spam emails in bulk, it takes more time to filter out the specific emails you want from your inbox and consumes a lot of system space and communication bandwidth. In addition to protecting users' data from spammers, effective spam filters can prevent users from engaging in online fraud. Spam filtering is a method to distinguish between necessary and spam emails to save time and effort (Khandelwal & Bhargava, 2021).

The main feature a spam filtering solution must possess, it should consistently prevent spam from entering a person's mailbox while also avoiding misrepresenting harmless business communication. Among other methods, AI is an effective method for spam protection. To define AI is the "capability of machines to think like humans and perform smart tasks without being specifically programmed to do so." It plays a crucial role in identifying and preventing undesired spam messages (*The Importance of AI Spam Filtering - Cii Technology Solutions*, n.d.).

The key features of AI in spam detection and filtration area:

i.   Keyword and content-based filtering: It includes the formation of rules, evaluation of keywords allocation, and frequency to filter spam emails. Techniques such as Neural networks, naive Bayesian classification, k-nearest neighbor (kNN), and other methods of machine learning are employed.

ii.  Similarity-based filtering: In this case, the kiln is used to classify emails depending on whether they are comparable to previously saved emails. New instances will be mapped as pointers based on email characteristics for upcoming emails.

iii. Sample-based filtering: In this method, machine learning algorithms get trained to detect whether new emails are genuine, or spam based on training data gathered from sample emails. Sample emails contain both legitimate and spam emails.

iv. Adaptive email spam filtering: Spam emails are classified in this procedure, and each category gets represented by a token or symbolic text. These collections of sample texts are composed of words, sentences, and even nonsensical strings. Based on its closeness to tokens or representative text, incoming email is categorized as spam or not spam (Dada et al., 2019).

## 4.5 Fraud Detection

Digitalization makes it easier for us to complete our daily tasks. We buy products online, pay our bills with banking apps, get insurance with a few clicks, and so on. On the contrary, online platforms provide thieves with anonymity. Due to greater anonymity, online fraudsters have a lower chance of being caught even when they make huge profits from fraud. As a result of its enhanced efficiency, artificial intelligence has emerged as a crucial instrument for combating major fraud. It can analyze large amounts of transactions to find fraud trends that help to detect and prevent fraud in real-time. AI models can be used to evaluate the probability of fraud, reject transactions, outright if it is suspected, or flag them for more investigation when the fraud has occurred. Thus, it allows investigators to concentrate their attention on the most promising cases. Using AI models to combat fraud is more effective than manually detecting and preventing it because it facilitates efficient data interpretation. Interpreting a large sample size is vital for fraud detection since larger datasets give better insights into client preferences, behaviour, and fraud patterns (*How Is AI Used in Fraud Detection? | Analytics Steps*, n.d.).

AI offers four key techniques to detect and prevent fraud. They are:

i. Integration of Supervised and Unsupervised AI/ML models:

A supervised model, which is the most common sort of machine learning throughout all fields, is a model that has been trained using a large number of accurately labelled transactions. Each transaction is either classified as fraudulent or not fraudulent. These models get trained by collecting massive amounts of labelled transaction data to uncover patterns that best depict legitimate activity.

Unsupervised models are designed to detect unexpected behavior when labelled transaction information is limited or non-existent. As a result, unsupervised models may seem to be better at recognizing new sorts of fraud schemes. These models discover behavioral anomalies by detecting transactions that deviate from the norm. Therefore, an organization can improve its defence against fraud by merging supervised and unsupervised AI/ML models.

ii.  The application of behavioral analytics:

In behavioral analytics, machine learning is implemented to evaluate and predict the behavior at the micro level across all parts of a transaction. The data is monitored by using profiles that reflect the habits of each user, merchant, account, and device. Companies can detect whether the transaction is fraudulent by examining data about how much money customers spend, where they spend it, the items, or services they tend to buy, the areas where they make transactions, and so on. When a customer's spending habits are out of the ordinary, the business may inform the customer, request more verification before continuing the transaction, or refuse the transaction altogether if the calculated risk is too high.

iii.  Creating Models from Large Datasets:

Each transaction possibly increases the size of the dataset. It is critical to keep data from multiple intervals to version the data and verify the performance of the ML model. When fraudsters invent a new fraud strategy, it is critical to incorporate it into the supervised ML model for the algorithm to become immune to novel frauds.

iv.  AI Self-Learning and Adaptive Analytics

Adaptive analytics is a type of predictive analytics in which real-time data is collected and analyzed rather than existing data. Some current fraud detection techniques are becoming outdated as fraudsters discover new ways to manipulate systems. In this context, it makes sense to prioritize particular fraud schemes based on current patterns. An efficient tool in this approach is adaptive analytics.

Similarly, data versioning can be an efficient method for emphasizing newer fraud techniques. Organizations could more effectively deploy resources against present fraud trends by removing outdated historical data that is no longer relevant (*How AI Can Improve Fraud Detection & Prevention in 2022?*, n.d.).

## 4.6 Malware Analysis and Incident Responses

Malware is malicious software that attempts to implement unauthorized commands on the target system. The malware can remotely access data, resulting in severe consequences for the victim. Malware is a growing problem with the increasing technology, but the process and plan for malware hunting are not enough due to the polymorphic nature of mutant malware (*GAVS Technologies | IT Process and Digital Transformation Solutions Powered by AIOps*, n.d.). In order to keep up with the continually changing nature of crimeware, malware detection technologies must constantly change. The transition from trapping to hunting is one of the most significant changes in malware detection. Threat trapping uses models of malicious behavior, such as signatures, to identify malware. Threat hunting uses good-behavior models to proactively look for suspicious and harmful activities that do not meet the models. Because advanced malware is so complex, it can easily circumvent security solutions that rely on bad-behavior models, such as signatures, this transition from trapping to hunting, or from bad-behavior to good-behavior modelling, is required.

Modern malware authors are very skilled at producing limited- or single-use malware that never gets noticed by vendors who make signatures. Conventional detection technologies that rely on bad-behavior models are considered worthless without signatures. They are incapable of detecting advanced malware. It is hard to develop reliable malware detection tools based on good-behavior modelling. A massive amount of data must be collected and analyzed. This never-ending task not only demands access to the data but also a tremendous amount of computing power. Behaviours are constantly evolving. Hence, behavior modelling is an ongoing process. It is never complete and quickly becomes outdated. It would be nearly hard to perform each of these good-behavior modelling tasks manually. However, AI, or machine learning, is particularly well adapted to this task. Artificial Intelligence never gets tired and has enormous scaling capabilities to handle large datasets. It can generate a basis for testing normal behaviour automatically (Vigna, 2020).

The key features of AI in malware analysis and incident response:

- It automates good-behavior modelling.
- It eliminates false positives.
- It combines bad behavior modelling with good behavior modelling.
- It drastically decreases reliance on humans.
- It reacts quickly to critical events.
- It classifies malware and analyses risks.

- It encourages better process management (*AI in Cybersecurity: Incident Response Automation Opportunities*, n.d.).

## 4.7 Vulnerability Management

Security professionals give top priority to vulnerabilities. Security teams are racing against the clock to identify, evaluate, and repair vulnerabilities before adversaries can exploit them. Due to the increasing number of risks and the lack of security personnel, conventional vulnerability management methods and techniques are useless. Due to the increasing number of risks and the lack of security personnel, conventional vulnerability management methods and techniques are useless. During vulnerability assessments, the environment is examined for obsolete or otherwise unpatched software and other exposure points. Traditionally, vulnerability assessment tools were used by security teams; however, older solutions are ineffective in remote environments, particularly hybrid setups with mobile and IoT devices. However, advanced attack vectors like phishing and credential problems are not considered by traditional vulnerability tools. The vulnerabilities are not prioritized in legacy solutions. It is up to security professionals to judge the severity of the vulnerabilities (*Is AI-Based Vulnerability Management Really That Efficient?*, n.d.).

Artificial intelligence, notably machine learning, analyses data in real time and prioritizes vulnerabilities based on risk levels. Threat and vulnerability management features in AI-powered solutions can scan and anticipate risk across hundreds of attack vectors and threats.

Application of AI techniques in vulnerability management includes:

- Enhancements to threat-detecting capabilities: Artificial intelligence (AI) technologies are helpful for identifying which assets are crucial to the business and require better protection. The system may compare various assets, creating a baseline of normalcy and highlighting unusual assets.
- Minimizing false positives in vulnerability detection: AI technology is used by security teams to determine the likelihood that the identified vulnerability is legit. The systems consider which detection mechanism flagged the vulnerabilities and also other variables.
- Contextual vulnerability risk assessment: It permits the creation of an accurate risk score by considering an in-depth understanding of an asset's context.

For example, it may detect if a potentially vulnerable asset gets disconnected from the network.

- Finding trends in vulnerability exploitation using sentiment analysis: Artificial intelligence (AI) technologies can gather data from social media platforms and cybersecurity chat rooms, evaluate it, and identify patterns in vulnerabilities to be exploited. The ability to recognize positive/negative sentiments and decipher the meaning of the text to assess risk is made feasible by AI techniques like neural networks and natural language processing.
- Enhancing remediation: Organizations can use context-driven list of vulnerabilities provided by AI technology to create remediation plan recommendations. It provides security teams with information about risk and vulnerability rankings that enhance remediation (*Vulnerability Management and Remediation: Leveraging AI to Modernize Your Program? | Secureworks*, n.d.).

## 4.8 Application Security

Application security refers to security controls used at the application level to protect data or code from being stolen or hijacked. It encompasses the protection of web, thick client, and mobile apps as they progress through the security development life cycle, including security design and secure coding (Maraju, 2018). Application security is crucial since current apps are frequently accessed through several networks and linked to the cloud, increasing their susceptibility to security breaches and threats. There is increasing demand and incentive to ensure network security and application security. The fact is that hackers are targeting apps with their attacks more frequently now than in the past (Curphey & Arawo, 2006; Enck et al., 2011). To improve application security, numerous AI domains, such as machine learning and expert systems, can be utilized to derive, anticipate, or apply inferences to foresee security risks, detect security vulnerabilities, and find security code corrective suggestions. These strategies can help security auditors automates the identification of attack threats and review code. The procedure entails creating multiple decision support and inference rules for different application security flaws, applying the rules to expert systems, and instructing the same systems using an algorithm with a wide range of application security attack scenarios and attack paths.

The following sub-fields of AI that is in use for application security:

- Decision-tree learning (DTL) in machine learning for threat identification.
- Code review guidance and security code review using expert systems—forward and backward chaining.

i.    DTL in machine learning for threat identification

DTL is a deductive learning technique that develops a generalizable hypothesis using a training set of instances. Additionally, it chooses the most advantageous attack routes (threats). A collection of training instances gets divided into smaller subsets, and a corresponding decision tree gets built gradually. Following the completion of the learning process, a decision tree comprising the training set develops.

ii.   Code review guidance and security code review using expert systems—forward and backward chaining.

Expert systems may interpret the information, advise, and derive a solution. Additionally, they offer potential solutions to the issue and forecast outcomes. An expert system consists of two parts: a knowledge base and an inference engine. The forward chaining - security code review inference engine can be used to forecast values, i.e., to deduce what might happen next. It will aid security code review engines in determining the nature of the attack. To diagnose the values, that is, determine what happened, one can utilize the Application security remediation guidance expert system with backward chaining. This expert system for application security remediation guidance assists the developer in determining various sub-goals (solutions) to resolve the vulnerabilities (Al-Ajlan, 2015).

# 5. LIMITATIONS OF AI IN CYBERSECURITY

Technology can be super simple or electronic complex. But every technology has its limits. Some limitations of application of AI in cybersecurity are shown in Figure 4.

*Figure 4. Limitations of AI in cybersecurity*

| | |
|---|---|
| **(1) ETHICALITY OF AI IN CYBER SECURITY** | • Hackers are the finest in the world at technology maturity. These people are seated in front of computers, recording data and performing complex analytics to find any opening or weakness they may exploit. There are advantages and disadvantages of using AI in cybersecurity. It is basically a competition to see who can create an algorithm that responds better to the data that is being shared online. In this regard, the employment of AI poses a serious security risk. Another problem is that, while a corporation studies and learns from data to identify dangers, a hacker studies the organization's cyber-defence procedures and policies to look for "open doors" that would allow it to carry out the intended assault. |
| **(2) SECRECY OF DATA** | • AI algorithms include the examination of massive volume of data, which is essential for the created algorithms to deliver reliable results. In addition to routine traffic from everyday transactions and operations, a company's data also includes sensitive customer information, such as biometric data and personal data. But when our data is sent to the AI agent, what is the secrecy of data? When using AI for cybersecurity purposes, data protection is crucial. No excuse should be given for jeopardising the confidentiality of the clients' data. |
| **(3) URGENCY OF DATA** | • Cybersecurity is an area that is continually changing, with new threats and assaults appearing periodically. In present, significant instances include browser-in-browser assaults and increasingly sophisticated ransomware operations. The AI programme requires data to do the correct training in order to detect assaults later on. The number of data needed to respond quickly to an assault will likely increase due to the more dynamic environment created by threats that are constantly appearing and changing. This approach to cybersecurity has many drawbacks, including the inability of AI to keep up with the exponential expansion of data and the lack of data available for the AI-algorithm to provide results. |

Limitations of AI in Cyber Security

# 6. CONCLUSION

In the digital age, cyber security has grown to be a big concern. Data breaches, identity theft, captcha cracking, and other similar issues frequently harm millions of people as well as corporations. Inventing the proper rules and processes and putting them into practise with pinpoint accuracy to combat cyberattacks and crimes has always been a problem. Recent advances in artificial intelligence have significantly increased the danger of cyberattacks and other crimes. In a variety of modern cyber security applications, efforts have been made to use artificial intelligence (AI) approaches. Instantaneous insights from artificial intelligence (AI) allow users to cut through the din of the hundreds of security warnings they get each day. Cybersecurity and artificial intelligence overlap in a variety of transdisciplinary fields (AI). On the one hand, deep learning and other AI technologies may be used in cyber security to build intelligent models for malware categorization, intrusion detection, and threat intelligence sensing. On the other hand, AI models will be exposed to a variety of cyber-attacks, which will interfere with its decision-making, learning, and sampling. Therefore, particular cyber security defence and protection solutions are required for AI models in order to counter adversarial machine learning, safeguard machine learning privacy, secure federated learning, etc.

# 7. FUTURE ASPECTS

In the future, AI will be crucial to cybersecurity. There are more data generated with the increasing numbers of cyber risks. Currently, Artificial intelligence aids in the process, that happens automatically and quickly over the human analysts complete a lot of duties solitary. AI can help in enhancing cyberattack defenses by predicting them and acting more quickly than humans.

The future of AI in cyber security will be follow:

1.   AI technologies would be used to detect security incidents on large scale.
2.   Firewalls using machine learning technology to detect anomalies.
3.   NLP (Natural Language Processing) techniques would be utilized to trace the source of cyberattacks.
4.   Automating rule-based procedures and tasks using RPA (Robotic Process Automation) bots
5.   Monitoring and investigating cyber threats on mobile endpoints.
6.   More secure transaction of net banking
7.   Prevention and investigation of Fraud in Credit and debit card.
8.   Make the more secure wireless devices by using the AI.
9.   Reduce the networks' vulnerability to prevent cyber threat.
10.  Boost the recovery rate of a cyber-attack.

AI will make the cyber security tool more sophisticated and more accurate in future and also the rate of false positive detection will be decreased in future. Risks are identified and analyzed, and information is also provided to analysts to assist in better decision-making. Deep Learning networks and machine learning algorithms would be use to improve AI over the time. It would be managed future threats that are more complex in nature.

The tasks of monitoring the website's security are generally assign to cybersecurity specialists. Human dominance over everything and its overall decision-making on cybersecurity restricts the scope of AI involvement in security matters. It becomes challenging to take a break for professionals during continuous process. On the other hand, AI can manage similar circumstances without pause since it is designed to handle high-risk situations without at problem.

# ACKNOWLEDGMENT

Authors are grateful to Dr. Kapil Kumar, Associate Professor, Department of Biochemistry & Forensic Science, Gujarat University, Ahmedabad, India, for his constant guidance, motivation and technical supports.

# REFERENCES

*AI in cyber security: predicting and quantifying the threat.* (n.d.). Retrieved November 29, 2022, from https://www.information-age.com/ai-in-cyber-security-predicting-quantifying-13818/

*AI in Cybersecurity: Incident Response Automation Opportunities.* (n.d.). Retrieved November 29, 2022, from https://www.sisainfosec.com/blogs/ai-in-cybersecurity-incident-response-automation-opportunities/

Al-Ajlan, A. (2015). The comparison between forward and backward chaining. *International Journal of Machine Learning and Computing, 5*(2), 106–113. doi:10.7763/IJMLC.2015.V5.492

Belani, G. (2021). *The Use of Artificial Intelligence in Cybersecurity: A Review.* Https://Www. Computer. Org/Publications/Tech-News/Trends/the-Use-Ofartificial-Intelligence-in-Cybersecurity

Benko, A., & Lányi, C. S. (2009). History of artificial intelligence. In *Encyclopedia of Information Science and Technology* (2nd ed., pp. 1759–1762). IGI Global. doi:10.4018/978-1-60566-026-4.ch276

Chan, L., Morgan, I., Simon, H., Alshabanat, F., Ober, D., Gentry, J., Min, D., & Cao, R. (2019). Survey of AI in Cybersecurity for Information Technology Management. *2019 IEEE Technology & Engineering Management Conference (TEMSCON)*, 1–8. doi:10.1109/TEMSCON.2019.8813605

Curphey, M., & Arawo, R. (2006). Web application security assessment tools. *IEEE Security and Privacy, 4*(4), 32–41. doi:10.1109/MSP.2006.108

Dada, E. G., Bassi, J. S., Chiroma, H., Abdulhamid, S. M., Adetunmbi, A. O., & Ajibuwa, O. E. (2019). Machine learning for email spam filtering: Review, approaches and open research problems. *Heliyon, 5*(6), e01802. Advance online publication. doi:10.1016/j.heliyon.2019.e01802 PMID:31211254

Enck, W., Octeau, D., McDaniel, P. D., & Chaudhuri, S. (2011). A study of android application security. *USENIX Security Symposium, 2*(2).

*GAVS Technologies | IT Process and Digital Transformation Solutions Powered by AIOps.* (n.d.). Retrieved November 29, 2022, from https://www.gavstech.com/

*How AI Can Improve Fraud Detection & Prevention in 2022?* (n.d.). Retrieved November 29, 2022, from https://research.aimultiple.com/ai-fraud-detection/

*How Does Artificial Intelligence Work? | CSU Global.* (n.d.). Retrieved November 28, 2022, from https://csuglobal.edu/blog/how-does-ai-actually-work

*How is AI used in Fraud Detection? | Analytics Steps.* (n.d.). Retrieved November 29, 2022, from https://analyticssteps.com/blogs/how-ai-used-fraud-detection

*Is AI-Based Vulnerability Management Really that Efficient?* (n.d.). Retrieved November 29, 2022, from https://aithority.com/machine-learning/is-ai-based-vulnerability-management-really-that-efficient/

Jouini, M., Rabai, L. B. A., & Aissa, A. (2014). Classification of security threats in information systems. *Procedia Computer Science*, *32*, 489–496. doi:10.1016/j.procs.2014.05.452

Khandelwal, Y., & Bhargava, R. (2021). Spam Filtering Using AI. *Artificial Intelligence and Data Mining Approaches in Security Frameworks*, 87–99.

Maraju, K. (2018). *Applying AI in Application Security.* https://www.isaca.org/resources/isaca-journal/issues/2018/volume-1/applying-ai-in-application-security

Mccarthy, J. (2007). *What is artificial intelligence?* http://www-formal.stanford.edu/jmc/

McCorduck, P., Minsky, M., Selfridge, O. G., & Simon, H. A. (1977). History of artificial intelligence. *IJCAI (United States)*, 951–954.

Morovat, K., & Panda, B. (2020). A Survey of Artificial Intelligence in Cybersecurity. *2020 International Conference on Computational Science and Computational Intelligence (CSCI)*, 109–115. 10.1109/CSCI51800.2020.00026

Nielsen, M. A. (2015). Neural networks and deep learning (Vol. 25). Determination Press.

*The Importance of AI Spam Filtering - Cii Technology Solutions*. (n.d.). Retrieved November 29, 2022, from https://ciinc.com/the-importance-of-ai-spam-filtering/

Toosi, A., Bottino, A. G., Saboury, B., Siegel, E., & Rahmim, A. (2021). A brief history of AI: How to prevent another winter (a critical review). *PET Clinics*, *16*(4), 449–469. doi:10.1016/j.cpet.2021.07.001 PMID:34537126

Truong, T. C., Zelinka, I., Plucar, J., Čandík, M., & Šulc, V. (2020). Artificial intelligence and cybersecurity: Past, presence, and future. In *Artificial intelligence and evolutionary computations in engineering systems* (pp. 351–363). Springer. doi:10.1007/978-981-15-0199-9_30

Ullah, F., Naeem, H., Jabbar, S., Khalid, S., Latif, M. A., Al-Turjman, F., & Mostarda, L. (2019). Cyber security threats detection in internet of things using deep learning approach. *IEEE Access : Practical Innovations, Open Solutions*, *7*, 124379–124389. doi:10.1109/ACCESS.2019.2937347

Veiga, A. P. (2018). *Applications of artificial intelligence to network security*. ArXiv Preprint ArXiv:1803.09992.

Vigna, G. (2020). *How AI will help in the fight against malware*. Retrieved from TechBeacon.

*Vulnerability Management and Remediation: Leveraging AI to Modernize your Program? | Secureworks*. (n.d.). Retrieved November 29, 2022, from https://www.secureworks.com/resources/wp-the-role-of-ai-in-modernizing-vulnerability-management

*What is a Data Breach & How to Prevent One*. (n.d.). Retrieved November 29, 2022, from https://www.kaspersky.com/resource-center/definitions/data-breach

*What is Endpoint Protection? - Check Point Software*. (n.d.). Retrieved November 29, 2022, from https://www.checkpoint.com/cyber-hub/threat-prevention/what-is-endpoint-security/

*What Is Next-Generation Endpoint Security? | Trellix*. (n.d.). Retrieved November 29, 2022, from https://www.trellix.com/en-us/security-awareness/endpoint/what-is-next-gen-endpoint-protection.html

Wirkuttis, N., & Klein, H. (2017). Artificial intelligence in cybersecurity. *Cyber, Intelligence, and Security*, *1*(1), 103–119.

Chapter 3
# AI Applications in Cybersecurity:
## Worldwide and Saudi Arabia Focus

**Ahmad Fahad Aljuryyed**
*Robert Morris University, USA*

**Sulaiman Sami Refaee**
*University of Jeddah, Saudi Arabia*

**Nawaf Ahmed Almufarriji**
*University of Jeddah, Saudi Arabia*

**Naif Ayub Hussain**
*University of Jeddah, Saudi Arabia*

**Rayan Saadullah Aziz**
*King Abdulaziz University, Saudi Arabia*

## ABSTRACT

*Since the creation of the internet, technology has evolved and continues to mass produce systems that humans can rely on and make their lives more productive. Artificial intelligence (AI) is one of those software as it is a tool that mimics human intelligence to perform tasks that we sometimes find repetitive and time-consuming. Another important use of this technology is the introduction of cybersecurity, which ensures the protection of a user's sensitive data online to prevent unauthorized use. When cybersecurity and AI interlay, an increment of protection shows a tangible result; it assures greater protection against cybercriminals. First, this chapter discusses and introduces terms related to cybersecurity and AI; then it goes on to widely explore multiple methods of how AI tools are being integrated within the*

DOI: 10.4018/978-1-6684-7110-4.ch003

*cybersecurity space, as well as what characteristics of AI pose a threat to the protection that cybersecurity offers. The main idea explored in this chapter is how AI tools are being used to improve and revolutionize the way cybersecurity works worldwide.*

# INTRODUCTION

As the world continues to evolve and change to keep up with the demanding needs of people, so does the internet. Moreover, with the constant evolution of the internet, security measures to protect data and privacy must evolve alongside all other changes to ensure users stay safe and protected online. While there are many ways to ensure user privacy and protection within cyberspace, this chapter looks at one of the most budding areas of improving data protection and privacy by integrating artificial intelligence and cybersecurity.

Artificial intelligence was not always met with open arms within the cybersecurity world due to its disadvantages and history of being used by cybercriminals to hack into and steal valuable information. Still, that view is rapidly changing as many experts and businesses benefit from the immersion of these two technological disciplines.

For example, "Pillsbury—a global law firm focusing on technology—and The Economist Intelligence Unit have noted in a report that 49 percent of world leaders think AI is the best tool to counter nation-state cyberattacks. Widespread machine learning and AI-powered systems across cybersecurity range from anomaly detection algorithms to detect malicious traffic or user behaviors in real-time to algorithms for zero-day malware and spam detection to AI systems prioritizing threats and taking automated remediation actions" (Mavrona & Csernatoni, 2022).

It is becoming increasingly clear that once the integrity of AI is kept, it can do better than harm in cybersecurity. This chapter explores all variables combining cybersecurity and AI, including examples of Artificial Intelligence-based cybersecurity and the main characteristic of AI that poses a cybersecurity threat. Particular emphasis is placed throughout this chapter on the Kingdom of Saudi Arabia and how combining these two technological disciplines benefits cyberspace within that country and emphasizes the positive aspects of collaboration with other countries.

# Cybersecurity and AI Overview

The landscape of cybersecurity is extensive, ranging from individuals to nations, and continuously evolves with new threats and countermeasures. This dynamic nature of cybersecurity makes it challenging to find an objective consensus on a definition. Definitions from a sample of sources include:

I. "The state of being safe from electronic crime and the measures taken to achieve this."
II. "The activity or process, ability or capability, or state whereby information and communications systems and the information contained therein are protected from and defended against damage, unauthorized use or modification, or exploitation."
III. "Cybersecurity is the collection of tools, policies, security concepts, security safeguards, guidelines, risk management approaches, actions, training, best practices, assurance and technologies that can be used to protect the cyber environment and organization and user's assets" (Kavak et al., 2021).

There are different concepts surrounding cybersecurity due to its journey through time; the constant evolution of cybercrimes has, without a doubt, increased the dynamism of cybersecurity. Furthermore, the constant apparencies of these crimes have forced users to be more active in their online protection, using cybersecurity and AI tools.

# AI Ethical Challenges in Cybersecurity

In recent years, Artificial Intelligence has a transformation from a specialized concept in research operations into an important but widely misunderstood technological development. Increased funding and consumer attention to these technologies raised a question about how they can be used. The ethical challenges for AI and Cybersecurity are complex, multifaceted, and enduring; in addition to technical solutions, ethical issues will require a deeper understanding of human nature.

At the same time, new tools for protecting privacy and security have been developed in conjunction with ethical considerations. The main ethical challenge for AI and cybersecurity is the use of data. The technology has come under scrutiny in recent years due to its uses, and ethical questions have been raised regarding how it's affecting privacy.

The greatest ethical challenge in AI is that many of its products are used by companies and governments with capabilities that use them for various purposes. A key aspect of addressing this challenge is understanding when AI is appropriate, how to make it effective, and how to control it. This includes ensuring its use is consistent with its purpose while allowing its benefits to be realized.

Concerning the ethical challenges of Artificial Intelligence, today, there are advanced technical mechanisms for AI that work to collect and analyze various data in intelligent systems related to all aspects of life, beginning with individuals' personal and family information, health and banking information, and ending with individuals' shopping information.

Big data is also accessible via the Internet and other systems in institutions, government organizations, companies, and the commercial sector. As a result, there are several places from which this information might be collected and used in unlawful, ethical, or other ways. Furthermore, no legal framework is presently in place to safeguard the ethical development of AI technology. The following are among the most significant ethical obstacles to artificial intelligence throughout the world:

- Complete distrust of artificial intelligence by many
- Lack of accountability and responsibility
- Lack of data quality
- Some functions have disappeared
- Lack of privacy, especially when using health, security, and other data
- Related security challenges
- Lack of integrity and sometimes data bias
- Possibility of criminal and malicious use
- Loss of freedom and individual autonomy as a result of constant machine surveillance
- Not allowing artificial intelligence systems to access many public and government services
- Reducing human contact, especially in the health field (Stahl, 2021).

Therefore, artificial intelligence ethics are the texts and legislation that enable us to know what is right and wrong while dealing with AI technology. In the first place, there has become an interest in many vital elements that help in the functioning of such legislation, such as the governance and identification of data that feeds smart systems and their ownership, classification, privacy, access, and utilization, as well as the protection and security of that data.

Another critical element in AI ethics is the need for the data used to feed intelligent machines to be high-quality and reliable.

According to Bernard Marr, a best-selling business author, following are some of the main 7 ethical challenges of artificial intelligence that could prove to be roadblocks to certain extents:

**Bias:** AI needs data, and we need to try our best to avoid any kind of biases in the data so that it can train the algorithm of the AI. One exact example to explain this challenge is the ImageNet database. It consists of more white face data as compared to the non-white face. Hence, it does not have a correct balance to give authentic results without any bias. As the result will not work for non-white faces, it shows that this database has a preference that will provide inauthentic results, which is wrong. We should enable the databases to avoid these biases as much as possible and produce accurate data for the AI algorithm to detect.

**Takeover and control of humankind:** Humans have to make the most dominant decisions, meaning that the AI intervention can only be so little. The most accurate example is the international convention where there is the use of an automatic drone. Now think if an automated drone can launch a missile. Then, there needs to be a human decision involved so that there is not much damage without the human element involved in the decision. The control challenge is quite vital. Another example would be the financial trades these days. AI and its algorithm make 90% of these decisions. There is almost no space for other parties, including humans, where AI is in control. In the case of automatic cars, AI is completely involved. It shows that AI control is such a huge ethical challenge that we need to deal with to avoid damages and issues in the future.

**Privacy of data:** Data and AI pose a lot of risks in people's lives. We must know where this data is coming from, where this data can be used, and by whom. An accurate example of the information and privacy leak risk can be the talking Barbie where your kid is talking to it. Other third parties can use the information fed inside the doll. There is a possibility that your data is being sold to other people. Hence, it shows that data privacy is a huge risk or challenge in the case of AI.

**Power balance:** Every megacorporation uses AI, like Amazon, Google, etc. China is a country that focuses on AI strategies quite passionately as the government backs it. It is said that whoever is good at AI has a higher chance of winning the race. So, the most important question arises: how can we bring a balance of power in such a race and competition? Will there be only a few countries ahead and the rest of the world behind? These questions show that we have to ensure that such wealth is distributed equally among the nations.

**Ownership:** Another major challenge of AI is about the one who will take ownership of all the things that are made through AI. People often use AI for the wrong purposes, like fake images, fake text, videos, etc. Then, who will be responsible if such fake things and fake news spread all across the internet? People also use AI for creating music and other arts. In such a situation, intellectual property rights might create a huge debate. Hence, ownership is the most significant concern in the AI trends and world.

**Environmental impacts:** People assume that whatever we are doing on our devices and computers does not have any environmental impact. These companies and cloud infrastructure consume a lot of power. AI training creates 17 times more carbon emissions than the average American in a year. How can we use this power generation to benefit the world and its issues? We should reconsider our priorities regarding AI and environmental safety.

**Inferiority complex:** With AI's power and efficiency, how can we act like a human with such speed and automation? Such superiority makes us feel isolated and disconnected from our essence and power. The increasing automation and AI are almost trying to replace us humans. But we hope it cannot replace us. How can we be beneficial as humans to become irreplaceable in such times? We must try our best to keep ourselves updated with new trends and technologies to work side by side with the latest machines and software's. It will enable us to swiftly transit towards the AI world without getting redundant.

Implementing ethics to AI requires eliminating biases, mending the inferiority complexes in humans regarding AI, creating a balance among the power, and having clarity on the ownership and other such matters that will improve AI and its ethical practices in the industry. *(Erma, Inc 2022).*

Cybersecurity is another important ethical issue that we need to consider. Organizations own personal information about their users and are ethically responsible for protecting that information from hackers. Unfortunately, in several high-profile data breaches, the organizations that have been hacked have had a percentage of the error. So, partial adoption of AI applications in cybersecurity will make the cyber defense even more robust and offer a strategic advantage to malicious users who rely extensively on AI to launch new attacks (CompTIA, 2022).

Ethical design and deployment of AI is the first necessary step in this direction, but more needs to be done, especially when considering state use of AI for cybersecurity purposes. Regulations are needed to ensure responsible behavior, protection of individual rights, and identify legitimate actors and targets" (Taddeo, 2019).

It's important to consider how we can strike a balance between the need for cybersecurity and the need for Artificial Intelligence. For example, how do we identify an organization's ethical obligation to preserve our information or respect our privacy, and how do we hold them accountable?

The most significant for all is step is to respect privacy as an end in itself. The moral belief that humans have intrinsic value and dignity underpins the notion that they deserve privacy. People with dignity have the right to privacy in person and online. Acting or thinking otherwise would be a violation of our most fundamental moral standards. This is the beginning point for a series of ethical discussions that should take place. We may never find a solution that pleases everyone. Still, at the very least, we will be asking the right questions and moving in the right direction: greater safety, security, and privacy for all of us.

## THE INTEGRATION AND INTERSECTIONS BETWEEN CYBERSECURITY AND AI

Many organizations are getting used to relying on AI-powered solutions and models in order to assist them in defending their networks; AI and its use in the context of achieving efficient cybersecurity goals have become an essential factor to organizations to identify cyber threats quickly; this way, they can disrupt these attacks and assist in detecting malicious patterns.

Cybersecurity and AI work together to achieve any organization's goals; it is worth mentioning that many areas need to be clarified linked to AI and what it can do in the cybersecurity context.

Advancements in cybersecurity technology have led to an increase in the number of complexes cyberattacks, threats, and vulnerabilities. AI advancements can help address complex security challenges. The technology allows data to be analyzed based on its attributes without the need for human intervention or even provides security personnel with better insights into what is happening on the network. Additionally, malicious pattern recognition and predictive intelligence in AI systems make it possible to identify aberrant activity before it causes harm to the system. The impact of AI in cybersecurity is clear and growing every day as attackers and malicious entities are continuously looking for vulnerabilities in the systems. However, the knowledge, human factor, and skill set required to utilize AI effectively will continue to be essential to organizations' success.

Today, many organizations have started integrating artificial intelligence into their cybersecurity practices to help manage a growing range of cybersecurity risks and technical challenges. According to Pupillo et al. (2021), AI can help security teams by improving a system's robustness, resilience and response. Is also with mentioning that according to market research firm Research and Markets, AI in cybersecurity market was 8.6 billion in 2019, which will reach 101.8 billion in 2030 (N. Kshetri, 2021).

System robustness-which is delegating to the machines the process of verification and validation, implies that AI can perform anomaly detection and profiling of anything that is generically different. Robustness can also be enhanced by incorporating AI in the system's development to increase security controls, for example, via vulnerability assessment and scanning.

Code review is another area of application for enhancing system robustness. Peer code review is a standard best practice in software engineering where source code is reviewed manually by one or more peers (reviewers) of the code author. There is a downside to human code reviews. There is a high degree of subjectivity, a study found that only 13% of pull requests are rejected due to technical reasons (Zanaty et al., 2018). Hence, Automating the process using AI systems can reduce time and allow more bugs to be discovered than ones discovered manually. Teams might get more actionable insights, analytics, and functionality by using AI code review or machine learning approaches that are not achievable without such algorithms. Some tools are already available (e.g., DeepCode, CodeGuru, etc.).

Automating the process using AI systems can reduce time and allow more bugs to be discovered than ones discovered manually.

When a system resists and tolerate an attack with a strategy of facilitating anomaly detection and threat is called system resilience. It implies some fundamental shift in the core actions of the systems, unlike system robustness, and this adapts to the new environment.

System response refers to enhancing the capacity of a system to react autonomously to attacks, identify vulnerabilities in other machines, operate strategically by deciding which vulnerability to attack and at which point, and launch more aggressive counterattacks.

With the continuous growth of new unique malwares every day, classification of recent threats by humans alone is becoming impossible while threats are becoming more complicated and better dissimulated. In the past, signatures were commonly used to classify malicious attacks, leveraging databases of known threats. However, such measures are becoming considerably less effective against the latest strains of advanced malware.

AI solutions for cybersecurity enable a fundamental shift from a signature-based detection to a more flexible and continuous network monitoring as it shifts from its normal behaviors. In addition, AI creates real-time, customer-specific analysis, improving the percentage of malware identified and reducing false positives. Hence, AI data processing helps cybersecurity threat intelligence become more effective.

AI can facilitate attack responses by deploying, for example, semi-autonomous lures that create a copy of the environment the attackers intend to infiltrate. These deceive them and help them understand the payloads (the attack components responsible for executing an activity to harm the target). AI solutions can also segregate networks dynamically to isolate assets in controlled areas of the network or redirect an attack away from valuable data (Pupillo et al., 2021).

With powerful automation, individuals can manage the complexity of operations and the scale of information to be utilized to secure cyberspace. Nonetheless, technology and software with traditional fixed implementations are difficult to build (hardwired decision-making logic) to safeguard against security threats. This condition can be dealt with using machine simplicity and learning methods in AI (Das & Sandhane, 2021).

As a result, businesses and industries have already embraced AI systems. Given that AI can thoroughly read and analyze unstructured data, statistics, voice patterns, and words, in addition to quickly scrolling through standardized data. Therefore, it can readily save time and money.

Businesses nowadays are faced with a wide range of cybersecurity challenges. It might be challenging to recognize and prevent these attacks. Cybersecurity experts have lately developed security models and made predictions using AI models to address these challenges.

AI models come in a wide variety; some work better to solve cybersecurity problems than others. Hence, it is important to relate that AI models can help strengthen any cybersecurity action plan.

Logistic Regression is a statistical AI model that provides binary results to predict the probability of events by considering historical data points.

A Decision Tree is also an AI model, which is the easiest to implement as it does not require data normalization to solve many cybersecurity issues. Decision Trees can help intrusion detection systems (IDS) to understand signatures and classify events in the network. One last model is Support Vector Machines (SVM) which is a widely used model among data scientists, as it offers a robust capacity for data classification that can be used to classify malware and benign software as an application in cybersecurity (EasyDmarc, 2022).

Based on the above two aspects, we review the intersection of AI and cyber security. There is a wide variety of interdisciplinary intersections between cybersecurity and artificial intelligence. For example, suppose you take deep learning, which subsets to machine learning, and at the same time, its subsets to AI technologies. In that case, it can be introduced into cybersecurity to construct smart models for implementing malware classification, intrusion detection, and threatening intelligence sense.

AI models need a specific cybersecurity protection method that involves the technology to fight adversarial machine learning since it will face several cyberthreats, which will interrupt their sample, learning and decisions.

Cyberspace security has imposed tremendous impacts on various critical infrastructures. Traditional security relies on the static control of security devices deployed on unique edges or nodes, such as firewalls, intrusion detection systems (IDSs), and intrusion prevention systems (IPSs), for network security monitoring according to the pre-specified rules. However, this passive defense methodology is no longer helpful in protecting systems against new cyber security threats, such as advanced persistent threats (APTs) and zero-day attacks.

Advanced Persistent Threats (APTs) are among the most dangerous cyberattacks. The term "APT" refers to a persistent, multi-stage attack that aims to compromise the target system and obtain information from it. It can cause significant physical harm and considerable financial loss. Currently, the problem of detecting APT attacks still faces many challenges. APT attacks are designed specifically for each target, so it is difficult to detect them based on experiences or predefined rules. Many different methods are researched and applied to detect early signs of APT attacks in an organization *(Cho, Lai, et al. 2020)*.

Using AI for detecting APT is one of the most efficient methods. Several artificial intelligence models to detect APTs, like a stacked autoencoder, a recurrent neural network, and a one-class state vector machine, show significant improvements in detection in the data exfiltration stage. According to APT-2020's authors, current models have the most considerable challenge specific to this stage. Den Helder introduced a method to successfully detect data exfiltration by analyzing the payload of the network traffic flow. Helder's flow-based deep packet inspection approach improves detection compared to other state-of-the-art methods (A. Dijk, 2021).

Moreover, as cyber threats become ubiquitous and sustainable, the diverse attack entry points, high-level intrusion modes, and systematic attack tools reduce the cost of cyber threat deployment. To maximize the security level of core system assets, it is urgent to develop innovative and intelligent security defense methodologies that can cope with diversified and sustainable threats. To implement new cyber security defense and protection, the system should obtain the history and current security state data and make intelligent decisions that can provide adaptive security management and control.

"Artificial intelligence is a fast-growing branch of computer science that researches and develops theories, methods, techniques, and application systems to simulate, extend, and expand human intelligence" (Li, 2018).

In recent years, the evolution of artificial intelligence technology has made great advancements, and deep learning technology is its most prominent manifestation. It is based on the development of artificial neural networks that mimic the way that the human brain works; thus, the networks can experiment, learn, and grow themselves without human intervention. Deep learning technology has demonstrated its strength to recognize images, to communicate, and to translate from one language to another.

Deep learning is a branch of machine learning that aims to develop a model that matches the level of the human brain in solving complex problems in the real world by utilizing artificial neural networks and simulation learning. The human brain consists of a group of neurons, and deep learning tries to reach the level of these neural connections by simulating the human brain through artificial neural network techniques, which is the core of deep learning.

Deep learning requires the use of high levels of cognitive skills such as analysis (compare, contrast) and synthesis (integrate knowledge in a new dimension).

The main features of deep learning are the intrinsic motivation that encourages learning as a source of satisfaction, meaning-centered learning, linking new knowledge with other subjects, merging expertise and real life, and promoting a critical spirit and analysis. Deep learning is characterized by the speed of learning, as it has the ability to learn from large amounts of data, which humans cannot handle. Therefore, deep learning may draw ideas and conclusions that humans cannot reach. Deep learning takes advantage of image recognition, weather forecasting, and agriculture. It has also been utilized in automotive technology and medical fields. Hence, artificial intelligence has been essential in supporting and enriching the lives of people and society (Aggarwal et al., 2022).

There are many approaches for implementing AI. People used a knowledge base to formalize their knowledge at a very early stage. However, this approach needs manual operations to precisely describe the world with complex rules. Therefore, scientists designed a pattern in which the AI system can extract a model from raw data, and this ability is called "ML." ML algorithms include statistical mechanisms, such as Bayesian algorithms, function approximation (linear or logistics regression), and decision trees (Hatcher & Yu, 2018).

# AI LEARNING MODELS THAT POSE A CYBERSECURITY THREAT

It is known in artificial intelligence that there are many types of learning that is present in machine learning. The focus of this chapter is only limited to two specific types of learning that could be used to cause a cybersecurity threat which are supervised learning and unsupervised learning.

Unsupervised machine learning is one of the many characteristics of artificial intelligence that is difficult to protect against cyberthreats. The unsupervised machine learning requires constant need for training and precision that places cybersecurity a top priority before all others which it can be used for surveillance, profiling, or other purposes related in that field.

The risks that are involved in the characteristics of artificial intelligence is not only limited to individuals, but is applicable to all users, therefore it is imperative to adapt and evolve artificial intelligence technologies to protect against vulnerabilities and mitigate them. This presents a particular challenge in the face of increasing global pressure on privacy and data protection standards. Since there are no standardized security controls that are built into artificial intelligence models and prototypes, they are deemed to be vulnerable to malicious use by third parties.

Firstly, the supervised learning method is the learning process where users insert a training input data with the desired output that is used for labelling to give a particular output. This type of learning is mostly used in the cybersecurity field that enables attackers to craft and launch an attack. However, the same concept could be used to detect an attack which is commonly present in security controls within the organization's network infrastructure (Jiang et al., 2020).

Moving over to the second method which is the unsupervised learning. This a process of self-training without knowing what is the desired output. This drastically increases the chance of wrong learning by filling the model with wrong training and testing data that increases a cyber-attack surface (IBM Inc., 2020).

However, self-learning capabilities introduces the possibility of false learning. False learning may be an issue when the artificial intelligence systems are not aware of its experience due to incorrect training methods, and it will only receive new experiences. Thus, the artificial intelligence systems can get trapped in a spiral of endless loop of sequences as a result. In a way, this might lead to overreactions by the model in various situations.

In addition, false learning may reflect as cyber threat in the artificial intelligence model, in which the attacker can use these vulnerabilities from false learning to attack the operations, which could damage the model's environment. Furthermore, when the artificial intelligence learns through given inputs that are specifically labelled to give a desired output, wrong labelling may introduce a cyber threat by making the artificial intelligence model learn inappropriately. It is possible to reduce false learning and prevent false data injection attack by implementing the model that was developed by "Distinguishing Between Cyber Injection and Faults Using Machine Learning Algorithms". Based on 6 different cases the average of the detection rate is 86.246% which was calculated noting that each case had different types of training and testing dataset (Amin et al., 2018).

Consequently, wrong learning is a consequence that comes from the artificial intelligence model's mistake and contributes to a cybercrime, that can be seen as a tool for attackers to achieve their purpose, which is to disrupt and sabotage the process, the same processes were the ones that artificial security was meant to solve.

Despite these risks, we can prevent these attacks by increasing the amount of data during the training process, these data should be separated into a training and testing phases so it must be reviewed, classified, and well tested by getting this dataset from trusted sources, and use the trusted dataset within testing phase, also when receive the data should be relevance to the need of the artificial intelligence model.

Secondly, there is a chance for getting a dataset from untrusted sources that could be made by attackers and training the machine learning with this dataset. However, attackers can manipulate the dataset of a machine learning model that could be used to recognize a threat, since the dataset are manipulated the machine learning model may unnoticed some threats and cause security risks within the organization that implement the model (Konstantinov et al., 2019).

Since the datasets are available on Kaggle or GitHub the attacker can access the model and take an advantage by altering the integrity of the data and can reuploads the data back from where he retrieved them. For example, spam detection application. These applications usually implement a "Mark as not Spam" function that is provided as feedback from the users. However, automated requests can still be sent by an attacker to mark certain message as not spam (This can be done by abusing APIs). Therefore, the attacker obtains indirect access to the model training pipeline which then the attacker can skew the model in the desired direction.

In a summary, and according to Quadri and Khan (2019), APT are sophisticated, professional, state-supported and systematic cyber-attack programs that continue for an extended period and in which a group of skilled hackers coordinates to design the attack with a particular motive, targeting specific information in high-profile companies and governments. They seek privilege escalation and perimeter expansion using malware-laden email or malware-infested USB drives and then hide inside the critical systems to collect intellectual property and other asset information for further sabotage or corporate espionage.

A dataset should be validated, curated, and maintained by the system providers directly, since the dataset collected it should isolate into a restricted area so no one can access without has a permission (Breck et al., 2019). Thus, insiders could have a chance for accessing artificial intelligence model and the ability of training and testing the data. However, implementing such policies such as (least privilege, separation of duties) for restricting any insider threats coming from an employee. Furthermore, more robust monitoring should be used in the beginning process of the implementation artificial intelligence model. Monitoring is necessary to ensure that divergence between the expected and actual behavior of a system is captured promptly and addressed adequately.

However, since there is a human mistake could be used to pose cyber threat there are an "Indirect criminological risk of using AI – the risk associated with unintended hazards in the context of the use of AI. These risks include:"

I.   "Random errors in the software of the AI system (errors made by the developer of the AI system that led to the commission of the crime)."
II.  "Errors made by the AI system during its operation" (Khisamova et al., 2019).

Meanwhile, "AI has made it possible to collect and process more data than ever before, allowing third-party companies to have even more data on us that leads to added privacy and protection issues" (Issquared Inc., 2021). As result, this led to having a cyber threat that focusing on the privacy and protection issues which can be used for cyber-attacks.

However, the secrecy of the information should not be used in unethical situation since artificial intelligence using algorithms for analysis of large of data, hence there is a normal traffic that related to normal activities, but also there is a traffics that holds a sensitive data related the employee and clients that includes their biometric and personal information. In addition, Advanced biometric methods that powered by artificial intelligence can provide accurate data on your appearance. While the data are accurate it used by the adversaries to track the privacy of the victim which led into data leak problem.

Due to the development and improvement of artificial intelligence in the world, this technology could be used in most sectors to facilitate and automate operations which reach us to a major security stage and causing cyber threats. In addition, Cyber-attacks aimed to break one part from three parts for achieving goals, the three parts are confidentiality, integrity, and availability. Recently attacks on the artificial intelligence system focusing for manipulating its behavior and gaining access that may impact critical infrastructure.

According to several studies, the main most active areas of AI implementation are medical applications (disease diagnosis programs), digital services – assistants, autonomous vehicles. At the same time, for example, an AI error in the program of diagnosis of diseases that has made an incorrect diagnosis can lead to incorrect treatment of the patient, and as a consequence, a possible violation of his health (Bikeev et al., 2019)

As results, professionals must pay attention to such matters and take them into account, especially that artificial intelligence can affect the infrastructure of countries, and this is a huge threat. Infrastructure of the countries have an important sector that used artificial intelligence and being targeted by hackers' especially health and oil sectors.

Furthermore, in the health sector, unappropriated training of model can cause a cyber threat and health disaster, because hospitals use artificial intelligence technologies in some delicate surgeries that do not accept any simple mistakes, causing by an attack or manipulating the model or the dataset at this stage is considered a disaster. for example according to IEEE "Heart disease is the leading cause of death worldwide. Currently, 33% of cases are misdiagnosed. Approximately half of myocardial infarctions occur in people who are not predicted to be at risk. The use of Artificial Intelligence could reduce the chance of error leading to possible earlier diagnoses which could be the difference between life and death for some" (Ankireddy et al., 2019). A cyber-attack could tamper with the dataset that deems to have inaccurate diagnosis. In addition, oil sector a damage by an attack or wrong training could cause disruption or tampering with the operation technologies by affecting the proportions of some components and causing changing in them, which reach the release of gas and the deadly explosion that will cause health disaster impact, including environmental impacts, social collapse, and economic collapse (Bikeev et al., 2019).

Finally, after providing some general characteristics of artificial intelligence that pose a cybersecurity threat, it is important to note that the artificial intelligence model used to make predictions must be based on a large and clean dataset, meaning that its integrity must be preserved. Integrity of the data is another important consideration when making predictions with AI, as it can prevent false positives or fail to provide accurate results if there are irregularities or uncontrolled data availability and processing. Based on this research paper "Sequential Detection of Cyber-attacks Using a Classification Filter" it is possible to implement their methods to reduce false positives, from the research paper it is stated "the experimental results show that when classification filter is 0.9, our proposed method can improve the detection performance well with detection rates of 93.94% (NSL-KDD'99) and 96.29% (CICIDS-2017), and our sequential detection system based on a classification filter can improve the detection rate by 11.81% while reducing the false positive rate and false negative rate by 18.16% and 20.97%" (Cai et al., 2021).

The supervised learning method was able to produce an excellent performance using small data sets while the unsupervised learning method was not so productive due to poor performance on larger datasets.

# AI BACKGROUND AND ITS RELATION WITH CYBERSECURITY

The start of AI is believed to be made by Alan Turing with his question "can machines think?" The Turing test, developed by Turing in 1950, is a test of a machine's ability to exhibit intelligent behavior equivalent to, or indistinguishable from, that of a human. The test set some requirements to build a truly intelligent machine that requires knowledge representation, natural language, machine learning, automated reasoning, vision, and robotics for the full test (Kayid, 2020).

Turing was a founding father of artificial intelligence and modern cognitive science, and he was a leading early exponent of the hypothesis that the human brain is largely a digital computing machine. He theorized that the cortex at birth is an "unorganized machine" that, through "training," becomes organized "into a universal machine or something like it."

Turing is reported as being "obsessed with the idea of speed on the machine". In Turing's lecture on the Automatic Computing Engine to the London Mathematical Society and his report on Intelligent Machinery he states that it is particularly important for a machine to have sufficient memory in order to be able to do interesting problems. The specifications that Turing was looking for in the ACE included memory capable of storing 200,000 binary digits. The reasons for such a demanding specification, effectively equivalent to many home computers in the 1980s, was to be able to tackle what he considered to be interesting problems rather than just being a demonstration of a stored program computing architecture. In particular, what he considered to be interesting problems were often inspired by biology, such as running "organized" and "unorganized" machines of neuron like processes to explore learning and how brains work (Bowen et al., 2018).

According to McCarthy's definition, intelligence is an ability, and so of course a system may possess that ability to various degrees. Thus the definition does not make an absolute distinction between systems that are intelligent and those that are not. A person, a thermostat, a chess-playing program, and a corporation all achieve goals to various degrees and thus can be thought of as intelligent to those degrees. McCarthy's definition also specifies that intelligence is the computational part of that ability, ruling out, for example, systems that achieve their goals merely by being physically strong, or by having superior sense organs (Sutton, 2020).

The global artificial intelligence market is projected to grow at a CAGR of 36.2% during the forecast period to reach USD 407.0 billion by 2027. Growth of data-based AI and advancement in deep learning and need to achieve robotic autonomy to stay competitive in global market are the major growth drivers (Markets and Markets Research, 2022).

In this section, we review the traditional ML schemes against cyberspace attacks and various DL schemes. The implementation process, experimental results, and efficiency of different programs in combating cyberspace attacks are discussed.

According to a Capgemini report, 51% of organizations highly utilize AI to detect cybersecurity threats. Also, according to the CISO of LogMeIn, AI and machine learning hold a grand promise for both defenders and attackers, making it one of the most important security trends (Al-Ghazawi, 2022).

Artificial Intelligence techniques and approaches like machine learning and deep learning show promise in enabling cybersecurity professionals to counter the constantly changing threats posed by adversaries. AI checks for behavioral anomalies that hackers are expected to display for starters, whether a password is written, or when the user logs in. AI can detect those little signs that otherwise would have gone undetected and stop the hacking group in their routes (Das & Sandhane, 2021).

Moreover, from an AI perspective, cyberattacks are malicious patterns that differ from legitimate Internet traffic. To distinguish malicious traffic from legitimate traffic, intrusion detection systems have been developed by using AI techniques because of their capability to examine a large amount of data and adapt to the changing nature of Internet traffic. Therefore, one of the most relevant AI applications to the cybersecurity area are in intrusion detection systems where artificial intelligence has the potential to intelligently analyze and automatically classify large amounts of Internet traffic (Zeadally et al., 2020).

In addition, it utilizes various machine learning approaches to separate the malicious from the regular traffic classes using the acquired internet traffic.

There are various cyber threats and attacks; common cyber threats are fraud detection, malware detection, spam classification, phishing, disabling firewall and antivirus, logging of keystrokes, malicious URL, and probing, to name a few (Shaukat, 2020).

Phishing is considered a critical threat to cyberspace. Phishing is the method of getting unauthorized access to data by pretending as a legitimate user. For example, sending a web page link posing as a legitimate page that navigates to other links to enter personal information is an example of phishing (Shaukat, 2020).

In 2021, 83% of organizations reported experiencing phishing attacks. In 2022, an additional six billion attacks are expected to occur. Also, roughly 90% of data breaches happen on account of phishing (CyberTalk, 2022).

Therefore, phishing emails are considered as one the most effective cyber threats on the targeted sectors and users. This means that more effective phishing detection technology is needed to curb the threat of phishing emails that have been growing at an alarming rate in recent years. Thus, techniques of phishing mitigation by Machine learning algorithms are prominent (Mughaid et al., 2022).

# Main Characteristics of AI That Pose a Threat to Cybersecurity

The problem of ensuring the security of confidential information is one of the keys for all digital economy subjects, including cybersecurity using AI (Wilner, 2018).

The world community is concerned about the use of AI for criminal purposes. Thus, in early 2017, the FBI held a major conference on the use of AI by law enforcement agencies and criminals. At the conference, it was noted: the data of Interpol, Europol, FBI, and law enforcement agencies of other countries, and the results of studies of leading universities indicate the lack of activity of criminal structures to create their developments in the field of AI.

Trusting artificial intelligence in cybersecurity is a double-edged sword, as artificial intelligence is playing an increasingly important role in cybersecurity good and can substantially improve cybersecurity practices; artificial intelligence can play a massive role in the bad, posing severe security threats. For instance, AI can be used to identify patterns in computer systems that reveal weaknesses in software or security programs, thus allowing hackers to exploit those newly discovered weaknesses, Finch said (Reporter, 2022).

In addition, attackers' misuse of largely distributed open-source data can cause numerous risks, including the malicious use of AI applications, as data is the primary input in AI. For example, cybercriminals can utilize AI to generate a various attempt of phishing and spear phishing emails to distribute malware or gather important data when paired with stolen personal information or open-source data such as social media public data and search engines.

According to Ovchinsky (2018), despite the lack of information about the development of cybercriminals in the field of AI, the potential for such a phenomenon exists. Cybercriminal has plenty to choose from to create their own powerful AI platforms. Almost all the development of AI with an open outcome code are containers.

Containers, such as Docker (n.d.) and Linux Containers (LXC) are standalone and self-contained units that package software and its dependencies together. Similar to Virtual Machines (VMs), containers are a virtualization technique that enable the resources of a single compute node to be shared between multiple users and applications. However, while VMs virtualize resources at the hardware level, containers do so at the operating system level. This makes them a lightweight virtualization approach that enables application environment isolation, fast and flexible deployment, and fine-grained resource sharing (Rodriguez & Buyya, 2020).

## CYBERATTACKS: PREVENTIVE MEASURES

Preventing a cyber-attack is part of applying a successful cybersecurity defense from the corporate or personal perspective. However, it is almost impossible to achieve a proper cyber-defense as long as systems remain connected to other systems via networks or the Internet. Therefore, we rely on preventive measures, which we categorize into three areas: technology, education, and policy.

"Technology" encompasses the tools, techniques, and software that detect, prevent, or stop an attack. A few of the common technologies include antivirus software, firewalls, automated updates, and IDSs. Antivirus software recognizes known malicious programs (e.g., computer viruses, worms, Trojans) using various techniques such as pattern-based detection and prevents their execution. Automated updates ensure that systems have the most up-to-date security to eliminate known vulnerabilities (Kavak et al., 2021).

Antivirus and anti-malware software use various methods to detect and prevent malware from infecting your device, such as these:

Signature-based detection: Signature-based detection is one of the oldest forms of antivirus protection. It compares files coming into devices to known malware, looking for signature matches. For the software to be effective, the antivirus database must stay up to date with the latest malware.

Heuristic-based detection: Heuristic-based detection is similar to signature-based detection in that it scans incoming files and programs for matches to known malware. However, while signature detection looks for exact matches, heuristic detection looks for similar tendencies or patterns in a file's code. As a result, it catches malware that signature detection may have missed.

Behavior-based detection: This form of detection examines how files and programs act, looking for anything out of the ordinary (Vigderman & Turner, 2022).

Technology is a prominent part of securing cyberspace. However, technology alone does not suffice. Over 90% of security incidents list human error as a factor. Therefore, to be effective, prevention measures must address the human component. Education and training are vital to cybersecurity. Training ranges from teaching users' basic security concepts like safe browsing, recognizing suspicious (phishing) messages, password security, understanding software permissions, and secure data disposal, to teaching security professionals how to recognize and react to a cyber threat.

Organizations must also be educated in cybersecurity. This occurs through the implementation and enforcement of policies and procedures. With cyberspace being such a critical component of almost all organizations, it is necessary to describe acceptable uses and responsibilities, explicitly. Documented best practices and formal policies shared throughout organizations can aid users and improve security. Additionally, governments are crafting laws and determining enforcement protocols for cyberattacks (Kavak et al., 2021).

# EXAMPLES OF AI/CYBERSECURITY TOOLS

Much like how AI can be utilized in cyber defense, it can also be used in the offense, whether for legit penetration testing or malicious targeting. In addition, the combination of AI and cyber-attacks enhances efficiency, which in turn can help avoid detection.

An efficient attack is an attack that requires less time or tries to achieve its purpose than traditional attacks with the same purpose, or it can help automate a process that is otherwise impossible to automate using traditional tools. Attackers, for example, can use the aid of AI in their reconnaissance of targets. In this phase, adversaries try to gather information on the target with passive or active scanning (Mitre, 2020).

One example of an AI-driven cyber scanning tool is Eyeballer, an open-source tool by Bishop Fox (2022). Eyeballer is meant for large-scope network penetration tests where you need to find "interesting" targets from a huge set of web-based hosts (Duc, 2021). Gowitness is a website screenshot utility written in Golang, that uses Chrome Headless to generate screenshots of web interfaces using the command line (Govanguard, 2020).

However, the process of going through Gowitness's screenshots and analyzing them is done manually by the user and can be pretty tedious in large-scale engagements. This is where Eyeballer comes into play. Eyeballer, with the help of AI, can identify possible targets in ways traditional automated HTML scanners cannot. For instance, soft 404 pages that host a 404 image on it will return a response code of 200 to users even if there is no actual content on the URL.

Most scanners cannot distinguish between an actual 200-page and a soft 404-page. Eyeballer with Gowitness supplements the automated scanners and distinguishes between pages with content and pages without content, regardless of the response code returned. Nevertheless, the most beneficial usage of Eyeballer is identifying old-looking web pages, one of the excellent findings a pen tester can come across. Old-looking web pages attract pen testers' attention because of the high probability that they contain legacy code, and legacy code is usually vulnerable and easier to exploit. Unfortunately, automatically identifying old-looking web pages was not possible before Eyeballer and its utilization of AI (Fox, 2019).

One of the most important elements of cyber security testing is the penetration test. Penetration tests show the extent to which IT security is threatened by attackers. Attacks and security measures can provide adequate IT security. Measures to improve IT security are needed to overcome the threats. In line with corporate IT security policy, all such measures are described in the

IT security concept for the entire organization. It is important to understand the process of penetration testing within cage protection and that it is not equal to public hacking. Penetration Test is a complex process that technically provides a comprehensive and realistic picture of the vulnerabilities of the info communication system (Armstrong et al., 2018).

The second example of an offensive cybersecurity tool that uses AI is DeepExploit by Isao Takaesu, which is a fully automated pen-testing tool linked with the Metasploit Framework (Takaesu, 2018). Metasploit is a flagship and open-source pen-testing framework developed by Rapid7, and contains a suite of offensive tools to carry out a cyber-attack on remote systems from start to finish. What DeepExploit brings to the table on top of Metasploit is more efficiency using ML and Reinforcement Learning (RL), an ML training method not dependable on human input, but instead on the outcome of previous tries as an input to the model that is used to make Metasploit targeting more efficient (MATLAB, n.d.).

Rockyou is a social media, social networking, and application vendor that was based in San Francisco [California]. Although they started off by making a slide show making software, they slowly branched to the world of social media and social networking. Rockyou was doing great until mid-December of 2009, where a hacker got unauthorized access into their account database. Typically, the hacker couldn't do much with the database due to the extensive encryption on the accounts. Unfortunately, Rockyou didn't encrypt their database, they stored it in plaintext. The hacker was able to gain access to over 32 million usernames and passwords via an SQL Injection attack (Cosmodium CyberSecurity, 2022).

There are many passwords lists available on the net, one example is the RockYou data breach that occurred in 2009. The company had stored their users' passwords in plaintext, and when hackers found a vulnerability in their database, the passwords were recovered and leaked onto the internet. An alternative approach to creating a password list is by analyzing the target to create a dictionary of words and phrases used on the target website, twitter feed, facebook feed or any other publicly accessible media (Hamra, 2020).

The RockYou2021 file was put into context by the cybersecurity expert Troy Hunt. On Twitter he explained that RockYou2021 is actually not a list of 8.4 billion breached credentials, and that the file does not offer anything new or unique. In fact, the 100GB file appears to be a compilation of old password leaks, probable and commonly-used passwords, and wordlists. According to Hunt, and as later confirmed by other experts, the compilation only contains a small portion of already-known breached passwords, while the majority of the 8.4 billion entries have never been passwords, and consist of wordlists and potential passwords. Wordlists have become popular tools used by cybercriminals to crack and guess passwords and take over online accounts. As the name suggests, these lists typically contain words from dictionaries with common character variations, in addition to common and previously exposed passwords. These tools can be used by bad actors to perform dictionary attacks, a brute-force technique where the attacker tries to guess a user's password by using common pre-selected words and phrases taken from the wordlist (WhiteBlueOcean, 2021). Due to cybersecurity issues like this, tools like Mentalist were created to help users remain safe online.

A mentalist takes password patterns as input and generates all possible passwords based on the pattern, making more accurate password guesses with patterns relevant to the target as the user sees fit. For example, birthday years are very common in passwords. Still, realistically, birthday years between 1960 and 2022 are magnitudes more frequently used than other years, which can cut down the number of guesses by thousands or millions depending on the complexity of the wordlist. Still, the manual generation of wordlists using intuition leaves much to be desired. That is until a promising method dependent on deep learning came into light in 2017: PassGAN. PassGAN uses a Generative Adversarial Network (GAN) to learn the statistical distribution of passwords from password dumps, and produces more accurate password guesses (Hitaj et al., 2019).

The method promises 51%-73% more successful password guesses with HashCat than without using PassGAN. In addition, an open-source Python tool based on the paper mentioned above was released by Brannon Dorsey with the ability to train a model on a custom dataset or use a pre-trained model on the RockYou wordlist, making it yet another useful AI-powered cybersecurity tool. DeepLocker, first introduced at Black Hat USA in 2018, takes malware stealthiness to a whole new level with AI. While most of the previous examples are for AI-aided cyber-attacks and focus on efficiency, DeepLocker is an AI-embedded attack, where the AI capability is embedded inside the malware itself and focuses on stealthiness (Kirat et al., 2018).

The Stuxnet worm illustrated how vulnerable control systems potentially are when it bypassed a number of security mechanisms to cause physical damage to an Iranian nuclear facility (Pretorius & van Niekerk, 2020).

Stuxnet destroyed approximately 1000 centrifuges at Iran's uranium enrichment facility in Natanz. The Stuxnet attack against the Iranian nuclear program demonstrates the critical impact that a sophisticated adversary with a detailed knowledge of I&C systems can have on safety-related infrastructures.

Attacks on Programmable Logic Controllers (PLCs) deployed in the safety protection system of NPPs would be especially critical because cyber threats on PLCs can cause problems related to safety (Choi et al., 2020).

Stuxnet would then control the machinery outside its safe performance levels, causing damage and failure. DeepLocker, on the other hand, does not rely directly and only on system attributes to identify its target, but rather on Deep Learning to achieve that. DeepLocker can identify its target in multiple ways, such as face recognition, voice recognition, geolocation, sensors, user activity, software and physical environment, and so on. Moreover, it conceals its malicious content on 3-levels. In the first level of concealment, the Target Class Concealment, it does not reveal what it is looking for, whether it is a face, a voice, or an utterly obscure object in the target environment.

The second level of concealment is the Target Instance Concealment, which hides the exact identity it is looking for, even if the Target Class is revealed. The third level is the Malicious Intent Concealment, which encrypts the final payload that decides how the attack is executed, where the decryption key generated with the target attribute match data.

Another primary difference between DeepLocker and previously discussed AI tools is how to defend against it. With the previously discussed and tools and their likes, the usual good and efficient mitigation can help against them, such as patching and rate limiting. DeepLocker, on the contrary, requires a new set of mitigation layers in order to achieve defense in depth against it. Unusual DeepLocker counter methods suggested by *IBM* researchers who invented it includes:

- Restricting access to sensors as a prevention approach.
- Preventing the code from retrieving the data required to identify the target.
- Decrypting the payload.

AI usage monitoring is another counter and detection method. However, AI usage by DeepLocker is different from typical AI usage because DeepLocker is trying to generate a decryption key constantly and in relatively large intervals because of the high computational cost of AI and to avoid suspicions.

# SAUDI ARABIA APPROACH IN CYBERSECURITY WITH AI

Great achievements in the field of fighting terrorism have been accomplished by Saudi Arabia, the country has been the target of terrorist attacks for a long time, at the same time it was able to improve the security and reduce crime to the lowest levels.

If you observe the geographical location of Saudi Arabia, been close to coasts and other resources, it makes it an important sector for logistics, it's worth mentioning that is one of the most secure countries.

Due to the high degree of digitization, the ports, airports, shipping, supply chain, internet and everything related to information technology will be highly important since it will be necessary for the modern economy.

A recent study from Capgemini Research Institute found two-thirds of businesses now believe AI is necessary to identifying and countering critical cybersecurity threats, and nearly three-quarters of businesses are using or testing AI for this purpose.

To help enterprises in Saudi Arabia secure their digital ecosystems, some companies have partnered with several leading information security consultancy firms and managed security services providers (MSSP) in the region. The new alliances will help to expand its advanced cyber threat intelligence and solutions to local organizations. Leveraging AI, these solutions allow organizations to automate the identification, assessment and triage of incoming cyber threats while staying ahead of cybercriminals using AI-driven tactics to attack companies at scale.

As critical research domains for the Riyadh R&D centre, some companies will invest in data science, artificial intelligence (AI) and cognitive security technologies to protect the region against emerging threats to protect smart cities and critical infrastructure. Cognitive security is the application of AI technologies patterned on human thought processes to detect threats and protect physical and digital systems.

Similar to how AI is used in financial services for fraud detection, AI can counteract cybercrime by identifying patterns of behavior that signify something out-of-the-ordinary may be taking place. Crucially, the use of AI means pattern identification can be made in systems that need to cope with thousands of events taking place every second, which is where cybercriminals will try to strike.

With rapid digitisation and with the appearance of Smart Cities, the complexity of cyberattacks and new security risks will only keep growing. The use of AI enables security teams to accelerate threat detection and preventive mechanisms (Arabian Business, 2022).

Canada, China, and the United States are among the countries in which many organizations began their AI journeys early, supported by government initiatives. Saudi Arabia is no different in terms of its commitment to becoming an AI powerhouse. As an extension of the country's Vision 2030, the Saudi Data and AI Authority (SDAIA) was established in 2019, followed by the release of the National Strategy for Data and AI in 2020. Given its strong focus on and dedication to fostering an AI ecosystem, Saudi Arabia is poised to see strong growth in overall AI spending, with a CAGR of 29% forecast for the 2021–2025 period that will see the market reach a value of $563 million in 2025.

According to a recent IDC survey of CIOs in the Kingdom, almost half the Saudi organizations that invest in AI technologies prefer to customize off-the-shelf solutions to meet their needs. This suggests an appetite among end users to work with local and global technology solution providers to meet their organizations' specific business requirements. In terms of in-demand AI applications, more than one-third of Saudi organizations are investing in digital assistants, chatbots, and conversational agents augmented by Arabic language capabilities. Recommendation engines, as well as prediction and forecasting, are other key investment areas that will be leveraged across various vertical markets.

Organizations in Saudi Arabia should approach AI as a strategic initiative rather than as a one-off project so they can drive organization-wide innovation and become AI disruptors. To understand an organization's AI readiness, five maturity traits of AI disruptors need to be evaluated. These are vision, people, process, technology, and data readiness. Responding to IDC's recent Saudi Arabia CIO Survey, 35% of organizations said that identifying and hiring talent and the cost of implementation were major challenges. The lack of a centralized strategy and unclear processes, the lack of alignment across business and IT functions, the lack of a single technology architecture and platform were also highlighted as major challenges.

Like all other emerging technologies, AI is also prone to cybersecurity threats. Threat actors and adversaries launch attacks to compromise the confidentiality, availability, and integrity of AI systems. Training data security, algorithm security, trained model security, and platform security, as well as model transparency, ethics, and responsibility, are the key focus areas for building a secure and sustainable AI practice (CIO, 2022).

# CRIMINOLOGICAL RISKS OF ARTIFICIAL INTELLIGENCE

Analyzing trends in the creation and use of AI allowed us to identify two types of criminological risks of using AI: direct and indirect. Direct criminological risk of using AI – the risk associated with an immediate effect on a person and a citizen of a danger caused by the use of AI.

These risks include:

1.  AI with the ability to self-training decided on actions/inactions constitutes a crime. A criminal act implies the deliberate commission by the AI system of a socially dangerous attack on human life and health; freedom, honor, and dignity of the individual; constitutional rights and freedoms of man and citizen; public security; peace and security of humankind, which have caused socially dangerous consequences.
2.  Intentional actions with the software of the AI system, which caused socially dangerous consequences. A criminal act implies illegally accessed to the system, resulting in damage or modification of its functions, as a result of which a crime was committed.
3.  AI was created by criminals to commit crimes. Criminals actively adopt AI and robotics. The IT threats that AI can generate were also analyzed in the recently published report The Malicious Use of Artificial Intelligence: Forecasting, Prevention, and Mitigation (Brundage et al., 2018), developed by a group of IT security experts working at Oxford, Cambridge, and Stanford universities, the Electronic Frontier Foundation and Open AI organizations, and several companies specializing in information security.

The researchers classified possible IT threats that could be created using AI in three ways:

a)  malware attacks,
b)  attacks using social engineering techniques,
c)  physical attack.

The first type of IT threat is based on making it easier for hackers to detect software vulnerabilities due to the capabilities of artificial intelligence in the speed and efficiency of software analysis of various types. The second type of IT threat is the use of "human thinking vulnerabilities" based, for example, on the use of artificial intelligence technologies for speech synthesis or the creation of "contextual" malware. These technologies will "lull the vigilance" of the person who clicks the link that its criminals need.

In the same group of IT threats, the researchers used AI to disorient people in the political sphere and monitor dissenters. In addition, AI can be used for personalized mass disinformation campaigns. The third type of IT threat is the organization of attacks on physical objects, for example, using combat drones controlled by artificial intelligence. Indirect criminological risk of using AI – the risk associated with unintended hazards in the context of the use of AI.

Another use of AI technics for cybersecurity offenses would be the automation of social engineering attacks, automation of ransomware tasks, and fake news using deep fake images, deep fake videos, deep fake voices, and deep fake text. *(2022, Dr. Daniel Al-Ghazaw)*

Malicious intelligence and cyber threats are becoming more sophisticated and rising exponentially; attackers are coming up with increasingly inventive and complex ways to carry out their attacks. Therefore, sophisticated cybersecurity countermeasures and strategies cannot be ignored; thus, organizations are using AI to bolster their protection and prevention systems and help reduce attack surfaces and cyber threats. AI has a ton of advantages in the context of cybersecurity, including but not limited to threat detection, threat hunting, vulnerability management, risk forecasting, and network traffic monitoring.

As a result, the increasing number of attacks such as distributed denial-of-service (DDoS) and data breaches, many of them highly costly for the impacted organizations, are generating a need for more sophisticated solutions. Therefore, the rise in cyberattacks is helping to fuel growth in the market for AI-based security products. A July 2022 report by Acumen Research and Consulting says the global market was $14.9 billion in 2021 and is estimated to reach $133.8 billion by 2030 (CNBC, 2022).

## CONCLUSION

This chapter explores how artificial intelligence technology mimics human actions and can replace us in time-consuming tasks, but most important, it's integration in cybersecurity and how it has enhanced the protection of its users. There is no doubt that AI in the cybersecurity landscape has encounter many challenges, from the definition itself, ethics, education, it's integration, learning models and many more other fields.

When we refer to ethical challenges, we need to understand that the increased funding and consumer attention to these technologies raised a question about how they can be used. A key aspect of addressing this challenge is understanding when AI is appropriate, how to make it effective, and how to control it. This includes ensuring its use is consistent with its purpose while allowing its benefits to be realized.

We detail on the chapter the main ethical challenges of AI and the consequences of an improper use. The content shows the advancements in cybersecurity technology, and specify how the technology allows data to be analyzed using this artificial intelligence. These advancements are being applied specially in organizations and getting excellent results on managing a growing range of cybersecurity risks and technical challenges. AI solutions for cybersecurity enable a fundamental shift from a signature-based detection to a more flexible and continuous network monitoring as it shifts from its normal behaviors.

In conclusion, cyberspace security has imposed tremendous impacts on various critical infrastructures. AI technology has made great progress in recent years thanks to the development of ultra-performance computing technology, it also has many other outstanding applications in the field of cybersecurity, such as malware monitoring and intrusion detection.

# REFERENCES

Aggarwal, K., Mijwil, M. M., Al-Mistarehi, A. H., Alomari, S., Gök, M., Alaabdin, A. M. Z., & Abdulrhman, S. H. (2022). Has the future started? The current growth of artificial intelligence, machine learning, and deep learning. *Iraqi Journal for Computer Science and Mathematics*, *3*(1), 115–123. Retrieved January 27, 2023, from https://journal.esj.edu.iq/index.php/IJCM/article/view/100/139

Al-Ghazawi, D. (2022). *How is artificial intelligence exploited in the offensive side of cybersecurity?* Information Security Association Protection. Extracted from: https://www.youtube.com/watch?v=2ER4P-yOiw4

Ankireddy. (2019). A Novel Approach to the Diagnosis of Heart Disease using Machine Learning and Deep Neural Networks. *2019 IEEE MIT Undergraduate Research Technology Conference (URTC)*, 1-4. https://ieeexplore.ieee.org/document/9660581 doi:10.1109/URTC49097.2019.9660581

Amin, A. (2018). Distinguishing Between Cyber Injection and Faults Using Machine Learning Algorithms. *2018 IEEE Region Ten Symposium (Tensymp)*, 19-24. https://ieeexplore.ieee.org/document/8691899 doi:10.1109/TENCONSpring.2018.8691899

Business, A. (2022). *Resecurity drives AI-powered cybersecurity in Saudi Arabia with new R&D centre*. https://www.arabianbusiness.com/industries/technology/resecurity-drives-ai-powered-cybersecurity-in-saudi-arabia-with-new-rd-centre

Armstrong, M. E., Jones, K. S., Namin, A. S., & Newton, D. C. (2018, September). The knowledge, skills, and abilities used by penetration testers: Results of interviews with cybersecurity professionals in vulnerability assessment and management. In *Proceedings of the Human Factors and Ergonomics Society Annual Meeting* (Vol. 62, No. 1, pp. 709-713). SAGE Publications. Extracted from: https://search.ebscohost.com/login.aspx?direct=true&profile=ehost&scope=site&authtype=crawler&jrnl=17881919&AN=132742665&h=NFF%2BpGs8uZcYYqZqqxCHH7bySrXe2wmxGfS2hdcME1i2303nm3AyUlXrKRIikSE1Ij96Uq9dTBFDyUy60Mv3EQ%3D%3D&crl=c

Bikeev, K. (2019). *Criminological risks and legal aspects of artificial intelligence implementation*. https://www.researchgate.net/profile/Pavel-Kabanov-3/publication/337883901_Criminological_risks_and_legal_aspects_of_artificial_intelligence_implementation/links/5e04ec92a6fdcc28374010af/Criminological-risks-and-legal-aspects-of-artificial-intelligence-implementation.pdf doi:10.1145/3371425.3371476

Fox, B. (2019). *BishopFox/Eyeballer: Convolutional neural network for analyzing pentest screenshots*. GitHub. Retrieved November 6, 2022, extracted from: https://github.com/bishopfox/eyeballer

Fox, B. (2022). *Bishop Fox Tool Eyeballer - Explained*. YouTube. Retrieved November 6, 2022, extracted from: https://www.youtube.com/watch?v=5Utfy8SuWeg

Bowen, J. P., Trickett, T., Green, J., & Lomas, A. (2018). Turing's Genius–Defining an apt microcosm. *Proceedings of EVA London 2018*. https://research.gold.ac.uk/id/eprint/24886/1/ewic_eva18_ha_paper4.pdf

Breck, P. (2019). *Data Validation for Machine Learning*. MLSYS. https://proceedings.mlsys.org/book/2019/file/5878a7ab84fb43402106c575658472fa-Paper.pdf

Brundage. (2018). *The malicious use of artificial intelligence: forecasting, prevention, and mitigation.* https://www.eff.org/files/2018/02/20/malicious_ai_report_final.pdf

Cai, F. (2021). Sequential Detection of Cyber-attacks Using a Classification Filter. *2021 IEEE Intl Conf on Dependable, Autonomic and Secure Computing, Intl Conf on Pervasive Intelligence and Computing, Intl Conf on Cloud and Big Data Computing, Intl Conf on Cyber Science and Technology Congress (DASC/PiCom/CBDCom/CyberSciTech)*, 659-666. 10.1109/DASC-PICom-CBDCom-CyberSciTech52372.2021.00111

Cho, L. (2020). *Detecting C&C Server in the APT Attack based on Network Traffic using Machine Learning. International Journal of Advanced Computer Science and Applications, 11(5).* doi:10.14569/IJACSA.2020.0110504

Choi, M. K., Yeun, C. Y., & Seong, P. H. (2020). A novel monitoring system for the data integrity of reactor protection system using blockchain technology. *IEEE Access, 8*, 118732-118740. https://ieeexplore.ieee.org/stamp/stamp.jsp?arnumber=9126779

CIO. (2022). *Capitalizing on Artificial Intelligence. Opportunities. The Journey to Building a World-Class Artificial Intelligence Practice.* Sponsored by SBM. Extracted from: https://www.cio.com/article/405700/capitalizing-on-artificial-intelligence-opportunities.html

CNBC. (2022). *Artificial intelligence is playing a bigger role in cybersecurity, but the bad guys may benefit the most.* Extracted from: https://www.cnbc.com/2022/09/13/ai-has-bigger-role-in-cybersecurity-but-hackers-may-benefit-the-most.html

Cosmodium CyberSecurity. (2022). *The Story of Rockyou.* Extracted from: https://www.cosmodiumcs.com/post/the-story-of-rockyou

CompTIA. (2022). *Ethical Issues in Cybersecurity.* Extracted from: https://www.futureoftech.org/cybersecurity/4-ethical-issues-in-cybersecurity/

CyberTalk. (2022). *Top 15 phishing attack statistics (and they might scare you).* Extracted from: https://www.cybertalk.org/2022/03/30/top-15-phishing-attack-statistics-and-they-might-scare-you/

Das, R., & Sandhane, R. (1964). Artificial Intelligence in Cyber Security. *Journal of Physics: Conference Series, 042072(4).* doi:10.1088/1742-6596/1964/4/042072

Dijk. (2021). Detection of Advanced Persistent Threats using Artificial Intelligence for Deep Packet Inspection. *IEEE International Conference on Big Data (Big Data)*, 2092-2097. https://ieeexplore.ieee.org/document/9671464 doi:10.1109/BigData52589.2021.9671464

Duc, H. N. (2021, May 7). *Eyeballer - A convolutional neural network for analyzing pentest screenshots by bishop fox.* Hakin9. Retrieved January 27, 2023, from https://hakin9.org/eyeballer-a-convolutional-neural-network-for-analyzing-pentest-screenshots/

EasyDmarc. (2022). *The Use of Artificial Intelligence in Cybersecurity.* Extracted from: https://easydmarc.com/blog/the-use-of-artificial-intelligence-in-cybersecurity/

Erma, Inc. (2022). *Artificial Intelligence and Its Ethical Challenges.* ERMA | Enterprise Risk Management Academy. https://www2.erm-academy.org/publication/risk-management-article/artificial-intelligence-and-its-ethical-challenges/

Govanguard. (2020, January 17). *Gowitness – a Golang, web screenshot utility using chrome headless.* GoVanguard Threat Center. Retrieved January 27, 2023, from https://govanguard.com/threat-center/2020/01/17/gowitness-a-golang-web-screenshot-utility-using-chrome-headless/

Hamra, S. (2020). *Ethical hacking: Threat modeling and penetration testing a remote terminal unit.* Extracted from https://www.diva-portal.org/smash/get/diva2:1517798/FULLTEXT01.pdf

Hatcher, W. G., & Yu, W. (2018). *A Survey of Deep Learning: Platforms, Applications and Emerging Research Trends* (Vol. 6). doi:10.1109/ACCESS.2018.2830661

Hitaj. (2019). PassGAN: A Deep Learning Approach for Password Guessing. *International Conference on Applied Cryptography and Network Security*, 217–237. Extracted from: https://arxiv.org/pdf/1709.00440.pdf

IBM, Inc. (2020). *Unsupervised Learning.* IBM Cloud Education. Extracted from: https://www.ibm.com/cloud/learn/unsupervised-learning

Issquared, Inc. (2021). ISSQUARED. *Pros and Cons of Artificial Intelligence in Cybersecurity.* Extracted from: https://www.issquaredinc.com/insights/resources/blogs/pros-and-cons-of-artificial-intelligence-in-cybersecurity

Jiang, T., Gradus, J. L., & Rosellini, A. J. (2020). *Supervised Machine Learning: A Brief Primer.* Behavior Therapy, U.S. National Library of Medicine. Extracted from: https://www.ncbi.nlm.nih.gov/pmc/articles/PMC7431677/

Kavak, H. (2021). Simulation for cybersecurity: state of the art and future directions. *Journal of Cybersecurity, 7*(1). doi:10.1093/cybsec/tyab005

Kayid, A. (2020). *The role of Artificial intelligence in future technology.* Retrieved January 25, 2023, from https://www.researchgate.net/profile/Amr-Kayid/publication/342106972_The_role_of_Artificial_Intelligence_in_future_technology/links/5ee257bd92851ce9e7d97e90/The-role-of-Artificial-Intelligence-in-future-technology.pdf

Khisamova, B. (2019). *Artificial Intelligence and Problems of Ensuring Cyber Security - ProQuest.* Extracted from: https://www.proquest.com/openview/a0f125d3f2115d338e180961818a409d/1?pq-origsite=gscholar&cbl=55114

Kirat. (2018). *DeepLocker - Concealing Targeted Attacks with AI Locksmithing.* Black Hat. Retrieved on November 6, 2022, from: https://i.blackhat.com/us-18/Thu-August-9/us-18-Kirat-DeepLocker-Concealing-Targeted-Attacks-with-AI-Locksmithing.pdf

Konstantinov, L. (2019). *Robust Learning from Untrusted Sources.* PMLR. https://proceedings.mlr.press/v97/konstantinov19a.html

Li, J. H. (2018). Cyber security meets artificial intelligence: A survey. *Frontiers of Information Technology & Electronic Engineering, 19*(12), 1462-1474. Extracted from: https://jzus.zju.edu.cn/oldversion/article.php?doi=10.1631/FITEE.1800573&refdsp=ALL&comnowpage=0

MATLAB. (n.d.). *What Is Reinforcement Learning?* MathWorks. Retrieved on November 6, 2022, from: https://www.mathworks.com/discovery/reinforcement-learning.html

Markets and Markets Research. (2022). *Artificial Intelligence Market by Offering – Global forecast to 2027.* Extracted from: https://www.marketsandmarkets.com/Market-Reports/artificial-intelligence-market-74851580.html

Mavrona, K., & Csernatoni, R. (2022). *The Artificial Intelligence and Cybersecurity Nexus: Taking stock of the European Union's approach.* Carnegie Europe. Accessed: November 23, 2022. Extracted from: https://carnegieeurope.eu/2022/09/15/artificial-intelligence-and-cybersecurity-nexus-taking-stock-of-european-union-s-approach-pub-87886

Mikalauskas, E. (2022). *RockYou2021: Largest Ever Password Compilation Leaked online with 8.4 billion entries.* Cybernews. Extracted from: https://cybernews.com/security/rockyou2021-alltime-largest-password-compilation-leaked/

Mitre. (2020). *Reconnaissance, Tactic TA0043 - Enterprise.* MITRE ATT&CK®. Retrieved on November 6, 2022, from: https://attack.mitre.org/tactics/TA0043/

Mughaid. (2022). An intelligent cyber security phishing detection system using deep learning techniques. *Cluster Comput, 25*, 3819–3828. doi:10.1007/s10586-022-03604-4

Kshetri, N. (2021). Economics of Artificial Intelligence in Cybersecurity. *IT Professional, 23*(5), 73-77. Extracted from: https://ieeexplore.ieee.org/document/9568267 doi:10.1109/MITP.2021.3100177

Ovchinsky, V. S. (2018). *Criminology of the digital world.* Extracted from: https://www.cybercrimejournal.com/pdf/KhisamovaetalVol13Issue2IJCC2019.pdf

Pretorius, B., & van Niekerk, B. (2020). Cyber-security for ICS/SCADA. *Cyber Warfare and Terrorism*, 613–630. doi:10.4018/978-1-7998-2466-4.ch038

Pupillo. (2021). *Artificial intelligence and cybersecurity.* Centre for European Policy Studies (CEPS). Extracted from: https://www.ceps.eu/wp-content/uploads/2021/05/CEPS-TFR-Artificial-Intelligence-and-Cybersecurity.pdf

Quadri, A., & Khan, M. K. (2019). *The G-War: Race for Technological Supremacy in 5G and 6G The G-War: Race for Technological Supremacy in 5G and 6G. Policy.* Extracted from https://www.abacademies.org/articles/Advanced-persistent-threats-apt-an-awareness-review-1533-3604-21-6-202.pdf

Reporter. (2022). *Hackers leveraging AI to launch phishing scams.* Cybersecurity Connect. Extracted from: https://www.cybersecurityconnect.com.au/commercial/8261-hackers-leveraging-ai-to-launch-phishing-scams#:~:text=Adding%20to%20cyber%20threats&text=%22For%20instance%2C%20AI%20can%20be,weaknesses%2C%22%20Finch%20further%20explained

Richard, S. (2020). *John McCarthy's Definition of Intelligence.* Extracted from: http://www.incompleteideas.net/papers/Sutton-JAGI-2020.pdf

Rodriguez, M., & Buyya, R. (2020). Container orchestration with cost-efficient autoscaling in cloud computing environments. *Handbook of Research on Multimedia Cyber Security*, 190–213. doi:10.4018/978-1-7998-2701-6.ch010

Shaukat, K. (2020). Performance comparison and current challenges of using machine learning techniques in cybersecurity. *Energies, 13*(10), 2509. Extracted from: https://www.mdpi.com/1996-1073/13/10/2509/pdf?version=1589770863

Stahl. (2021). *Ethical Issues of AI*. Extracted from: https://link.springer.com/chapter/10.1007/978-3-030-69978-9_4?error=cookies_not_supported&code=09313d7e-2c23-4bbd-9ffc-4d1ce6eac90b

Taddeo. (2019). *Three Ethical Challenges of Applications of Artificial Intelligence in Cybersecurity. Minds and Machines*. Extracted from: https://www.researchgate.net/publication/333580685_Three_Ethical_Challenges_of_Applications_of_Artificial_Intelligence_in_Cybersecurity doi:10.1007/s11023-019-09504-8

Takaesu, I. (2018). *DeepExploit*. GitHub. https://github.com/13o-bbr-bbq/machine_learning_security/tree/master/DeepExploit

Vigderman, A., & Turner, G. (2022, October 17). *How does antivirus software work?* Security.org. Retrieved January 27, 2023, from https://www.security.org/antivirus/how-does-antivirus-work/

WhiteBlueOcean. (2021, July 6). *Is rockyou2021 really a password leak?* Retrieved January 27, 2023, from https://www.whiteblueocean.com/newsroom/is-rockyou2021-really-a-password-leak/

Wilner, A. (2018). Cybersecurity and its discontinuities: Artificial intelligence, the Internet of things, and digital misinformation. *International Journal, 73*(2), 308-316. Extracted from: https://journals.sagepub.com/doi/abs/10.1177/0020702018782496

Zanaty. (2018). An empirical study of design discussions in code review. In *Proceedings of the 12th ACM/IEEE International Symposium on Empirical Software Engineering and Measurement (ESEM '18)*. Association for Computing Machinery.

Zeadally, A. (2020). *Harnessing Artificial Intelligence Capabilities to Improve Cybersecurity* (Vol. 8). doi:10.1109/ACCESS.2020.2968045

# Chapter 4
# Artificial Intelligence for Information Security

**Lubana Isaoglu**

ⓘ https://orcid.org/0000-0001-5193-1380
*Istanbul University-Cerrahpaşa, Turkey*

**Derya Yiltas-Kaplan**

ⓘ https://orcid.org/0000-0001-8370-8941
*Istanbul University-Cerrahpaşa, Turkey*

## ABSTRACT

*The internet is becoming a widely used source of both online services and information. The primary function of the internet is to move data between nodes. It is a vast collection of interconnected devices and computers, and it has become the target of different cybercrimes. Due to the rapid development of the internet and the increasing number of cyber-attacks, the detection of these attacks has become more important. The traditional security methods are not enough to face these threats; thus, researchers have been developing smarter techniques such as deep learning and machine learning to address these problems. This chapter explores the various aspects of deep learning and machine learning on information security. It also focuses on the challenges and motivations of this new technology. This chapter reviewed previously conducted surveys and papers in the last two years in the field; thus, it can be used by researchers who are interested in learning more about the various aspects and trends of deep learning and machine learning in information security.*

DOI: 10.4018/978-1-6684-7110-4.ch004

# INTRODUCTION

With the development of technology, people are becoming more reliant on it in all aspects of their lives, such as social communication, education, health, business fields, and even shopping. This high dependence means a large volume of data that is used and stored in various institutions and organizations. Weak data security can lead to key information being lost or stolen, that's why the protection of information is crucial to the strength and growth of any organization.

Information security (InfoSec) management can be defined as; the process of protecting information from unauthorized use, unauthorized disclosure, unauthorized destruction, unauthorized alteration, damage to information, or preventing unauthorized access to information (Onyango, 2021).

In other words, it is the process of preserving information. Confidentiality, Integrity, and Availability are the basis for the development of security systems, and they form a model called the "CIA triad". This name comes from the first letters of the three standards. Confidentiality aims to make sensitive data disclosed only to authorized parties who have a right to access and view data. While Integrity aims to protect sensitive data from being deleted or modified by an unauthorized party, if such data is deleted as a cause of human error by an authorized party, then the damage can be reversed. On the other hand, Availability is to ensure that sensitive data can be accessed by the right people, albeit through secure access channels safeguarded by authentication systems. When all those three standards have been met, security is stronger and better equipped to handle a threat and this is the main goal of computer security research.

Data breaches, fraud, and cyber-security attacks are all becoming more common as the amount of information that is being used is increased. Over the years researchers have worked on different ways to protect information. Recently, with the development of research on artificial intelligence (AI), researchers are encouraged to use it for enhancing InfoSec. AI enables the computer to think like humans, allowing it to solve complex problems just like a human. Machine Learning (ML) is a subset of AI that helps in building AI-driven applications. Deep Learning (DL) is a subset of ML. It uses huge amounts of data and complex algorithms to train a model. AI has evolved significantly over the past few years. Although it has become popular, it is actually as old as computer technology. Its development has created a wide range of useful applications. Such as voice recognition, image processing, and natural language processing. And InfoSec is one of the applications.

The use of AI can assist organizations in protecting themselves against internet threats, detecting malware, setting security standards, and improving their prevention and recovery procedures. For this reason, in this paper, the studies in InfoSec using AI are reviewed. To examine the most recent trend in this field, this paper focused on research that has been published in the last two years.

The rest of this paper is organized as follows. The literature review will start with a background of AI. Then a classification of the cyber-attacks will be presented. After that, the most common datasets for cyber security will be reviewed. Additionally, the InfoSec field will be discussed in detail. Also, Different ML and DL models used in InfoSec applications will be discussed in this section with the benefits of using them and the cyber threats that they can face. After that, the open problems and future research direction is discussed. Then some discussions will be presented. Finally, the paper will be concluded in the conclusion.

# LITERATURE REVIEW

In this section, the background of AI will be presented. Additionally, cybersecurity threats and attacks will be presented. The focus will be on the application of ML and DL in InfoSec.

## Artificial Intelligence Background

AI is the theory and development of computer systems that can be able to perform tasks normally requiring human intelligence, such as visual perception, speech recognition, decision-making, and translation between languages. This term was first introduced after a workshop held in 1956 at Dartmouth Summer Research Project on Artificial Intelligence at Dartmouth College in New Hampshire (Haenlein and Kaplan, 2019). That workshop was held by two scientists Marvin Minsky and John McCarthy, which are known now as the founding fathers of AI. The Dartmouth Conference was followed by a period of nearly two decades that saw significant success in the field of AI. Now AI becomes a promising solution for many different problems in many different fields.

AI contains many subfields. ML is a subset of AI, and it is used in many different applications. It contains a series of widely used data analysis techniques that automates the construction of analytical models. Approaches based on ML have the strength to learn from data, identify patterns, and make decisions with minimal human intervention (Wang and Ji, 2020). ML is usually divided into three categories: supervised learning, unsupervised learning, and reinforcement learning (Gupta et al., 2022).

A supervised learning algorithm constructs a set of mathematical models that contain both the desired outputs and the inputs of a training program. These data, which are referred to as training data, are represented by a variety of training examples. Each of these examples has one or more inputs that are required for the program to perform properly. The training examples are represented by a vector or array in the mathematical model, while the data is presented in a matrix. Through an iterative optimization process, the learning algorithm can then predict the output of the new inputs. An optimal function can help the learning algorithm determine the correct output for the inputs that were not included in the training data. It can improve its accuracy by learning to perform this task over time.

There are various types of supervised-learning algorithms, such as regression and classification. In the case of regression, the relationship between the input and output variables is considered a factor that can be used to predict the future outcomes of a continuous variable. Some popular regression algorithms that are commonly used in this type of computation are linear regression, non-linear regression, and Bayesian linear regression. When a variable is categorical, classification algorithms can be used to determine the appropriate output for the given class. Some popular platforms for this type of computation include Logistic Regression, Decision Trees, and Support Vector Machines (Xin et al., 2018).

Unsupervised learning is a method of analyzing and clustering unlabeled datasets. It can find hidden patterns and data groupings without requiring the intervention of humans. This is ideal for analyzing customer segmentation, image recognition, cross-selling techniques, and exploratory data analysis. The two main tasks of unsupervised learning are clustering and dimensionality regression. In clustering, the data is analyzed and grouped according to its similarities and differences. This method is mainly used to process unclassified information. When there are too many dimensions or features in a given dataset, a method known as dimensionality reduction can be used. This process can help to reduce the number of data inputs and preserve the integrity of the data. It is commonly used during the preprocessing phase of data analysis. There are a variety of methods that can be used to perform this process, such as autoencoders and principal component analysis.

Reinforcement learning is focused on learning the best possible behavior to obtain the most reward from an environment. This process is similar to learning how to learn by interacting with the world around us. Without supervision, a learner must perform a trial-and-error search to find the sequence of actions that will maximize their reward. The quality of the actions is evaluated based on their immediate reward and delayed gratification. With the help of a reinforcement learning algorithm, a learner can learn the actions that lead to success in an unsupervised setting. The most important learning models used in reinforcement learning are known as Q-learning, deep Q-learning, and the Markov Decision Process.

DL is a subset of ML that uses artificial neural networks (ANNs). It can be performed on various tasks, such as learning complex models with a deep structure. Compared to generic ML models, DL models perform better in terms of performance. Unlike traditional ML techniques, DL models are designed to learn complex tasks without requiring any programming. They can perform these tasks efficiently by using layers of artificial neurons. Neural networks have been used in the past to perform various tasks such as voice recognition and facial recognition.

In the past couple of years, the development of DL models has led to the emergence of neural networks that have started to play various roles in society. Various DL models such as deep neural networks (DNNs), deep belief networks (DBNs), deep reinforcement learning, recurrent neural networks (RNNs), convolutional neural networks (CNNs), and Transformers have been used in different fields, such as speech recognition, machine translation, and natural language processing (Geetha and Thilagam, 2021). They have been able to perform better than human experts in some cases.

DL refers to the process of using multiple layers in a network. In earlier studies, it was shown that a linear perceptron cannot be considered a universal classifier. However, a network with a non-polynomial activation function and an unbounded number of layers can be considered a DL model. This variation of the technique allows for optimal implementation and practicality. In DL, the layers are allowed to deviate from the biologically informed models to improve their efficiency and understandability. This is called the structured part of the process (Geetha and Thilagam, 2021).

DL algorithms are based on a DNN. These are large networks that are capable of learning autonomously. They can be classified into two groups: supervised and unsupervised DL algorithms. There are three types of supervised DL algorithms. The first one is called Feedforward Neural Network (FNN), which is a flexible and general-purpose algorithm for classification tasks. It can be used for tasks that require a minimal computational cost. The other two are called DNNs and are like the ones that are used for learning. One of the most common types of DNNs that are used for learning is a CNN. This type of network is very effective at analyzing spatial data. It can be used for various tasks that require a minimal computational cost. Another type of DNN is RNN, which is a sequence generator. It is very hard to train with FNN because its neurons send their output to the previous layers.

DL algorithms that are unsupervised have two different networks. One of them is DBN, which is a class of DNNs that are designed without an output layer. This type of network can be used for training. It can be useful when training with unlabeled datasets. The other type of DNN that is used for learning is called the stacked autoencoders. This is a class of networks that are composed of several autoencoders. It performs similarly to DBN but is better suited for small datasets.

These various types of ML and DL techniques encouraged the researchers to apply them in the cyber security field to enhance the security detection and protection facing different kinds of attacks.

## Cyber-Attacks Classification

As the network's diversity increased, attacks and threats evolved, becoming more sophisticated and non-repetitive. Cyber-attacks are acts of exploitation of computer networks and systems. They can be carried out through malicious code and can lead to various types of crimes, such as identity theft and fraud. Due to the rise of digital technology, cyber-attacks increased.

There are two types of cyber-attacks: Web-based and System-based cyber-attacks (Halbouni et al., 2022b). One of the most common types of web-based attacks is injection. This attack involves taking advantage of the data stored in a web application to perform various operations. Some of these include SQL injection, log injection, and XML injection. Another type of computer security attack is DNS spoofing. This occurs when data is introduced to a DNS resolver's repository, which causes the name server to send an error message and reroute traffic to the attacker's computer. It can lead to various security issues as the attacker can remain undetected for a long time.

Moreover, a type of security attack known as session hijacking is usually carried out when a user's session is protected by a network. An attacker can access the user's data by stealing the cookies that are stored in a web application. Another type of attack is phishing, which tries to steal a user's credit card number and login credentials. It occurs when an individual tries to trick a user into entering their personal information. A brute force attack is usually carried out through a trial-and-error method, which generates many guesses. It can be used by criminals to access a user's data, or it can be used by security experts to test an organization's security. Another type is the denial-of-service attack is usually carried out to prevent a network or server from being able to access the users. It can be done through a combination of methods, such as sending traffic to the target and causing a crash (Shaukat et al., 2020).

One more is a volume-based attack which is usually carried out to saturate the available bandwidth of a website. A protocol attack is carried out to consume the resources of a server. An application layer attack is conducted to crash a web server. A dictionary attack is carried out to validate the credentials of a commonly used password. A URL interpretation attack is another type that is carried out to allow an attacker to modify the parts of a web page that are not allowed to be accessed by a user. File inclusion attacks are also known to allow an attacker to access essential or unauthorized files on a web server. A malicious link is executed on a web server using the included functionality. Also, A man-in-the-middle attack is carried out when an attacker intercepts a connection between a client and a server. It allows the attacker to perform various actions on the intercepted connection.

System-based attacks are some of the most common types of attacks that occur. Some examples of system-based attacks can be viruses, worms, trojan horses, and backdoors. One of the most common types of malicious software is a virus, which is a self-replicating program that can spread through computer files. It can modify the files in its directory and execute instructions that are harmful to the system. A type of malware known as a worm is designed to replicate itself to infect uninfected computers. It typically arrives in email attachments that look like they are from trusted senders. Another type of malware is the Trojan horse which is designed to perform unusual activities on a computer even when it should be idle. It can mislead the user by displaying a normal application, but when it is opened or executed, it will start running malicious code. A backdoor is a method that allows a developer to bypass the authentication process. It can be used to access an operating system or application for certain purposes. Bots are automated processes that interact with various network services. Some of these programs are programmed to automatically run and execute certain commands.

# Most Common Datasets for Cyber Security

When it comes to implementing and testing cyber security systems using DL and ML, one must consider the datasets that are used to ensure that the system is accurate. As networks and applications grow, the right tools must be used to protect them. Following the most used datasets in cyber security will be discussed.

KDD CUP 1999 is the most popular dataset for analyzing cybersecurity threats and it is based on the DARPA dataset. This includes various details about the connections between networks and applications, such as their connection window and IP addresses. It also contains over 20 different attacks and a record for a test subset (Podder et al., 2021). However, in this dataset, the data is distributed unevenly. It is a common dataset for intrusion detection, where there are 391,458 instances in the DoS class and only 52 instances in the U2R class (Wang and Ji, 2020). The NSL-KDD is an improved version of the KDD dataset, which features a large amount of redundancy. It also has an advanced sub-dataset. Four attack categories that are included in this are DoS, U2R, R2L, and probe (Sarker, 2021).

The Australian Center for Cyber Security created the UNSW-IDS15 dataset in 2015. It was collected from various real-world websites, such as Symantec Corporation, Microsoft, and CVE. The samples contained both malicious and normal traffic. The nine attack families that are included in this are DoS, worms, and fuzzers (Yavanoglu and Aydos, 2017). The CIC-IDS2017 dataset was created in 2017 by the Canadian Institute for cybersecurity. It contains various attack scenarios and an abstract behavior for 25 individuals using different protocols such as HTTP, HTTPS, and SSH (Halbouni et al., 2022b).

The PU-IDS derivative was created to take advantage of the NSL-KDD data. It then produces new synthetic instances by extracting a statistic from the input data. The attributes and format of this data are similar to those of the NSL-KDD (Yavanoglu and Aydos, 2017). The data collected at the University of Victoria by researchers in Information Security and Object Technology (ISOT) formed the ISOT10 dataset which consisted of both non-malicious and malicious datasets. They gathered the data from a decentralized botnet, and they were able to extract non-malicious traffic from it (Sarker, 2021). Another dataset called CTU-13. This dataset contains 13 captured scenarios of various types of infections in a botnet. Each scenario is stored in a file known as pcap. The file contains all the packets of traffic (Podder et al., 2021).

UNSW-NB15 is a network intrusion dataset which was proposed in 2015 by (Moustafa and Slay, 2015). It contains nine different types of attacks. The original network packet for the UNSW-NB15 dataset was created using the IXIA PerfectStorm tool. This tool is from the Australian Centre for Cyber Security network-wide laboratory. It is mainly used to generate real modern normal behavior, as well as current synthetic attack activities.

The ISCX2012 public benchmark dataset contains the complete details of the network's interaction and payload. It includes various multi-stage attacks that have realistic background traffic. Around 41000 intrusive samples and 1.4 million benign ones can be found in the ISCX2012 data. Some of the commonly used intrusive samples in the dataset include DDoS, BFSSH, and HTTP (Shiravi et al., 2012). Another dataset is the DARPA1998 dataset which consists of benign samples and four types of intrusive samples including DoS, Probe, U2R, and R2L (Lippmann et al., 2002). The DARPA1998 dataset contains 3.5 million samples.

ECML PKDD dataset was presented at the 2007 PKDD/ECML conference. It contains information about the 6 components of an HTTP request, such as the protocol, URI, query parameter, method, body, and headers. There are 52296 requests in 8 classes, including 7 types of web attacks and validation (Sriraghavan and Lucchese, 2008).

Another dataset that is used for intrusion detection studies is CICSIDS2017. The latest version of this dataset features 11 new attacks (Sharafaldin et al., 2018). Some of these include DoS, Brute Force, and PortScan. It is additionally used to monitor the various types of malicious and benign traffic.

## Information Security

As mentioned before, the primary focus of InfoSec is on the integrity, confidentiality, and availability of data. and the ultimate goal of computer security research is to meet the "CIA triad" three standards, thus the security is stronger and better equipped to handle a threat.

Wang and Ji (2020) discussed various security strategies that can be used to protect information. These include surveillance, detection, deception, and prevention. These strategies can help prevent systems from getting affected by security risks. The goal of the prevention strategy is to prevent unauthorized access, modification, replication, destruction, and disclosure of information. It has little tolerance for unauthorized individuals, and this strategy is often utilized to prevent information leakage. This strategy is carried out through the surveillance of information, which is designed to monitor the changes in environmental conditions. It allows decision-makers to develop effective measures to prevent InfoSec threats.

The goal of the detection strategy is to identify security behaviors that can affect an organization's information systems. This strategy differs from the surveillance method, which is designed to monitor the overall environment. Instead of focusing on the overall status of the system, the detection strategy focuses on specific events. The response strategy follows a two-phase process. It involves identifying and implementing corrective actions to prevent further attacks. The first phase of the process is called the reaction phase, while the second phase is called the recovery phase. Deception is a process that involves taking various steps to mislead an attacker so that they will not take actions that will affect the security of an organization's information. In other words, it uses decoys to distract the attacker's attention so that they will not perform the actions that are required to keep the information secure. There are two types of this strategy: active and passive. The former focuses on performance while the latter aims to hide (Wang and Ji, 2020).

The last few years witnessed a wide application of AI in InfoSec. Some of the early adopters of AI in InfoSec are Google, IBM, and Balbix (Onyango, 2021). These companies use AI to improve the efficiency and effectiveness of their operations. For instance, in Gmail, Google uses this technology to provide suggestions and filter messages. With AI, IBM has been able to consolidate its data in a cognitive learning platform, which it then uses in threat detection. Balbix, on the other hand, uses this technology to analyze and predict the risks associated with an organization's data. By this technology, Balbix has been able to create a proactive approach to its security measures. This has allowed its team to focus on addressing and preventing various types of attacks.

Onyango (2021) has categorized AI into three categories as applied to InfoSec: Artificial General Intelligence (AGI), Artificial Super Intelligence (ASI), and Artificial Narrow Intelligence (ANI). ANI is designed to perform a single task in a specific region. It learns the task by implementing built-in intelligence. It then continues to perform the task without fail. This technology is very useful in our lives as it helps to receive information on smartphones where it is present as Siri or Cortana. AGI is capable of thinking in general. It's developed using past learning to make decisions. It's similar to the human brain in that it can learn and improve while carrying out various tasks. This technology can also be used in healthcare. The complexity of ASI is considered to be greater than that of human intellect. This type of AI is the most efficient of AI since it can perform better in everyday scenarios. It can also think critically and mitigate abstractions. Unlike humans, AI is perfect because it can develop mitigation strategies and predict the errors that it will make. One example of this is the Alpha 2 robot.

# Different ML and DL Models Used in Information Security Applications

Wang and Ji (2020) have surveyed to analyze the various aspects of AI and its applications in the security of information. They found that two main approaches are known to be useful in identifying and preventing threats: the neural network and the fuzzy logic. The researchers believe that the use of fuzzy logic can help improve the performance of InfoSec techniques. It can be used to develop effective rules that are designed to protect an organization's information. Two main research goals are currently being pursued by the researchers: improving the adaptive and learning capabilities of algorithms that are designed to automatically design fuzzy rules. They also want to enhance the readability and comprehensibility of the methods by applying them to various ML techniques.

Using fuzzy logic, an organization's InfoSec system can smooth the separation between normal and abnormal situations. This is particularly useful in detecting and preventing threats. The paper analyzed the various aspects of the research that was conducted on the use of ANNs in the security of information. Since these networks are capable of processing limited and noisy data, researchers have been developing them as effective tools for analyzing and preventing threats. Due to the complexity of the security issues faced by organizations, more research has been conducted on the development of DNNs (Wang and Ji, 2020).

Gupta et al. (2022) analyzed over 170 papers and presented various models that were related to the use of AI in the security of information. Then, they came up with a list of recommendations that are aimed at improving the performance of security techniques. They divided the process of developing DL models and ML models into six phases. These include problem conceptualization, data aggregation, data preparation, preprocess data, model development, and deployment and evaluation.

In the problem conceptualization phase, the statements are identified then the relevance according to the theme is defined also the problem statement is formulated. The required datasets are gathered and stored, and the related samples are collected in the data aggregation phase. In the data preparation phase, the data are retrieved and explored, and the datasets are cleaned and arranged. The next phase is preprocessing data where the data is analyzed and transformed, and the useful attributes are identified. After that, the model is developed and trained, the insight from training results is gathered, and the stability of the modules is validated. The last phase is deployment and evaluation where the results are evaluated and the models are exported and the model is monitored in real-time usage (Gupta et al., 2022).

In 2021, Kim conducted a study to answer the question: "How can AI be used to improve InfoSec?". His review showed that most of the studies that were conducted on the use of AI in InfoSec were focused on using ANNs. Some of these include ANN and CNN, in addition to using Decision Trees frequently (Kim, 2021).

The objective of Roponena et al. (2021) is to review the various ML techniques and technologies that can be used to maintain high-level cyber security. Numerous supervised ML algorithms are used for both regression and classification tasks. Some of these include the AdaBoost, Classification and Regression Trees, DNN, Decision Tree, Logical Regression, Long-Short-Term Memory (LSTM), Naïve Bayes, Neural Networks, Random Forest, and Support Vector Machines. Most of the studies that were reviewed in their paper focused on the classification of IP and DNS addresses. Unsupervised clustering is a method that can be used for various tasks, such as network traffic clustering and anomaly detection. Most of the studies that were reviewed in their paper focused on the clustering techniques used for traffic analysis and botnet detection. Some of these include the Agglomerative algorithm, the density-based spatial clustering of applications with noise, the Self-Organizing Map, and the X-means.

Sarker (2021) conducted a comprehensive review of cybersecurity utilizing DL techniques and ANNs. He then discussed their applications in different scenarios. In his study, he discussed various deep-learning techniques that are commonly used in cybersecurity. These include reinforcement learning, supervised learning, and unsupervised learning. Some of these networks are Multi-layer Perceptron, CNN, LSTM-RNN, Self-organizing Map, Auto-Encoder, Restricted Boltzmann Machine, DBN, Generative Adversarial Network, Deep Transfer Learning, and Deep Reinforcement Learning. According to him, the security model should have the necessary DL modeling to analyze the data collected by it. Before it can be used to make intelligent decisions, the system needs to be trained on the data related to its target application (Sarker, 2021).

Zeng et al. (2020) studied various aspects of DL application in network InfoSec. They analyzed seven aspects of DL that are used in network InfoSec. They showed that malware detection and network intrusion detection are two significant improvements in InfoSec cases by DL networks. DL has shown more significant improvements than rules-based and classic ML solutions. Zeng et al. (2020) introduced the network information concepts and current development status in China as a case study.

Due to the increasing amount of data collected and stored globally, the need for effective and efficient Intrusion Detection Systems (IDS) has become more critical. The actions that can threaten a source's confidentiality, availability, or integrity are referred to as intrusion. Such violations can cause various issues, such as the loss of data or unauthorized access to online resources. An IDS can be defined as an automated system that monitors activities and generates alarms when it detects a potential security issue. This type of monitoring system can then help an incident response team to identify and respond to the issue (Efe and Abacı, 2022). Lansky et al. (2021) explored the various frameworks that are used in DL-based intrusion detection which was published between 2010 and 2020. They provide a comprehensive analysis of the techniques that are used in the detection process. They also describe the types of DL networks that are used in the detection of this issue. They also provide an overview of the various security services that are offered by each scheme. Another survey was published by Gümüşbaş et al. (2021), in which the authors analyzed the various aspects of DL-based intrusion detection and its applications in cybersecurity. They focused on the most recent techniques which are based on DL.

Since using DL for InfoSec is still a hot topic, there are more studies that proposed DL models that have not been reviewed in the previously mentioned surveys. In Table 1, we tried to collect all the studies that have been published about newly proposed models in the last three years. Table 1 is ordered according to the published year of the paper.

## Benefits of Artificial Intelligence Applications in Information Security

AI can be beneficial in security. According to Onyango (2021), there are many benefits to implementing it. First Information Technology Asset Inventory can perform various tasks such as analyzing and categorizing data with AI. It can also help in making it easier for organizations to manage their inventory. Also, with AI-based systems, organizations can get up-to-date information about their global and company-specific security threats. This information can then be used to adjust their systems to prevent attacks. To maintain a stable and effective security posture, organizations must first understand how

*Table 1. Recently proposed models*

| Reference | Deep Learning Architecture | Purpose | Dataset |
|---|---|---|---|
| (Gu et al., 2019) | Intrusion detection framework based on SVM ensemble with feature augmentation | Effective intrusion detection framework | NSL-KDD dataset |
| (Thirumalairaj and Jeyakarthic, 2020) | Develop an application that detects intrusions and attacks, and protects computer systems | MLP and PID | CICIDS2017 dataset |
| (Tian et al., 2020) | An intrusion detection approach based on improved DBN | Mitigate the following problems in the existing intrusion detection systems: overfitting, low classification accuracy, and high false positive rate | NSL-KDD and UNSW-NB15 public datasets |
| (Zhong et al., 2020) | The Big Data based Hierarchical Deep Learning System | Enhance the performance of machine learning based IDS | ISCX2012 dataset DARPA1998 dataset CICIDS2017 dataset |
| (Karacan and Sevri, 2021) | Bi-LSTM based web application security models | Detect web attacks and classify them into binary or multiple classes using HTTP requests | CSIC-2010 HTTP Dataset ECML PKDD Dataset |
| (Liu et al., 2021) | The k-means and the random forest algorithms for the binary classification, Then, using the CNN, LSTM, and other DL algorithms. | Intrusion detection model that combines ML with DL | The NSL-KDD and CISIDS2017 datasets |
| (Nasir et al., 2021) | DL based insider attack detection scheme | Insider threat detection through behavioral analysis of users | CMU CERT synthetic insider threat dataset r4.2 |
| (Yan et al., 2021) | A deep convolution generative adversarial networks (DCGAN) based privacy protection method | Protect the information of collaborative DL training and enhance its stability | MNIST dataset |
| (Halbouni et al., 2022a) | A hybrid IDS model CNN and the LSTM Network | Increase the IDS detection rate and accuracy | CICIDS 2017, UNSW-NB15, and WSN-DS |

various processes and tools affect their overall security. With the aid of AI, they can create an efficient and stable InfoSec program.

Aside from monitoring and controlling the effectiveness of their assets, AI can also predict when and where a breach might happen. This method helps organizations plan their strategy and allocate resources to prevent a potential security issue from happening. According to a study conducted by a cybersecurity expert, using AI can help an organization's security department improve its efficiency and control its processes. In the long run, this method can help improve the company's cyber resilience. One of the most important factors that AI can help with when it comes to security is the response to incidents. With the help of this method, security officials can quickly identify the cause of the incident and prevent it from happening again. The ability to explain concepts and recommendations using AI systems is also beneficial for security. According to a cybersecurity expert, this process helps the management communicate with other stakeholders and employees involved in the security program (Onyango, 2021).

According to Kim (2021), AI can help security agencies detect and respond to malware and cyber-attacks by analyzing historical data. This technology, which can be used in combination with data mining, can be more efficient than humans when it comes to identifying harmful threats. In addition to analyzing data, this technology can also help security analysts identify threats within the organization. The lower the costs associated with a data breach, the faster it can be discovered. Using intelligent orchestration and safety automation, security organizations can improve their ability to respond to hazards and detect breaches (Li et al., 2019). AI applications are commonly used in various applications, such as spam filters and secure user authentication. These applications are designed to detect and respond to malware based on the behavior of the users in previous sessions. According to IBM, the cost of a data breach can be reduced by implementing automated security solutions. The cost of a security breach is typically higher in an automated organization than in a non-automated one. This is because the lack of automation in the security process can lead to significant financial losses.

Additionally, Onyango (2021) showed that by using AI, security experts can now isolate compromised data and prevent further attacks from happening in their networks. This process is very important as it can help organizations prevent their systems from being exploited by malware. Through its intelligence, the technology can then detect anomalous activities in the cyber environment.

# Information Security, Cyber-Attacks, and Their Defenses

According to Gupta et al. (2022), a cyber-attack is a type of attack that occurs when a network flaw or system is exploited by various vulnerabilities. It can be a daunting task to learn about new technologies and security trends. Even though the target may not be aware of all the types of cyber-attacks that are out there, they can still implement a strategy to prevent them from happening. The cause of such attacks can be either a residual or inherent risk. Some attack types that could threaten InfoSec are malware, phishing, password attacks, man-in-the-middle, SQL injection, and DoS.

According to Onyango (2021) to effectively address the various threats that can affect their operations, organizations must be able to implement AI in their security management processes. This can be done by using AI at three levels. The first level is prevention and mitigation. AI-based systems can be equipped with hidden defenses that can prevent unauthorized access, data errors, and losses. These systems use flexible algorithms to improve the management's decision-making process. When a new system is introduced, detection and prevention occur automatically. The second level is detection. AI systems are designed to analyze and understand the activities of a system. They are usually based on the system's signature. Each system has its own set of rules that are dependent on the recognition and update of its signatures. According to researchers, these systems can detect subtle changes in the data transmission and storage environment. A monitoring software uses advanced techniques to analyze and monitor the flow of packets and ensure that they are protected from various privacy and security violations. The third level is the response, which determines the efficiency of the AI in overcoming the threats it encounters. With the help of ML and natural language processing, AI can automate manual tasks such as searching logs. It can also create valuable activities using knowledge and shared learning. This allows it to respond efficiently to attacks originating from either an external or internal perimeter. An effective use of AI is to create duplicate environments that can be used to lure attackers into a trap. It can also identify gaps in the system and provide a solution to protect it. With network segmentation, some systems can be programmed to redirect attackers to safer areas. Through its advanced capabilities, AI can also help improve the security management of organizations by identifying and sealing the weakest points in the system (Onyango, 2021).

Miao et al. (2022) showed that one of the most important factors that can affect the success of a data-driven cybersecurity solution is the implementation of effective countermeasures. They summarized it into three main groups. The first group is detection which aims to identify and prevent unauthorized access to the data collected by the security algorithms. The second group is the disruption Which aims to disrupt the data in a cost-effective manner. The third group is isolation aims to limit access to data sources (Miao et al., 2022).

# OPEN PROBLEMS AND FUTURE DIRECTIONS

The study conducted on DL-based and ML security analytics revealed several research issues related to cybersecurity. This section aims to summarize the challenges faced by researchers in this field and provide them with future directions to improve the security of networks.

The performance of DL-based and ML security solutions depends on their characteristics and the nature of the security data. To effectively collect and analyze the security data in cybersecurity, it is very important that the learning algorithms can perform well in their respective domains. The current state of the cyber world enables the production of large amounts of data. Besides analyzing the security data, the researchers can collect useful data related to the target applications such as smart city applications. This can be done through the development of effective data collection methods. Unfortunately, the data collected by the security algorithms can contain various characteristics, such as missing values and outliers. The availability of training materials and the quality of the data are additionally important factors that affect the performance of the security model. If the security data is not good, the models may not be able to perform well. Quality and relevance of the data collected by the security algorithms are two of the most important factors that can affect the performance of a model. Besides the security features, other factors such as spatial context and temporal context can also considered to improve the model's performance.

There are numerous DL algorithms and neural networks that can be used to analyze security data. Unfortunately, choosing the right learning algorithm for the cybersecurity task is very challenging. The results of different learning algorithms depend on the data attributes they are handling. Selecting the wrong learning algorithm can lead to unexpected results and loss of effort. In addition, it can also affect the model's accuracy and effectiveness. In terms of model building, there is much research that provided numerous techniques that can be used to solve various security issues. However, one of the most important factors that can affect the performance of a model is the design of hybrid networks. This can be done by combining multiple learning algorithms and methods in one model.

ML models are often used to solve complex problems in the real world, but they can also be very inefficient. For instance, models that are used on a single device often require a lot of data to run properly. Instead of having to use a lot of resources to train them, implementing generalized algorithms that are designed to run on a small amount of data can help us make informed decisions.

During the last two years, most of the incidents that happened were related to network scanning, viruses, phishing, and website defacement. Every year, there are more incidents and new vulnerabilities. These attacks tend to leave the users with a lot of questions about the system. Despite the increasing number of attacks, the time it takes to respond to them is often not enough to prevent them from happening. Therefore, it is important that the various technologies that are used to protect the system are continuously updated.

Today, businesses rely on the Internet and internal computer systems to conduct their operations. Due to the increasing number of devices and their connectivity, network security is becoming more critical. Therefore, it is important that organizations adopt a strategy that enables them to manage their network security. This strategy should not only eliminate the privacy-sensitive features of acquired data but should also enable them to upload the data to remote clouds. Due to the rapid emergence and evolution of the internet and technology, it is important that people become more aware of the importance of security and privacy. One of the most effective ways to do this is by implementing a privacy-preserving mechanism. This type of system can help protect the messages sent and received between users.

In addition, various types of biometric and privacy-respecting databases can be integrated into security systems to provide convenient and secure storage of data. This approach clearly shows the potential threat to the privacy of data collected in the field of big data analytics. Despite the importance of protecting the privacy of data, it is still important to balance the quality of the analysis and the computational models used in the process.

Network topology is also important when it comes to security. Because of this, scalability issues in the model can be eliminated to reduce its inefficiencies. Unfortunately, due to the existence of privacy and economic concerns, the number of security incidents has been under-reported. One of the most effective ways to improve the security ecosystem is by developing a better technique for dealing with sudden and unexpected threats.

Current models can be used in certain scenarios to keep vital details abstract. Due to the emergence of AI and ML techniques, cyber security will be more sophisticated in the near future. Although an evaluation of existing security models is likely to be the best solution, it should still be considered with caution.

# DISCUSSION

AI can detect both present and future threats. as it is shown in this paper ML algorithms are popular for cybersecurity solutions because of the method's capability to detect advanced attacks and learn patterns. ML is a powerful tool for big data that can be used to analyze and improve the efficiency of various operations, such as forecasting and demand generation. There are already several methods that are being developed to improve the performance of ML. It is important to not only create a classification model but also to select the most suitable features from the dataset to achieve good performance.

The results of the analysis revealed that most of the studies focus on detecting specific attacks and abnormal network behaviors. On the other hand, the use of malware and software vulnerabilities is still marginal. Although the use of supervised DL techniques such as CNN is still prevalent, it is important to note that other DLN architectures are being used as well. In addition, the scope of applications that are being used is often too generic. Also, the number of datasets that are being used is still not public. The increasing number of publications about the chosen topic has created great room for the development of new DL techniques in the future.

AI has put forward many effective solutions to solve the security problems of infosec, but this does not mean that the security in this field has been properly solved. There are still many challenges to be faced in data, algorithms, and architecture. More research is required to develop viable solutions for other security concerns such as physical threats, network attacks, and encryption attacks. Communication systems also need to be more efficient, with more protective measures.

The training data of ML models can be exploited, especially those that are hosted on cloud-based systems, such as those used in fraud detection applications. For instance, ML models are confidential due to the security mechanisms that are built into these systems. Also, it is important to take in mind that the ML model itself can be vulnerable to attacks. An attacker can perform a different attack in two different attack modes. In the first, they aim to create an ML model as a tool to perform an efficient and accurate stealing attack. In the second, they target the model itself.

# CONCLUSION

Due to the increasing number of cyberattacks, the need for effective and efficient security measures has become more prevalent. The use of traditional security systems is no longer enough to prevent these attacks. This paper aims to provide a comprehensive overview of the various aspects of AI technology. Through this review, we aim to bridge the gap between the concepts of ML and threats to InfoSec. The paper discusses the applications of ML techniques and DL techniques in Infosec. Due to the varying characteristics of cyber threats, it is difficult to predict which model will be most effective in fighting them.

We have also discussed the various foundations of DL and ML, as well as the significant techniques that are required for a beginner to understand this technology. The paper presents a summary of the various attacks that are currently threatening infosec. It also discusses the existing techniques that are used to fight these threats. We have additionally discussed the security datasets that are commonly used by researchers.

With the help of AI, organizations can now identify and respond to threats immediately. This is very important as it allows them to develop effective incident response strategies. In the past few years, the use of AI has become a vital component of InfoSec management as it allows organizations to analyze, protect and detect their dynamic information systems. Due to the lack of traditional technologies to protect their systems, organizations can now benefit from the capabilities of AI. Using AI, organizations can now identify and prioritize the risks that they are facing in their networks. This allows them to develop effective incident response strategies and improve their efficiency. In addition to threat detection, AI also has applications in other areas such as inventory management and response to incidents.

We do hope that this review can benefit scholars involved in this area. Our future work will focus on a more in-depth analysis of ML and DL approaches for InfoSec.

# REFERENCES

Efe, A., & Abacı, İ. N. (2022). Comparison of the host based intrusion detection systems and network based intrusion detection systems. *Celal Bayar University Journal of Science*, *18*(1), 23–32. doi:10.18466/cbayarfbe.832533

Geetha, R., & Thilagam, T. (2021). A review on the effectiveness of machine learning and deep learning algorithms for cyber security. *Archives of Computational Methods in Engineering, 28*(4), 2861–2879. doi:10.100711831-020-09478-2

Gu, J., Wang, L., Wang, H., & Wang, S. (2019). A novel approach to intrusion detection using SVM ensemble with feature augmentation. *Computers & Security, 86*, 53–62. doi:10.1016/j.cose.2019.05.022

Gümüşbaş, D., Yıldırım, T., Genovese, A., & Scotti, F. (2021). A comprehensive survey of databases and deep learning methods for cybersecurity and intrusion detection systems. *IEEE Systems Journal, 15*(2), 1717–1731. doi:10.1109/JSYST.2020.2992966

Gupta, C., Johri, I., Srinivasan, K., Hu, Y. C., Qaisar, S. M., & Huang, K. (2022). A systematic review on machine learning and deep learning models for electronic information security in mobile networks. *Sensors (Basel), 22*(5), 2017. doi:10.339022052017 PMID:35271163

Haenlein, M., & Kaplan, A. (2019). A brief history of artificial intelligence: On the past, present, and future of artificial intelligence. *California Management Review, 61*(4), 5–14. doi:10.1177/0008125619864925

Halbouni, A., Gunawan, T. S., Habaebi, M. H., Halbouni, M., Kartiwi, M., & Ahmad, R. (2022a). CNN-LSTM: Hybrid deep neural network for network intrusion detection system. *IEEE Access : Practical Innovations, Open Solutions, 10*, 99837–99849. doi:10.1109/ACCESS.2022.3206425

Halbouni, A., Gunawan, T. S., Habaebi, M. H., Halbouni, M., Kartiwi, M., & Ahmad, R. (2022b). Machine learning and deep learning approaches for cybersecurity: A review. *IEEE Access : Practical Innovations, Open Solutions, 10*, 19572–19585. doi:10.1109/ACCESS.2022.3151248

Karacan, H., & Sevri, M. (2021). A novel data augmentation technique and deep learning model for web application security. *IEEE Access : Practical Innovations, Open Solutions, 9*, 150781–150797. doi:10.1109/ACCESS.2021.3125785

Kim, T. (2021). A study on the influence of artificial intelligence research on the development of information security research. *Asia-Pacific Journal of Convergent Research Interchange, 7*(12), 41–53. doi:10.47116/apjcri.2021.12.05

Lansky, J., Ali, S., Mohammadi, M., Majeed, M. K., Karim, S. H. T., Rashidi, S., Hosseinzadeh, M., & Rahmani, A. M. (2021). Deep learning-based intrusion detection systems: A systematic review. *IEEE Access : Practical Innovations, Open Solutions*, 9, 101574–101599. doi:10.1109/ACCESS.2021.3097247

Li, R., Tian, B., Li, Y., & Qu, Y. (2019). Information security evaluation based on artificial neural network. *International Journal of Performability Engineering*, 15(11), 2908–2915. doi:10.23940/ijpe.19.11.p9.29082915

Lippmann, R. P., Fried, D. J., Graf, I., Haines, J. W., Kendall, K. R., McClung, D., Weber, D., Webster, S. E., Wyschogrod, D., Cunningham, R. K., & Zissman, M. A. (2002). Evaluating intrusion detection systems: the 1998 DARPA off-line intrusion detection evaluation. In *Proceedings DARPA Information Survivability Conference and Exposition (DISCEX'00)* (pp. 12–26). IEEE. 10.1109/DISCEX.2000.821506

Liu, C., Gu, Z., & Wang, J. (2021). A hybrid intrusion detection system based on scalable K-means+ random forest and deep learning. *IEEE Access : Practical Innovations, Open Solutions*, 9, 75729–75740. doi:10.1109/ACCESS.2021.3082147

Miao, Y., Chen, C., Pan, L., Han, Q., Zhang, J., & Xiang, Y. (2022). Machine learning-based cyber attacks targeting on controlled information: A Survey. *ACM Computing Surveys*, 54(7), 1–36. doi:10.1145/3465171

Moustafa, N., & Slay, J. (2015). UNSW-NB15: a comprehensive data set for network intrusion detection systems (UNSW-NB15 network data set). In *Proceedings of 2015 Military Communications and Information Systems Conference (MilCIS)*. IEEE. 10.1109/MilCIS.2015.7348942

Nasir, R., Afzal, M., Latif, R., & Iqbal, W. (2021). Behavioral based insider threat detection using deep learning. *IEEE Access : Practical Innovations, Open Solutions*, 9, 143266–143274. doi:10.1109/ACCESS.2021.3118297

Onyango, O. (2021). Artificial intelligence and its application to information security management. doi:10.13140/RG.2.2.12066.09921

Podder, P., Bharati, S., Mondal, M. R. H., Paul, P. K., & Kose, U. (2021). Artificial neural network for cybersecurity: A comprehensive review. *Journal of Information Assurance and Security*, 16(1), 10–23. doi:10.48550/arXiv.2107.01185

Roponena, E., Kampars, J., Gailitis, A., & Strods, J. (2021). A literature review of machine learning techniques for cybersecurity in data centers. In *2021 62nd International Scientific Conference on Information Technology and Management Science of Riga Technical University, Proceedings (ITMS)* (pp. 1–6). IEEE. 10.1109/ITMS52826.2021.9615321

Sarker, I. H. (2021). Deep cybersecurity: A comprehensive overview from neural network and deep learning perspective. *SN Computer Science, 2*(3), 154. Advance online publication. doi:10.100742979-021-00535-6 PMID:33778771

Sharafaldin, I., Lashkari, A. H., & Ghorbani, A. A. (2018). Toward generating a new intrusion detection dataset and intrusion traffic characterization. In *Proceedings of the 4th International Conference on Information Systems Security and Privacy (ICISSP 2018)* (pp. 108–116). SCITEPRESS. 10.5220/0006639801080116

Shaukat, K., Luo, S., Varadharajan, V., Hameed, I. A., & Xu, M. (2020). A survey on machine learning techniques for cyber security in the last decade. *IEEE Access : Practical Innovations, Open Solutions, 8*, 222310–222354. doi:10.1109/ACCESS.2020.3041951

Shiravi, A., Shiravi, H., Tavallaee, M., & Ghorbani, A. A. (2012). Toward developing a systematic approach to generate benchmark datasets for intrusion detection. *Computers & Security, 31*(3), 357–374. doi:10.1016/j.cose.2011.12.012

Sriraghavan, R. G., & Lucchese, L. (2008). Data processing and anomaly detection in web-based applications. In *2008 IEEE Workshop on Machine Learning for Signal Processing* (pp. 187–192). IEEE. 10.1109/MLSP.2008.4685477

Thirumalairaj, A., & Jeyakarthic, M. (2020). Perimeter intrusion detection with multi layer perception using quantum classifier. In *2020 Fourth International Conference on Inventive Systems and Control (ICISC)* (pp. 348–352). IEEE. 10.1109/ICISC47916.2020.9171159

Tian, Q., Han, D., Li, K.-C., Liu, X., Duan, L., & Castiglione, A. (2020). An intrusion detection approach based on improved deep belief network. *Applied Intelligence, 50*(10), 3162–3178. doi:10.100710489-020-01694-4

Wang, R., & Ji, W. (2020). Computational intelligence for information security: A survey. *IEEE Transactions on Emerging Topics in Computational Intelligence, 4*(5), 616–629. doi:10.1109/TETCI.2019.2923426

Xin, Y., Kong, L., Liu, Z., Chen, Y., Li, Y., Zhu, H., Gao, M., Hou, H., & Wang, C. (2018). Machine learning and deep learning methods for cybersecurity. *IEEE Access : Practical Innovations, Open Solutions, 6,* 35365–35381. doi:10.1109/ACCESS.2018.2836950

Yan, X., Cui, B., Xu, Y., Shi, P., & Wang, Z. (2021). A method of information protection for collaborative deep learning under GAN model attack. *IEEE/ACM Transactions on Computational Biology and Bioinformatics, 18*(3), 871–881. doi:10.1109/TCBB.2019.2940583 PMID:31514150

Yavanoglu, O., & Aydos, M. (2017). A review on cyber security datasets for machine learning algorithms. In *IEEE International Conference on Big Data (Big Data)* (pp. 2186–2193). IEEE. 10.1109/BigData.2017.8258167

Zeng, H., Liu, Z., & Cai, H. (2020). Research on the application of deep learning in computer network information security. *Journal of Physics: Conference Series, 1650*(3), 032117. doi:10.1088/1742-6596/1650/3/032117

Zhong, W., Yu, N., & Ai, C. (2020). Applying big data based deep learning system to intrusion detection. *Big Data Mining and Analytics, 3*(3), 181–195. doi:10.26599/BDMA.2020.9020003

# Chapter 5
# Hardware and Software Cyber Security Tools

**Tamalika Das**
*Pailan College of Management and Technology, India*

**Nabonita Nath**
*Pailan College of Management and Technology, India*

**Kshounish Acharyya**
*Pailan College of Management and Technology, India*

**Shirsa Chakraborty**
*Pailan College of Management and Technology, India*

**Parag Chatterjee**
*Pailan College of Management and Technology, India*

## ABSTRACT

*The issue of cybercrime is becoming crucial in society. This is partly a result of the widespread adoption of technology in both essential government infrastructure and our daily lives. Due to an overreliance on technology, hackers and other people with bad intentions now have more ways to exploit systems and access databases containing sensitive data, including records relating to people's personal, financial, educational, and medical records. The importance of cybersecurity can be understood through research. Cyber security follows real-time information on the latest IT data. So far, various methods have been proposed by researchers around the world to prevent cyber-attacks or reduce the damage caused by them.*

DOI: 10.4018/978-1-6684-7110-4.ch005

# INTRODUCTION

The Internet has contributed significantly to international communication for more than two decades and is now a part of almost everyone's daily life. The availability, use, and performance of the Internet have substantially improved thanks to innovations and low cost in this sector; as a result, there are currently about 3 billion Internet users globally by Tan et al. (2021).

Currently, the majority of international economic, commercial, cultural, social, and governmental interactions and activities—including those of individuals, non-governmental organisations, governments, and governmental institutions—are conducted in cyberspace by Aghajani and Ghadimi (2018).

This place plays a crucial role in both the material and spiritual capital of nations and in the material success and spiritual growth of their population by Amir and Givargis (2020). Therefore, the question that arises is how to defend against cyber attacks.

Because they were typically constructed before current cybersecurity requirements, essential infrastructure like power plants, nuclear facilities, the electric grid, and dams are particularly susceptible to assaults. Our civilization is a prime target for cybercrime because of these expanding opportunities as well as hackers' greater motivation and access to resources.

Particularly, information warfare and cyberterrorism show the enormous effect of harmful attacks in action. Despite the fact that these attacks might not happen as frequently as other cybercrimes like cyberstalking, cyberbullying, identity theft, or data breaches, they have the capacity to bring down entire country's infrastructures and cripple vital resources. These attacks are frequently state-sponsored and are regarded as Advanced Persistent Threats (APT).

The only effective strategy to lowering future cybercrimes is to solve the underlying issue. While some cybercriminals may be driven by monetary gain, others may be motivated by social or political issues. One single policy might not be able to fully address all of these issues, therefore by concentrating on these many sorts of offenders, we can offer policymakers more appropriate answers.

For the cyber security and privacy of a corporation or an individual, a cybersecurity software is a must. The technique used to defend against cyberattacks on the network, system, or applications is known as cybersecurity. It serves as protection against identity theft, cyberattacks, and illegal data access. The various components of cybersecurity include application security, information security, network security, disaster recovery, operational security, etc. It must be kept up to date to protect against numerous cyberthreats, including social engineering, malware, phishing, and ransomware.

The term "hardware security" also describes protecting physical systems from harm. Attacks that aim to destroy equipment, for instance, concentrate on computing and networked non-computing equipment, such as that used in machine-to-machine or internet of things (IoT) contexts. Large numbers of hardware devices that need to be secured using either hardware- or software-based security are connected and communicate in these environments. Severe new security concerns have been identified and researched recently. These include IP (Intellectual Property) theft and reverse-engineering attacks on ICs (Integrated Circuits) by Torrance et al. (2009), hardware Trojan attacks by Tehranipoor et al. (2010) in an untrusted design house or foundry, side-channel attacks (Zhou et al., 2005) where secret information of a chip can be extracted through measurement of side-channels (such as power, delay, and electromagnetic emission), Modchip attacks (PCBs). These attacks show the necessity of hardware security. The vast scope also suggests that college students would need experimental equipment and tools that could support a variety of practice applications and were flexible enough for prospective improvements in the future at a lower cost. These tools would facilitate learning and application practice for students about hardware security topics.

Study says, security metrics are heavily used by 27% of large enterprises, 20% of mid-sized organisations, and 17% of small businesses. According to the same report, the cybersecurity market generated $91.4 billion in revenue in 2018 and had growth of 10.2%.

# CYBER SECURITY POLICIES

The ability to increase uniformity, which saves time, money, and resources, is the finest thing about having a policy. The policy should explain to the employees their specific responsibilities as well as what they are allowed and prohibited to do with confidential company information.

When a human error compromises system security, the organization's security policy will support any disciplinary action and serve as evidence in court if necessary. The company's policies serve as a contract that attests to the fact that the company has taken precautions to safeguard both its clients' and customers' intellectual property.

During a business transaction involving the transfer of their sensitive information, corporations are not required to give other vendors a copy of their information security policy. When working with smaller organisations that have less sophisticated security systems in place, it is true that larger businesses guarantee their own security interests are protected.

A well-written security policy can also be viewed as a teaching tool that informs readers of the significance of their role in safeguarding sensitive company data. It includes selecting the appropriate passwords and outlining procedures for file transfers and data storage, all of which raise employee understanding of security in general and how it may be reinforced. To govern the security of our network, we utilise security policies.

# WELL KNOWN CYBER SECURITY TOOLS

Our IT infrastructure needs to be protected above everything. Cybersecurity must be taken very seriously by every firm. Hacking assaults come in many forms and harm companies of all sizes. Viruses, spyware, and hackers are a few of the genuine security risks in the online world. Every organisation needs to be aware of the potentially harmful security assaults and take security precautions. The cyber defence may need to take into account a variety of factors.

**Antivirus Software**: Virus and other malware attacks on individual computers, networks, and IT systems can be prevented, detected, and eliminated with the help of antivirus software. Additionally, it guards against various threats and viruses as Trojan horses, worms, keyloggers, browser hijackers, rootkits.

**Penetration Testing:** By carefully attempting to exploit vulnerabilities, penetration testing, also known as pen-testing, is a crucial method for assessing the security of an IT infrastructure and the security of our company's security systems. Operating systems, services, and applications, poor setups, or dangerous end-user behaviour all contain these vulnerabilities. Cybersecurity experts will leverage criminal hackers' methods and techniques in penetration testing to look for vulnerabilities and potential dangers.

It stimulates he kind of cyber assault that might be made against a company, including password cracking, code injection, and phishing. A simulated real-world attack on a network or application is what it entails. In order to systematically assess servers, online applications, network devices, endpoints, wireless networks, mobile devices, and other components, these tests can be carried out using either manual or automated technologies.

**Firewall:** The firewall serves as the foundation of security measures and is among the most crucial ones. Its task is to stop unauthorised users from accessing or leaving a private network. It can be put into practise as software, hardware, or a combination of the two. Unauthorized internet users are prevented from accessing private networks linked to the Internet via firewalls. The firewall is the point of entry and exit for all messages to and from the intranet. Each message is examined by the firewall, which then rejects any that do not adhere to the established security standards. Although the Firewall is highly helpful, it also has certain drawbacks. A knowledgeable hacker was capable of producing data and programmes that acted as reliable firewalls.

**MDR:** Modern cybercriminals and hackers breached corporate security using increasingly sophisticated methods and technologies. Therefore, it is essential for all firms to employ stronger cybersecurity defences. Threat detection, threat intelligence, security monitoring, incident analysis, and incident response are all features of the advanced security service known as MDR. It is a service that develops out of the demand for organisations (that lack resources) to increase risk awareness and enhance their capacity to identify and address hazards. In addition, MDR employs AI and machine learning to do research, automatically identify threats, and coordinate responses for quicker outcomes.

**Rootkit Unhooker**: It is a simple tool that allows you to check for and get rid of rootkits from your system. In addition, it enables you to end drivers and other operations. You are welcomed by a typical window with a well-organized layout following a quick and uneventful setup process that doesn't demand particular user attention. Despite being unattractive, it is simple to navigate. Multiple panels devoted to SSDT, shadow SSDT, processes, drivers, stealth code, files, code hooks, and a report can be found in the main window. You can disconnect one or more chosen files, forcefully or gracefully end processes, see associated DLLs, dump all process memory, wipe or copy the file, and conduct BSOD.

# PASSWORD AUDITING TOOLS

**Wireshark**: A console-based cybersecurity tool called Wireshark was once known as Ethereal. The good network protocol analyzer Wireshark is used to do real-time network security analysis. To detect vulnerabilities, Wireshark examines network protocols and continuously sniffs the network. Wireshark is a helpful tool for examining every aspect of network traffic at various levels, from the connection level to every individual data packet. To capture data packets and examine the properties that individual data packets exhibit, security experts utilise Wireshark. The information acquired makes it simple to pinpoint security flaws in the network.

**Cain and Abel**: One of the first cybersecurity programmes to find flaws in Windows operating systems was Cain and Abel. Security experts can find holes in the password security of systems using the Windows operating system with the help of Cain and Abel. It is a free password recovery tool for cybersecurity. It provides a wide range of features, including the capacity to record VoIP conversations. Additionally, Cain and Abel can examine routing protocols to find out if compromised data packets are routed.

Furthermore, Cain and Abel use brute force attacks to decrypt encrypted passwords in addition to revealing cached passwords and password boxes. Additionally, the programme is very efficient at cryptoanalysis and can decipher passwords that have been scrambled. Cain and Abel should be used as the foundation for all packet sniffing procedures, according to businesses.

**Tcpdump**: It is used by cybersecurity experts to log and monitor TCP and IP traffic transmitted over networks. The command-based software tool tcpdump examines network traffic between the computer it runs on and the network it traverses. By capturing or filtering TCP/IP data traffic sent over or received over the network on a specified interface, Tcpdump precisely verifies the security of a network. Tcpdump uses a variety of formats, depending on the command, to describe the packet contents of network traffic.

## ENCRYPTION TOOLS

**Tor browser** can be an excellent choice to encrypt your internet traffic and shield your browsing habits from prying eyes if you wish to surf the Internet anonymously. Popular browser plugins like Flash, RealPlayer, Quicktime, and others that can be tricked into revealing your IP address will be blocked by Tor Browser. It is advised against adding any more add-ons or plugins to the Tor browser because doing so could lead Tor to be bypassed and put your privacy and security at risk. Anyone who wants to hide any surfing activities from prying eyes can use the unique Tor browser, which has been created for this purpose. The release candidate for the most recent version of this browser, Tor Browser 0.4.0.4, which is available for download, fixes a number of issues from earlier versions.

**LastPass,** arguably one of the most well-liked password manager software available, is free to use with a few features but will still protect your passwords and personal information. You won't need to remember or write down a password in a notepad or any other physical location if you use encryption software like this. With its user-friendly and straightforward interface, LastPass can make things simpler for you. The popular web browsers, including Mozilla Firefox and Google Chrome, each have extensions.

**TrueCrypt** is regarded as one of the most widely used encryption software. It is made for instantaneous encryption. The application can create virtual encrypted discs in a file or encrypt an entire storage device or storage medium. Additionally, TrueCrypt, which is a disc encryption technology, enables security experts to encrypt multilayer content using two separate access control types. This is one of the reasons TrueCrypt is still a widely used encryption programme even after its developers stopped giving it the necessary updates.

**KeePass** is primarily used by cybersecurity professionals for identity management. It is extremely applicable to various business contexts. It enables system users to log into all of their work-related accounts using a single password. KeePass is superior to other identity management tools because it balances security and usability. The application, for instance, enables system users to establish distinctive passwords that they can use to secure several accounts. Once the master password has been entered, KeePass will automatically fill in the password for the account being accessed. KeePass removes this threat because poor password management is the main cause of system or network intrusions. Security experts address security threats brought on by human factors with KeePass.

# NETWORK SECURITY TOOLS

**Splunk**: A quick and flexible network monitoring tool is Splunk. One of the applications with a more user-friendly UI. The robust search capabilities of Splunk make application monitoring simple. There are free and premium versions of the application Splunk. The free version has restrictions. If you have a limited budget, this is a great tool to add to your list. Independent contractors frequently exercise caution while purchasing expensive tools. Splunk is an excellent investment. Any information security expert with a sizable clientele should purchase Splunk.

**P0f**: P0f is widely used because the application was almost perfect when it was released, there haven't been many changes in more than ten years. P0f is efficient and streamlined, producing no extra traffic. Any host with which it communicates can use it to determine the OS system on that host. Numerous tools in this category generate inquiries of various types, including probes and name lookups. P0f runs smoothly and is light. A must for experienced users, but not the simplest for the team's newcomers to grasp.

## VULNERABILITIES AND EXPOSURE

As the number of vulnerabilities discovered and reported grows, so does the scarcity of experts in secure software development. When publicly known vulnerabilities are reported, a unique identifier is assigned by MITRE's CVE (Common Vulnerabilities and Exposures) program. CVE Numbering Authorities (CNA), which includes major IT companies such as Microsoft, Oracle, and RedHat, as well as CERT Coordination Centers, have contributed to this repository. Custom-built software is not included in the database. Figure 1 depicts the number of CVE identifiers assigned and a rising trend.

*Figure 1. Number of CVE IDs per year*

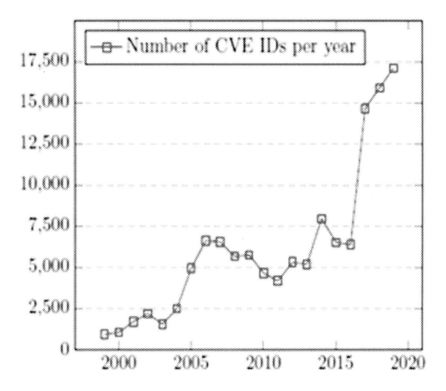

The (ISC)2 Cybersecurity Workforce Study 2019 estimates that the current worldwide cybersecurity workforce gap is around 4.07 million ((ISC)2 2019). According to the Frost & Sullivan (2017) report for the Center for Cyber Safety and Education, the most high-value skills in short supply are intrusion detection, secure software development, and attack mitigation. A study by the Center for Strategic and International Studies (2016) in partnership with Intel Security also indicated secure software development as the second most scarce skill in cybersecurity.

The current situation is both a challenge and an opportunity for higher education institutions. Universities must address a genuine need for businesses and society, which allows us to propose academic programmes that provide a concrete career path in cybersecurity. It is worth noting in this regard that formal security education can enable new specialists to compete with more experienced professionals in solving well-formalized but relatively new security tasks by Allodi et al. (2018).

The following educational questions are pertinent to software security:

What role can higher education play in software security education?
Which pedagogical approaches are available, and which teaching and learning
    theories can they be based on?
How to effectively teach the design and development concepts and techniques.

## SOFTWARE SECURITY EDUCATION

According to Schneider (2013), there are two distinct perspectives on how to develop university cybersecurity courses. The first is to teach adversarial thinking in order to allow designers to see their systems through the eyes of attackers. The second is to concentrate on the principles and abstractions required to build secure systems. Authors such as Bishop and Frincke (2005), Dark, Belcher et al. (2015), Pothamsetty (2005), and Walden and Frank (2006) advocate that academia and industry should focus on training software engineers to consider security in all aspects of the development process, including requirements, design, implementation, testing, and deployment. Pothamsetty (2005), in particular, observes that on many occasions, much more effort is put into.

Jøsang *et al.* (2015) remark that many IT experts still have insufficient understanding of security and "it is irresponsible to offer IT programs at university without compulsory modules in information security".

According to Bishop and Frincke (2005), adding security mechanisms to existing systems or fixing vulnerabilities is difficult because it necessitates a thorough understanding of many aspects of these systems. Furthermore, they recommend that one of the primary goals of an undergraduate computer science curriculum be to teach students how to write secure code.

Because there is a significant applicative aspect in disciplines such as computer science, principles and practise are frequently blended. On the one hand, this meets employers' expectations that graduates understand both theory and practise. On the other hand, there is concern that educators will focus on teaching specific programming languages, techniques, and environments at the expense of teaching concepts and principles that can be applied to new situations because of the need for software security.

There is a conflict between the need to learn how to solve specific current problems and the ability to tackle new ones in the future. Some scholars, such as Bishop (2000), believe that undergraduate education should focus on broad principles and their application, rather than specific technologies, because the main goal should be to enable the understanding of general principles that can be abstracted and applied across many situations and systems.

Others, such as Johnstone (2013), believe that a thorough understanding of how systems operate in practise is unavoidable. They believe this is also true when it comes to teaching secure coding to beginners, because, while some vulnerabilities can be mitigated with simple programming techniques, the most significant exploits are carried out by individuals who have spent a significant amount of time learning how software behaves and how to exploit it. To determine whether such vulnerabilities exist, students must first understand how these exploits work.

Williams et al., (2014) argue that students should learn secure code principles alongside other aspects of computer programming, but Johnstone (2013) points out that some instructors are concerned that teaching programming secure software systems will be another barrier to learning to code. He agrees that students should learn secure coding practises in order to avoid writing insecure programmes, but he recognises that explaining how different exploits work may be difficult due to a lack of understanding of how computer systems work.

Another question concerns the application of research to security education. According to some authors, such as Bishop (2002) and Dark, Bishop et al., (2015), students are rarely exposed to research until they begin working on their dissertation. In accordance with the research-led teaching approach, they propose providing continuous exposure to scholarly work throughout the course of studies (Griffiths, 2004). The goal is to apply research findings and methodologies to real-world problems in a practical setting. This approach assists students in connecting theory to practise and in incorporating cutting-edge techniques into their future work. However, from an educational standpoint, the technical complexity of security research makes this task extremely difficult.

## Rationale for the Design of a Course on Security Protocols Design and Implementation

We can now discuss the rationale for designing a course on programming security protocols based on the background work presented in the previous sections. They are important because they play an important role in protecting data exchanged over a network infrastructure that can be controlled by an adversary, and as we have seen, programming security protocols is difficult and error-prone.

The course's main pedagogical goal is to teach how to build secure distributed applications using common cryptographic primitives (symmetric and asymmetric encryption, digital signature, hashing, message authentication codes) while abstracting from their low-level details. This course is designed to assist students in quickly grasping key security concepts and effectively applying them to the development of distributed programs that can ensure security goals such as authentication and confidentiality.

It should be noted that our goal is not simply to transfer knowledge, but to effect cognitive change in the learner. As a result, the course is also designed to familiarise students with techniques such as formal modelling and verification of security protocols, as well as Model Driven Development when time allows (MDD)

For the development of this course, we identified the needs to be addressed as a series of design and pedagogical questions, inspired by Ben-constructivist Ari's approach (2001).

For the reasons stated in Section 3, we focus primarily on constructivism, specifically in the works of Ben-Ari (2001, 2006) and Hadjerrouit (1998, 1999, 2005). In summary, constructivism enables the development of a viable mental model and aids in the early detection of misconceptions.

To that end, the selection of tools, as well as the pedagogical reasons, is critical in this context. This choice, however, can be flexible, as teachers can generally consider their own preferences and interests in terms of software tools for modelling and verification, as well as specification/programming languages, as long as the choice of tools is coherent and consistent with the approach and the learning objectives. As a result, the concrete example of the course we propose should be viewed as a proof-of-concept, inspired by our research interests and practise as well. As a result, when necessary, we briefly introduce the tools that will be discussed in greater detail in Section 6.

*Figure 2. Abstract and concrete model*

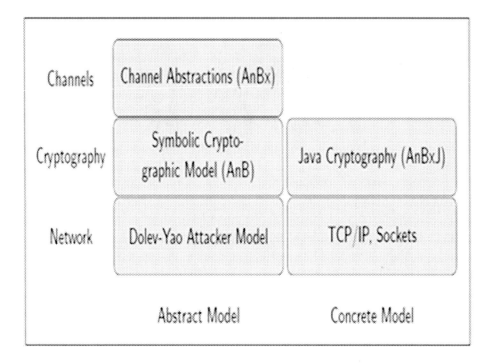

## What Is the Appropriate Model of the "System"?

First and foremost, from a constructivist standpoint (Ben-Ari, 2001; Hadjerrouit, 1998), we must consider what is the appropriate model of the "system." There are two main approaches to security protocols: computational and symbolic (Blanchet, 2012). Messages are bitstrings in the computational model, and cryptographic primitives are functions that map bitstrings to bitstrings. The model takes into account the computational properties of cryptography primitives (for example, key size), and the adversary is any probabilistic Turing machine..

The cryptographic primitives are represented by function symbols in the symbolic model, as in the Dolev and Yao (1983) adversary model, assuming perfect cryptography. The opponent is limited to using only such primitives. Figure 3 depicts the intruder rules, and the fact knows(m) indicates that the intruder is aware of the term m. Every communication between honest agents is assumed to be mediated by the intruder, i.e. it occurs via knows facts. The model assumes the existence of a set of function symbols (each with an associated arity) divided into public and private subsets. The first rule applies to both asymmetric encryption and signing, whereas the second assumes that a ciphertext can be decrypted if the corresponding decryption key is known.

# What Is the Suitable Level of Abstraction?

Along with the adversary model, we must teach how to model cryptographic primitives and their properties in the symbolic model. This is required so that the learner can understand the actions that honest agents take during protocol execution. This is necessary in order to comprehend the model and define a level of abstraction upon which the learners can build their knowledge. At this point, we should recall Ben-(2001) Ari's recommendation about explicitly presenting a viable model one level below the one we are teaching. To that end, we propose a set of learning activities aimed at building simple security protocols in a real programming language (Java in our case).

The logic of this approach is supported by Sivilotti and Lang (2010), who propose separating interface concerns from implementation concerns. According to Alexandron et al. (2012), one potential challenge is that some programmers may perceive the appropriate level of abstraction as the one that corresponds to their programming experience. This can cause cognitive dissonance, which can "even lead to a negative attitude toward the high-level abstraction."

*What Is a Language Suitable for the Specification of Security Protocols?*

We propose the Alice and Bob language (AnB) (Mödersheim, 2009), a simple and intuitive notation for describing messages exchanged between agents and allowing the formal specification of security goals in a human readable format. Messages can be composed using symbolic cryptographic functions. This notation simplifies (and compacts) the coding of security protocols compared to other formal languages (e.g., process calculi (Abadi and Fournet, 2001; Abadi and Gordon, 1997) or real-world programming languages. This simple language enables students to create their own security protocol models and experiment with them using tools that support such notation, such as the model checker OFMC.

# HARDWARE SUPPORT FOR SOFTWARE SECURITY

Attackers find it simpler to penetrate software. One single objective of compromised software is to overuse computational resources. Such mistreatment might occur in different ways.

forms, such as the alteration of crucial code or data, the theft of private information, and eavesdropping on or involvement in system operations. Cyber-physical systems should be resilient and continue to function properly even in the face of harmful attacks. We look at computer hardware's role in preventing harmful assaults from compromising software in the parts that follow. We begin by discussing attacks and defences that rely on software, then go on to how hardware enhances crypotography's performance and security, and finally, we examine defences against physical attacks that rely on hardware access.

Accessing memory from another application is a straightforward attack. Attackers are drawn to try gaining unrestricted access in order to run harmful software or steal sensitive data because of code and data vulnerabilities. Traditional defences against memory-based attacks isolate execution contexts, such as processes and virtual memory address spaces, to stop one context from unauthorised accessing the data and code of another.

Discuss tried-and-true and cutting-edge methods for hardware-supported memory isolation.

even when using strong passwords, robust cryptography, and physically guarded hardware, as well as when isolating each programme in a system.

Despite the fact that cryptographic accelerators make cryptography more efficient and aid in preventing side-channel attacks, there is still a chance that the device will end up in the hands of the attacker. An attacker having physical access to hardware can steal data or undermine security mechanisms even with fairly sophisticated technology. Secure coprocessing is one method for protecting against physical assault.

In general, a secure coprocessor must be able to safeguard sensitive data, such as cryptographic keys, from physical attack, offer side-channel-resistant cryptographic operations to the host system, and offer a secure environment for software execution. Physical protection methods such as fuses, temperature sensors, and other tamper detection methods that can result in the destruction of all secrets are often used to meet the first condition.

# Memory Protection

The use, modification, and sharing of a computing system's resources are governed by security policies. In the past, an operating system (OS) was used to specify security policies and rely on hardware to help enforce them.

This section examines how hardware supports system security by isolating and managing resources.

## Memory Security in Common Systems

Think of an abstract computer that has two main parts: the CPU and the memory. To run programmes, the processor retrieves code and data from memory.

A programme could mistakenly or maliciously corrupt or steal another program's data from memory or prohibit any other programme from accessing the processor if both components are shared by all applications (denial-of-service).

The kernel holds the highest privilege ring and hence has complete control over all computing resources. Any memory address can be read or written to, any command supported by the processor can be carried out, all hardware events can be received, and all peripherals can be operated. User applications, which are at the lowest level of privilege, can only access peripherals by using OS services, have restricted memory access (which is now enforced by virtual memory), and cannot execute privileged instructions.

Bits in a specialised register, referred to as the programme status word generally and as the Program Status Register in ARM architectures, the Hypervisor State Bit in PowerPC architectures, the Privileged Mode in the Processor State Register in SPARC architectures, or the Current Privilege Level in the Code Segment Register in Intel architectures, distinguish between the kernel and the user.

The middle rings are architecture-specific and frequently omitted in practise.

The privileged status also specifies memory separation in straightforward designs. A straightforward policy might allow privileged code to access all memory, while user code is limited to a specific range, such as 0xF000 to 0xFFFF. Privileged code can control memory allocation and division across application tasks using one or more fixed memory divisions. Static memory partitioning is not feasible for all applications, save from embedded and highly customised ones.

*Figure 3. Rings of privilege (levels). The OS or hypervisor often uses the innermost ring, which has the maximum privilege level at which software can run. The lowest privilege is in the outermost ring, which is typically utilised by application software.*

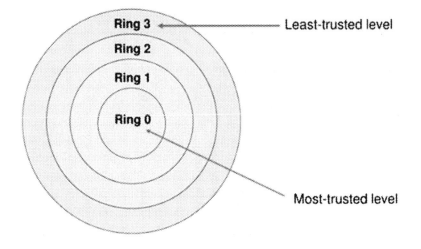

Dynamic memory management is necessary in a multiprocessing system with dynamic tasks because it prevents memory fragmentation and maintains resource balance. Each dynamic task has unique (and frequently statically unknown) memory and execution requirements.

## Hardware Trojan Detection

Hardware Trojans are more dangerous to computer systems since they can't be simply removed by firmware updates, unlike software viruses and software Trojans. Attackers create hardware Trojans to modify the design with undesirable capabilities. There is no set method for creating hardware Trojans because it depends on the objectives and resources of the attacker.

Despite this, experts in hardware security have classified several Trojans. As an illustration, authors in classified Trojans into implicit payload and explicit payload depending on the actions the Trojan took when it was activated provide a more thorough taxonomy of the Trojan family.

Based on the stealth of hardware Trojans and the potential damage they may do, many Trojan designs were also put forth.

A different well-liked solution is side-channel fingerprinting. Even though a hardware Trojan can avoid functional testing since it is difficult to activate during testing, the installed Trojan still needs to change the parametric profile of a contaminated circuit. This method's efficacy depends on the capacity to distinguish between side-channel signals from circuits with and without Trojans.

In order to generate side-channel fingerprints by removing the growing process variation and measurement noise, complex data analysis techniques are used. For fingerprint formation and Trojan identification, a number of side-channel characteristics and their combinations are used, such as path delays, global power traces, local power traces, and global power traces.

# Proof-Carrying Hardware

An way to guaranteeing the reliability of hardware is Proof-Carrying Hardware. The PCH approach draws its inspiration from G. Necula's proof-carrying code (PCC).

Unreliable software vendors and developers certify their software code via the PCC process.

After that, the vendor gives the user a PCC binary file that contains the formal proof of the safety features encoded in the software's executable code. When the PCC binary file is promptly validated in a proof checker, the customer is given confidence in the security of the programme code.

This method's effectiveness in cutting down on customer validation time caused it to be used in a variety of applications. Despite its benefits, the PCC technique required a sizable, reliable computing base (TCB).

Authors in suggested a preliminary Proof-Carrying Hardware (PCH) for dynamically reconfigurable hardware platforms, which was modelled after the PCC framework concept. Utilizing runtime combinational equivalences testing between the design specification and the design implementation on reconfigurable platforms is the important concept in this situation.

With the exception that the resolution proof traces are taken as proofs for the functional equivalence, this approach, despite being called PCH, is actually a SAT solver-based combinational equivalence checking.

In this approach, the security attribute and the imposed safety policy are unrelated.

Instead, the conjunctive normal form, which is used to describe combinational functions, is the bitstream format that both bitstream providers and IP consumers have agreed to use.

A new PCH framework was created, which was based on the development and use of the CAP, in order to apply the proof-carrying approach to secure generic pre-synthesis register-transfer level (RTL) IP cores other than the post-synthesis FPGA bitstreams.

The new PCH framework uses the Coq functional language for proof building and makes use of the Coq platform for automatic proof validation, similar to FPCC and CAP framework.

Utilizing the Coq platform makes it possible to streamline the evidence validation process and ensures that IP sellers and consumers will use the same deductive principles.

However, the Coq platform is unable to natively detect the HDLs used by commercial devices.

A formal temporal logic model was created to represent hardware circuits in the Coq environment in order to address this issue.

## Hardware-Assisted Computer Security

Hardware platforms may be included in software-level protection plans in addition to circuit-level IC supply chain protection techniques. Researchers in the field of cybersecurity frequently use layered security protection techniques and have created a number of strategies to safeguard a higher abstract layer (such as the guest OS) by strengthening security at a lower abstract layer (such as the virtual machine monitor or hypervisor).

Cybersecurity defence mechanisms have been pushed from guest OS to hypervisors through this chain.

Following this pattern, new techniques are being developed for directly supporting advanced security policies through modifications to the hardware infrastructure, making system-level protection systems more effective. In reality, security-enhanced hardware enabling cybersecurity defences has recently gained a lot of popularity in both industrial and academic research.

## ARM TrustZone

In order to enable trusted computing, the TrustZone concept relies on a trusted platform, where a hardware design upholds and enforces a security infrastructure across the system.

The TrustZone architecture ensures system-wide security that is extended to any component of the system, as opposed to safeguarding assets in a specific hardware block.

The TrustZone architecture essentially attempts to offer a security framework to enable the creation of a programmable environment that allows the confidentiality and integrity of application assets against a variety of assaults.

The hardware and software resources on the SoC are divided into two worlds—one that is secure and one that is not—in order for the TrustZone implementation to work. For the handling of secure and non-secure applications, as well as their interaction and communication, hardware supports access control and permissions.

## Intel SGX

Extensions to the Intel architecture known as the Intel SGX (software guard extension) are used to enforce memory access regulations and permissions. Applications can now operate in the native operating system (OS) environment with confidentiality and integrity thanks to these changes.

Instruction set architecture (ISA) extensions are used to create hardware-enforceable containers at a developer-specified granularity, either fine or coarse, to achieve userspace compartmentalization.

With the aid of these extensions, an application is able to create an enclave, a protected container that designates a secure region within the application's address space. Despite being invisible to the OS, these containers are nevertheless under its control. Software that is not resident in the enclave cannot attempt to access the memory area of the enclave.

## CHERI

With software compatibility intact, the CHERI (capability hardware enhanced RISC instruction) addition aims to provide fine-grained memory compartmentalization in hardware.

Previous methods that used software virtualization to provide fine-grained compartmentalization result in significant performance overhead. Hardware compartmentalization has historically only offered coarse-grained security through reducing overhead.

Two compartmentalization examples that achieve a compromise between better efficiency while still providing virtualized security, but at the sacrifice of granularity, are the stack frame and memory management unit (MMU) page protection.

The CHERI project adds byte granularity memory protection to the 64-bit MIPS ISA (instruction set architecture) via a hybrid, capability-based addressing approach that supports MMU virtual memory. The CHERI extension is supported by updates to the LLVM compiler and FreeBSD operating system.

# CONCLUSION

Employees working from home use systems that have not been patched, completed, or protected by the company's IT department. It expands the company's attack surface and allows hackers to enter the system from within, bypassing border security. Critical business data is being stored on these systems, increasing the risk of a data breach.

More and more businesses are implementing IoT devices and applications to collect data, remotely control and manage infrastructure, improve customer service, and other purposes. Many IoT devices lack strong security, making them vulnerable to attack. Hackers can increase the mechanism of botnet strategies for practise and influence IoT faintness to gain network access.

The future of cybersecurity will be like the present: difficult to describe and potentially limitless as digital skills interact with humans across virtually all aspects of policies, society, the family, and the outside world. We built this project on the premise that the "cyber" and "security" mechanisms of the concept "cybersecurity" would be in high gear throughout the second half of the 2010s. That gesture is more likely to quicken than slow, but its manner varies greatly depending on our circumstances.

# REFERENCES

Abadi, M., & Fournet, C. (2001). Mobile values, new names, and secure communication. In C. Hankin & D. Schmidt (Eds.), *Conference Record of POPL 2001: The 28th ACM SIGPLAN-SIGACT Symposium on Principles of Programming Languages*. ACM. doi:10.1145/360204.360213

Abadi, M., & Gordon, A. D. (1997). A calculus for cryptographic protocols: The Spi calculus, In *CCS '97, Proceedings of the 4th ACM Conference on Computer and Communications Security*. ACM. doi:10.1145/266420.266432

Aghajani, G., & Ghadimi, N. (2018). *Multi-objective energy management in a micro-grid Energy Rep.* Academic Press.

Alexandron, G., Armoni, M., Gordon, M., & Harel, D. (2012). The effect of previous programming experience on the learning of scenario-based programming. In Proceedings of the 12th KOLI Calling International Conference on Computing Education Research. ACM. https://doi.org/10.1145/2401796.2401821.

Allodi, L., Cremonini, M., Massacci, F., & Shim, W. (2018). *The Effect of Security Education and Expertise on Security Assessments: the Case of Software Vulnerabilities*. Academic Press.

Amir, M., & Givargis, T. (2020). Pareto optimal design space exploration of cyber–physical systems. *Internet Things, 12*.

Ben-Ari, M. (2001). Constructivism in computer science education. *Journal of Computers in Mathematics and Science Teaching, 20*(1), 45–74.

Ben-Ari, M., & Yeshno, T. (2006). Conceptual models of software artifacts. *Interacting with Computers, 18*(6), 1336–1350.

Bishop, M. (2000). Education in information security. *IEEE Concurrency, 8*(4), 4–8.

Bishop, M. (2002). Computer security education: Training, scholarship, and research. *Computer, 35*(4), 31.

Bishop, M., & Frincke, D. A. (2005). Teaching secure programming. *IEEE Security and Privacy, 3*(5), 54–56.

Blanchet, B. (2012). Security protocol verification: Symbolic and computational models. In *Proceedings of the First International Conference on Principles of Security and Trust*. Springer-Verlag.

Center for Strategic and International Studies. (2016). *Hacking the skills shortage. A study of the international shortage in cybersecurity skills*. Author.

Dark, M., Belcher, S., Bishop, M., & Ngambeki, I. (2015). Practice, practice, practice... secure programmer! *Proceeding of the 19th Colloquium for Information System Security Education*.

Dolev, D., & Yao, A. (1983). On the security of public-key protocols. *IEEE Transactions on Information Theory, 2*(29).

Frost & Sullivan. (2017). *2017 Global information security workforce study. Benchmarking workforce capacity and response to cyber risk*. Academic Press.

Griffiths, R. (2004). Knowledge production and the research-teaching nexus: The case of the built environment disciplines. *Studies in Higher Education, 29*(6), 709–726.

Hadjerrouit, S. (1998). A constructivist framework for integrating the java paradigm into the undergraduate curriculum. In *ACM SIGCSE Bulletin*. ACM.

Hadjerrouit, S. (1999). A constructivist approach to object-oriented design and programming. In *ACM SIGCSE Bulletin*. ACM.

Hadjerrouit, S. (2005). Constructivism as guiding philosophy for software engineering education. *ACM SIGCSE Bulletin, 37*(4), 45–49.

(ISC)2. (2019). *Global information security workforce study 2019. Cybersecurity professionals focus on developing new skills as workforce gap widens*. Academic Press.

Johnstone, M. N. (2013). Embedding secure programming in the curriculum: Some lessons learned. *IACSIT International Journal of Engineering and Technology, 5*(2), 287.

Jøsang, A., Ødegaard, M., & Oftedal, E. (2015). Cybersecurity through secure software development. In *IFIP World Conference on Information Security Education*. Springer.

Mödersheim, S. (2009). Algebraic properties in Alice and Bob notation. *International Conference on Availability, Reliability and Security (ARES 2009)*. doi:10.1109/ARES.2009.95

Pothamsetty, V. (2005). Where security education is lacking. In *Proceedings of the 2nd Annual Conference on Information Security Curriculum Development*. ACM. https://doi.org/10.1145/1107622.1107635

Schneider, F. B. (2013). Cybersecurity education in universities. *IEEE Security and Privacy, 11*(4), 3–4.

Sivilotti, P. A., & Lang, M. (2010). Interfaces first (and foremost) with Java. In Proceedings of the 41st ACM Technical Symposium on Computer Science Education. ACM. https://doi.org/10.1145/1734263.1734436.

Tan, S. (2021). Attack detection design for dc microgrid using eigenvalue assignment approach. *Energy Rep., 7*, 469-476.

Tehranipoor, M. M., & Koushanfar, F. (2010). A Survey of Hardware Trojan Taxonomy and Detection. *IEEE Design & Test of Computers*, 27.

Torrance, R., & James, D. (2009). *The State-of-the-Art in IC Reverse Engineering.* . doi:10.1007/978-3-642-04138-9_26

Walden, J., & Frank, C. E. (2006). Secure software engineering teaching modules. In *Proceedings of the 3rd Annual Conference on Information Security Curriculum Development*. ACM. https://doi.org/10.1145/1231047.1231052.

Williams, K. A., Yuan, X., Yu, H., & Bryant, K. (2014). Teaching secure coding for beginning programmers. *Journal of Computing Sciences in Colleges*, *29*(5), 91–99.

Zhou, Y., & Feng, D. (2005). Side-Channel Attacks: Ten Years After Its Publication and the Impacts on Cryptographic Module Security Testing. *IACR Cryptology ePrint Archive, 388.*

# Chapter 6
# Zero Day Vulnerabilities Assessments, Exploits Detection, and Various Design Patterns in Cyber Software

**Vidhanth Maan Thapa**
*University of Petroleum and Energy Studies, India*

**Sudhanshu Srivastava**
*University of Petroleum and Energy Studies, India*

**Shelly Garg**
*University of Petroleum and Energy Studies, India*

## ABSTRACT

*In this technology-driven era, software development and maintenance is a rapidly growing domain and is predestined to thrive over the coming decade. But the growing demand for software solutions also brings its own implications. Software vulnerabilities are the most crucial of these. Software Vulnerabilities can be referred to as weaknesses or shortcomings of the software solutions which increase the risks of exploitation of resources and information. In the past few years, the number of exploits has been increasing rapidly, reaching an all-time high in 2021 affecting more than 100 million people worldwide. Although, even with the presence of existing vulnerability management models and highly secure tools and frameworks, software vulnerabilities are harder to identify and resolve as they may not be independent, and resolving them may cause other vulnerabilities. Moreover, a majority of the exploit are caused due to known vulnerabilities and zero-day vulnerabilities..*

DOI: 10.4018/978-1-6684-7110-4.ch006

# 1. INTRODUCTION

Zero-day vulnerabilities are the vulnerabilities that were previously unknown to the vulnerability management team[1]. They have a high risk of being exploited even before identification. These turn into zero-day exploits, if vulnerabilities are exploited before mitigation[2]. 2021 experienced exponential growth in these exploits with an estimate that more than 40 percent of these attacks occurred in the last year. From the 2006 Stuxnet attack to the 2019 Facebook and 2021 LinkedIn zero-day attacks, zero-day vulnerabilities are the cause of the majority of cyber attacks compromising the resources and information of millions of users[3-8].

## 1.1 Causes of Increased Zero-Day Exploits/Vulnerabilities

A major reason for an increasing number of zero-day vulnerabilities is the rising number of software solutions and updates that occur regularly. Although, these vulnerabilities are harder to detect before being exploited due to their unknown nature but often times devs don't really resolve these implications even identification as it may break other existing programs. This usually occurs due to ineffective design patterns or the existence of anti-patterns in the software solution. Moreover, large software solutions have hundreds (if not thousands) of existing vulnerabilities which may have higher risks of exploitation[9].

Furthermore, as a result of the increasing number of private companies that provide offensive cyber tools and services and malware vendors, global ransomware activity has escalated to a massive extent. This accessibility to developed exploit kits has hiked the number of zero-day exploits over the past few years[10].

## 1.2 Handling Zero-Day Vulnerabilities

Due to the unknown nature and increasing existing presence in legacy and current software solutions, it's impossible to completely eradicate zero-day vulnerabilities but with specific practices and tools, we can reduce their growth, and codependencies and tackle these exploits much more effectively in the long run[11].

For a secure software solution in regard to vulnerabilities and exploits we should successfully incorporate the following steps:

1.  Preventing zero-day vulnerabilities to occur in the first place.
2.  Finding Existing Zero-day Vulnerabilities.
3.  Quick Recovery from zero-day exploits.

## 1.3 Preventing Zero-Day Vulnerabilities To Occur In The First Place

One of the major reasons for the existence of zero-day vulnerabilities in software solutions is the implementation of improper or too co-dependent software/ architectural design patterns which often hinder troubleshooting or debugging processes. A suitable architectural design pattern can help mitigate security vulnerabilities. The basic procedure to choose a secure architectural design pattern for your software solution[12].

## 1.4 Secure Design Patterns

Secure design patterns help in minimizing the accidental insertion of vulnerabilities into the codebase and mitigate the consequences of these vulnerabilities.

Secure design patterns addressing security issues during the architectural design phase and the code-implementation phase[13].

A design pattern is a reusable solution partial solution to a commonly occurring problem in the designing phase. Secure design patterns differ a lot from security patterns which deal with access control, authorization, and authentication (AAA). These assist in the facilitation of secure development processes and govern the existence and configuration of current security systems.

There are three general classes of secure design patterns:

*   **Architectural level design patterns**: Architectural level design patterns primarily focus on high-level administration of roles and responsibilities between different components of the software solution and also define the interaction between these components. Distrustful Decomposition, Privilege Separation, and Defer to Kernel are some of the most widely used architectural-level secure design patterns[14-20].
*   **Design level Patterns:** Design level patterns help in addressing internal design issues of these high-level components and not the interaction between these components. Example: Secure State Machine and Secure Visitor[21].

- **Implementation Level patterns:** Implementation level patterns involve low-level security issues and are usually applicable for implementing a specific functionality or feature to the software solution. Secure Directory, Pathname Canonicalization, and RAII (Runtime Acquisition Is Initialization) are some of the widely used Implementation level patterns[22].

There can be many secure design pattern solutions depending on software susceptibilities and problem statements, although for preciseness and to avoid divergence from the current subject matter we will cover the following secure design patterns in detail[23-30].

## 1.5 Distrustful Decomposition

Distrustful decomposition is an architectural-level secure design pattern that primarily focuses on dividing the system into many small independent processes where each process has its own set of privileges. IPC mechanisms (Inter-Process communication) such as Remote Procedure calls (RPCs) and Unix domain sockets help in facilitating communication between these processes. The primary objective of the Distrustful decomposition design pattern is to move separate functions into mutually untrusting programs[31].

This helps in reducing the attack surface and prevents other processes to be affected when one or more processes are compromised. This prevents the attacker from compromising the entire system due to the exploitation of the single process/component because no other process trusts the information dispatched by the compromised component[32].

Incorporating a Distrustful Decomposition pattern during the software development cycle can largely reduce the number of zero-day exploits by minimizing co-dependencies between processes and also by containing the attack only at a single component level. This not only minimizes damages from zero-day exploits but also provides a better environment for troubleshooting and fixing vulnerabilities as each component is independent and directly doesn't affect other components without the use of IPC protocols[33].

Some of the prominent known application of the Distrustful decomposition pattern was in Windows vista for running applications safely with administration privileges, in the mail system, and also inspired the creation of a similar pattern used in the Postfix mail system[34].

# 1.6 PrivSep (Privilege Separation)

Privilege Separation (PrivSep) is another architectural-level pattern whose intention is to avoid limiting the overall functionality of the program while largely reducing the amount of code running with special privileges[35]. The primary goal is to ensure that only a small, safe necessary subset of the entire code base requires elevated privileges code base, while the remaining larger set of complex and error-prone operations runs on standard user privileges[36].

This pattern is useful for services that require users to authenticate themselves and then run the standard system operations with normal user privileges. This helps in reducing exploits like SQL injections and reducing the scope of zero-day exploits by limiting the attacker to only access user privileges and preventing exploitation of resources using elevated user access[37]. This basically means that if an adversary gain controls over the child's processes, it is only confined to the current set of privileges that may not be of a higher degree and fails to gain control over the parent, thereby minimizing the amount of damage that an attacker could inflict[38]. PrivSep Secure design pattern was implemented in OpenBSD, X Window server, and other Linux/Unix-based applications[39].

# 1.7 Defer to Kernel

Defer to Kernel is a secure design pattern that utilizes and takes advantage of existing verification kernel functionality and focuses on separating functionalities that require elevated user privileges from the existing user privileges. The primary objective of this secure design pattern is to reduce or avoid the use of user elevated privileges that are much more susceptible to privilege escalation attacks. The Key difference between the Privilege separation pattern is that the Differ to kernel pattern primarily utilizes existing kernel functionalities for user verification. Before execution of any operations that require root or super user privileges, the system needs to verify and validate whether the current user is allowed to execute functionality or not. The following secure design pattern is widely used in Linux/Unix-based systems and also in securable objects in windows. The Defer to Kernel pattern has a client-server architecture. Existing applications must be re-architectured as a client-server system which adds ups additional complexity to the system because of communication between the client and the server. The server receives the request from the client which also includes the identity of the client, which is then validated by the existing verification functionalities of the kernel, which further determines whether to authorize the user's request or to reject it[40-43].

## 1.8 Vulnerability Anti-Patterns

Anti-patterns are poor software practices of implementing certain design patterns that can have negative consequences. Developers should have operating knowledge of these anti-patterns to successfully avoid their inclusion in the codebase. These are highly error-prone and are susceptible to creating loopholes thereby making the program more vulnerable[44].

Many well-known anti-patterns can increase the risks of exploitable bugs and vulnerabilities. A few of these are:

## 1.9 God Object Anti-Pattern

The anti-pattern refers to the excessive concentration of functions in a single class, allowing the object of that class to have multiple functionalities. It supersedes the idea of "single responsibility". This means the responsibilities of too many functionalities are designated to a single class or object. This makes the code hard to debug, test, and maintain. From a zero-day perspective, it becomes very difficult to recover from zero-day exploits as functionalities are codependent,i.e fixing a bug can transpose other parts of the code. Moreover, if an attacker gains control over a god object, it will comprise the security of the entire system[45].

## 1.10 Boat Anchor Anti-Pattern

Boat anchor anti-pattern is another common software anti-pattern. It happens when developers leave a lot of unused (non-functional) code in the codebase for future use-case purposes. It overtime piles up, ending up creating a hulky mess of obsolete code in the code base which makes it harder to debug and unit test. This often leads to another design pattern known as "dead code". It not only hinders the patching process but also slows down execution speed due to excessive technical debt. Moreover, these boat anchors (obsolete codes) often contain a backdoor to the re-invented functionalities which an attacker can exploit and compromise certain parts of the program, if not the entire system[46-48].

# 2. FINDING EXISTING ZERO-DAY EXPLOITS

It is quite challenging to successfully identify and unravel zero-day vulnerabilities due to their unknown nature, but with optimal techniques and resources, it is possible to detect and identify exploitable zero-day vulnerabilities[49].

## 2.1 Common Vulnerability and Exposure Database and Third-Party Associations

Common Vulnerability and Exposure database (CVE) is an open-source project by MITRE corporation whose primary goal is to define, recognize and categorize publicly disclosed vulnerabilities. These vulnerabilities are reported to the database by bug hunters, security activists, and white-hat hacker groups. This acts as a formal notice to the manufacturer of the software informing them to fix those exploitable vulnerabilities. Another popular database is the National Vulnerability Database (NVD) which harmonizes with the MITRE CVE list[50].

But often, big tech giants prefer getting information from third parties or directly from bug hunters offering a higher incentive and keeping a non-disclosure agreement until the vulnerabilities are fixed. Companies like google have one of the finest security teams called *Project Zero* whose mission is to detect and catalog zero days vulnerabilities. Project Zero internally has a Threat Analysis Group (TAG) which tracks parties involved in government-backed hacking, disinformation campaigns, and financially motivated abuse. Once it is suspected that bad actors are using exploitable bugs, they report it to the manufacturer for quick recovery. Google's thread analysis group (TAG) doesn't only addresses zero-day vulnerabilities in google's tool but also discloses zero-day exploits in other software solutions too, with a primary objective of creating a secure world. For example, google recently disclosed a zero-day vulnerability targeting Windows operating system and reported it to Microsoft.

## 2.2 Monkey Testing (Extensive Fuzzing)

Monkey testing refers to the execution of random actions or inputs in a program until a crash or error occurs exposing any exploitable vulnerabilities. The idea behind monkey testing is if we generate random inputs (text prompts or either simulating random touches on the screen) it can cover all possible test cases given that we do it long enough and with enough randomness.

The figurative "monkey" refers to the infinite monkey theorem that states that if an army of monkeys is hitting random inputs on a typewriter for an infinite amount of time, it will eventually type out the entire works of William Shakespeare. Although apart from time and randomness, the intelligence of the monkey also plays a vital role in generating valid enough inputs that are not directly rejected by the parser but do create unforeseen behaviors that are invalid enough to expose or trigger some exploitable part of the code. So, the ultimate zero-day tool kit revolves around having a supercomputer powerful enough to bombard an application with all possible combinations of actions/inputs.

In the real world, monkey testing is practiced through a popular penetration testing framework known as fuzzing. Fuzzing is an automated software testing method that breaks the system by injecting random, malformed, and invalid inputs to find exploitable vulnerabilities. A fuzzer is a tool that allows us to inject these sem-random or random inputs. Google OSS-Fuzz, FuzzDB, Ffuf (fuzz faster u fool), Google ClusterFuzz, and radamsa are some of the open-source fuzzing tools prominently used by software testers.

## 2.3 Prominent Use-Cases

*One-Fuzz:* Microsoft open-sourced its fuzzing tool "One Fuzz" which is used by Microsoft edge to identify exploitable vulnerabilities. The fuzzer can create thousands (if not millions) of web pages and load them in the web browser. It was used to load all possible combinations of HTML and JavaScript files to see how the Microsoft Edge browser responds to it. After running the automated fuzzer for a certain amount of time says days or weeks the organization would log thousands of crash reports that exposed some exploitable vulnerabilities in the browser.

*OSS-FUZZ:* Google's open-source fuzzing tool which routinely examines over 700 critical open-source projects for vulnerabilities was launched in 2016. It is widely known for its effort to detect almost all Log4shell vulnerabilities over a certain amount of time. It continues to improve java fuzzing and has successfully reported over 10,000 exploitable vulnerabilities in open-sourced projects.

## 3. IMPLEMENTATION

In the upcoming Discussion, we will try to imitate monkey testing (Extensive fuzzing) using an open-source fuzzer called radamsa. It functions by reading samples of valid file inputs and generating similar test cases. The main objective is to break the program using semi-random inputs and find any exploitable vulnerabilities.

We tried to generate test-suite (set of test cases) for a simple c program which we will try to break (input sanitization) by giving random inputs for N number of test cases or until a crash occurs.

In order to achieve this, we created a basic shell script for creating random inputs (numbers) is fed to the above-mentioned C file and test-cases are recorded accordingly for errors.

Our objective behind this implementation is to provide a general idea of a zero-day toolkit which revolves around having a super computer powerful enough to bombard the system with all possible combinations of inputs in a relatively small times (say days or weeks).

*Figure 1. Handling Zero Day Exploits*

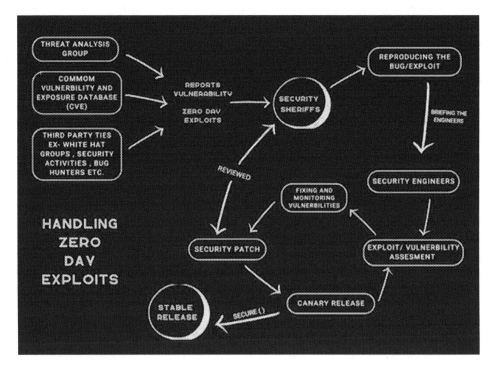

## 3.1 Quick Recovery From Zero-Day Exploits

Due to the unforeseen nature of zero-day exploits, it is not possible to provide an optimal model or pipeline for handling zero-day exploits. Most organizations follow the traditional way method of fixing exploits. Zero-day exploits need to be handled in a tightly bounded time frame in order to reduce the amount of damage that is inflicted during the lifecycle of the exploit which can incur heavy financial and technical debts to the system. Large Tech giants like Google have designated teams for solely handling zero-day vulnerabilities. Google has a queue of security sheriffs which facilitates the overall bug-fixing process and guides the security engineers.

Due to the lack of a concrete way for handling zero-day exploits, we proposed our own general model to handle these exploits which is based on google's zero-day project. Although, optimal results cannot be achieved as each zero-day attack may differ from the other.

## 3.2 General Zero-Day Model

Explanation:

The organization receives reports of a zero-day attack or exploitable vulnerabilities from threat analysis groups (TAG), CVE databases, or other third-party ties like white-hat hacker groups and bug-hunters. These reports are accessed by the Security sheriffs who are responsible for resolving these vulnerabilities and securing the software along with security engineers. The security sheriffs try to reproduce the bug in a secure environment to gain major information and brief the security engineers about the issues.

The security engineers then follow the standard exploit measures, essentially starting with a vulnerability assessment. Vulnerabilities are fixed and monitored in the next stage to ensure that it does not affect other parts of the code. A security patch is released which undergoes automated testing and is reviewed by the security sheriffs. After this, a canary release is deployed. After a few iterations of these processes authenticating the security standard of these patches, a stable release is deployed for the general public.

## 4. CONCLUSION AND FUTURE SCOPE

Even with potent present-day technological growth zero-day exploits still continues to be an impenetrable feat. Although, many tech companies have fabricated their own solutions with hopes of mitigating the damages inflicted by them but have failed to provide an optimal solution. An exponential growth related to supercomputers and mainframes is required to significantly improve present-day solutions to zero-day exploits. Although, it is possible to facilitate hassle-free patching of these vulnerabilities and significantly reduce zero-day vulnerabilities by implementing secure design patterns and avoiding poor software practices like anti-patterns. Moreover, organizations like google's threat analysis group (TAG) and Common vulnerabilities and exposure (CVE) database have continued their quest to create secure software solutions by regularly identifying and reporting exploitable vulnerabilities.

The success of any zero-day model relies largely on continuous adaptability as each zero-day exploit can bring forth unanticipated challenges oftentimes making prior principles and practices susceptible.

As for us, we should recognize that there are no optimal solutions to zero-day problems as strategies, principles, and practices can always be improvised to accommodate uncertain events. There is no golden model or pipeline that works for every organization as each organization may face different zero-day exploits depending on its software solution, therefore each needs to analyze its requirements and ongoing hazards to amalgamate strategies from different methodologies to figure out what works for them.

# REFERENCES

Abri, F., Siami-Namini, S., Khanghah, M. A., Soltani, F. M., & Namin, A. S. (2019, December). Can machine/deep learning classifiers detect zero-day malware with high accuracy? In 2019 IEEE international conference on big data (Big Data) (pp. 3252-3259). IEEE.

Afianian, A., Niksefat, S., Sadeghiyan, B., & Baptiste, D. (2019). Malware dynamic analysis evasion techniques: A survey. *ACM Computing Surveys*, *52*(6), 1–28. doi:10.1145/3365001

Ahmed, O. (2022). *Behaviour Anomaly on Linux Systems to Detect Zero-day Malware Attacks* (Doctoral dissertation, Auckland University of Technology).

Anand, P., Singh, Y., & Selwal, A. (2022). Learning-Based Techniques for Assessing Zero-Day Attacks and Vulnerabilities in IoT. In *Recent Innovations in Computing* (pp. 497–504). Springer. doi:10.1007/978-981-16-8248-3_41

Aoudni, Y., Donald, C., Farouk, A., Sahay, K. B., Babu, D. V., Tripathi, V., & Dhabliya, D. (2022). Cloud security based attack detection using transductive learning integrated with Hidden Markov Model. *Pattern Recognition Letters*, *157*, 16–26. doi:10.1016/j.patrec.2022.02.012

Aryal, K., Gupta, M., & Abdelsalam, M. *(2023). Analysis of Label-Flip Poisoning Attack on Machine Learning Based Malware Detector.* arXiv preprint arXiv:2301.01044.

Bilge, L., & Dumitraş, T. (2012, October). Before we knew it: an empirical study of zero-day attacks in the real world. In *Proceedings of the 2012 ACM conference on Computer and communications security* (pp. 833-844). 10.1145/2382196.2382284

Blaise, A., Bouet, M., Conan, V., & Secci, S. (2020). Detection of zero-day attacks: An unsupervised port-based approach. *Computer Networks*, *180*, 107391. doi:10.1016/j.comnet.2020.107391

Blumbergs, B., Dobelis, E., & Paikens, P. (2023). WearSec: Towards Automated Security Evaluation of Wireless Wearable Devices. In *Secure IT Systems: 27th Nordic Conference, NordSec 2022, Reykjavic, Iceland, November 30– December 2, 2022* [). Springer Nature.]. *Proceedings*, *13700*, 311.

Chen, C., Cui, B., Ma, J., Wu, R., Guo, J., & Liu, W. (2018). A systematic review of fuzzing techniques. *Computers & Security*, *75*, 118–137. doi:10.1016/j.cose.2018.02.002

Dionísio, N., Alves, F., Ferreira, P. M., & Bessani, A. (2019, July). Cyberthreat detection from twitter using deep neural networks. In 2019 international joint conference on neural networks (IJCNN) (pp. 1-8). IEEE. doi:10.1109/IJCNN.2019.8852475

Dougherty, C., Sayre, K., Seacord, R. C., Svoboda, D., & Togashi, K. (2009). *Secure design patterns*. Carnegie-Mellon Univ Pittsburgh Pa Software Engineering Inst.

Efstathopoulos, G., Grammatikis, P. R., Sarigiannidis, P., Argyriou, V., Sarigiannidis, A., Stamatakis, K., ... Athanasopoulos, S. K. (2019, September). Operational data based intrusion detection system for smart grid. In *2019 IEEE 24th International Workshop on Computer Aided Modeling and Design of Communication Links and Networks (CAMAD)* (pp. 1-6). IEEE. 10.1109/CAMAD.2019.8858503

Garg, S., & Baliyan, N. (2019). A novel parallel classifier scheme for vulnerability detection in android. *Computers & Electrical Engineering*, *77*, 12–26. doi:10.1016/j.compeleceng.2019.04.019

Garre, J. T. M., Pérez, M. G., & Ruiz-Martínez, A. (2021). A novel Machine Learning-based approach for the detection of SSH botnet infection. *Future Generation Computer Systems*, *115*, 387–396. doi:10.1016/j.future.2020.09.004

Jaber, A., & Fritsch, L. (2023). Towards AI-powered Cybersecurity Attack Modeling with Simulation Tools: Review of Attack Simulators. In *International Conference on P2P, Parallel, Grid, Cloud and Internet Computing* (pp. 249-257). Springer, Cham.

Jacobs, J., Romanosky, S., Adjerid, I., & Baker, W. (2020). Improving vulnerability remediation through better exploit prediction. *Journal of Cybersecurity*, *6*(1), tyaa015. doi:10.1093/cybsec/tyaa015

. Kaushik, B., Sharma, R., Dhama, K., Chadha, A., & Sharma, S. (2023). Performance evaluation of learning models for intrusion detection system using feature selection. *Journal of Computer Virology and Hacking Techniques*, 1-20.

Khan, H. A., Sehatbakhsh, N., Nguyen, L. N., Prvulovic, M., & Zajić, A. (2019). Malware detection in embedded systems using neural network model for electromagnetic side-channel signals. *Journal of Hardware and Systems Security*, *3*(4), 305–318. doi:10.100741635-019-00074-w

Khan, S., & Mailewa, A. B. (2023). Discover Botnets in IoT Sensor Networks: A Lightweight Deep Learning Framework with Hybrid Self-Organizing Maps. *Microprocessors and Microsystems*, *97*, 104753. doi:10.1016/j.micpro.2022.104753

Kim, T., Kim, C. H., Rhee, J., Fei, F., Tu, Z., Walkup, G., ... Xu, D. (2019). {RVFuzzer}: Finding Input Validation Bugs in Robotic Vehicles through {Control-Guided} Testing. In *28th USENIX Security Symposium (USENIX Security 19)* (pp. 425-442).

Kumar, R., & Subbiah, G. (2022). Zero-Day Malware Detection and Effective Malware Analysis Using Shapley Ensemble Boosting and Bagging Approach. *Sensors (Basel)*, *22*(7), 2798. doi:10.339022072798 PMID:35408413

Le, T. H., Chen, H., & Babar, M. A. (2022). A survey on data-driven software vulnerability assessment and prioritization. *ACM Computing Surveys*, *55*(5), 1–39. doi:10.1145/3529757

Liu, X., Lin, Y., Li, H., & Zhang, J. (2020). A novel method for malware detection on ML-based visualization technique. *Computers & Security*, *89*, 101682. doi:10.1016/j.cose.2019.101682

Malhotra, P., Singh, Y., Anand, P., Bangotra, D. K., Singh, P. K., & Hong, W. C. (2021). Internet of things: Evolution, concerns and security challenges. *Sensors (Basel)*, *21*(5), 1809. doi:10.339021051809 PMID:33807724

Martins, I., Resende, J. S., Sousa, P. R., Silva, S., Antunes, L., & Gama, J. (2022). Host-based IDS: A review and open issues of an anomaly detection system in IoT. *Future Generation Computer Systems*, *133*, 95–113. doi:10.1016/j.future.2022.03.001

Meira, J., Andrade, R., Praça, I., Carneiro, J., Bolón-Canedo, V., Alonso-Betanzos, A., & Marreiros, G. (2020). Performance evaluation of unsupervised techniques in cyber-attack anomaly detection. *Journal of Ambient Intelligence and Humanized Computing*, *11*(11), 4477–4489. doi:10.100712652-019-01417-9

Mercaldo, F., & Santone, A. (2020). Deep learning for image-based mobile malware detection. *Journal of Computer Virology and Hacking Techniques*, *16*(2), 157–171. doi:10.100711416-019-00346-7

. Mohammed, V. (2022). Automatic Static Vulnerability Detection Approaches and Tools: State of the Art. *Advances in Information, Communication and Cybersecurity: Proceedings of ICI2C'21, 357*, 449.

. Mubaiwa, T. G., & Mukosera, M. (2022). A Hybrid Approach To Detect Security Vulnerabilities In Web Applications.

Nafees, T., Coull, N., Ferguson, I., & Sampson, A. (2018, November). Vulnerability anti-patterns: a timeless way to capture poor software practices (vulnerabilities). In *24th Conference on Pattern Languages of Programs* (p. 23). The Hillside Group.

Nagendran, K., Adithyan, A., Chethana, R., Camillus, P., & Varshini, K. B. S. (2019). Web application penetration testing. *International Journal of Innovative Technology and Exploring Engineering*, *8*(10), 1029–1035. doi:10.35940/ijitee.J9173.0881019

Park, N. E., Lee, Y. R., Joo, S., Kim, S. Y., Kim, S. H., Park, J. Y., Kim, S.-Y., & Lee, I. G. (2023). Performance evaluation of a fast and efficient intrusion detection framework for advanced persistent threat-based cyberattacks. *Computers & Electrical Engineering, 105,* 108548. doi:10.1016/j.compeleceng.2022.108548

Pérez-Díaz, N. W., Chinchay-Maldonado, J. O., Mejía-Cabrera, H. I., Bances-Saavedra, D. E., & Bravo-Ruiz, J. A. (2023). Ransomware Identification Through Sandbox Environment. In *Proceedings of the Future Technologies Conference* (pp. 326-335). Springer, Cham.

Redini, N., Machiry, A., Wang, R., Spensky, C., Continella, A., Shoshitaishvili, Y., ... Vigna, G. (2020, May). Karonte: Detecting insecure multi-binary interactions in embedded firmware. In *2020 IEEE Symposium on Security and Privacy (SP)* (pp. 1544-1561). IEEE. 10.1109/SP40000.2020.00036

Redino, C., Nandakumar, D., Schiller, R., Choi, K., Rahman, A., Bowen, E., ... Nehila, J. *(2022). Zero Day Threat Detection Using Graph and Flow Based Security Telemetry.* arXiv preprint arXiv:2205.02298. doi:10.1109/ICCCIS56430.2022.10037596

Schwarz, M., Lackner, F., & Gruss, D. (2019, February). JavaScript Template Attacks: Automatically Inferring Host Information for Targeted Exploits. In NDSS.

Schwarz, M., Weiser, S., & Gruss, D. (2019, June). Practical enclave malware with Intel SGX. In *International Conference on Detection of Intrusions and Malware, and Vulnerability Assessment* (pp. 177-196). Springer, Cham.

Singh, U. K., Joshi, C., & Kanellopoulos, D. (2019). A framework for zero-day vulnerabilities detection and prioritization. *Journal of Information Security and Applications, 46,* 164–172. doi:10.1016/j.jisa.2019.03.011

Suciu, O., Nelson, C., Lyu, Z., Bao, T., & Dumitraş, T. (2022). Expected exploitability: Predicting the development of functional vulnerability exploits. In *31st USENIX Security Symposium (USENIX Security 22)* (pp. 377-394).

Vetterl, A., & Clayton, R. (2019, November). Honware: A virtual honeypot framework for capturing CPE and IoT zero days. In *2019 APWG Symposium on Electronic Crime Research (eCrime)* (pp. 1-13). IEEE. 10.1109/eCrime47957.2019.9037501

Vishwakarma, R., & Jain, A. K. (2019, April). A honeypot with machine learning based detection framework for defending IoT based botnet DDoS attacks. In *2019 3rd International Conference on Trends in Electronics and Informatics (ICOEI)* (pp. 1019-1024). IEEE. 10.1109/ICOEI.2019.8862720

Wang, Y., Jia, X., Liu, Y., Zeng, K., Bao, T., Wu, D., & Su, P. (2020, February). Not All Coverage Measurements Are Equal: Fuzzing by Coverage Accounting for Input Prioritization. In NDSS.

Yang, S., Dong, C., Xiao, Y., Cheng, Y., Shi, Z., Li, Z., & Sun, L. *(2023). Asteria-Pro: Enhancing Deep-Learning Based Binary Code Similarity Detection by Incorporating Domain Knowledge.* arXiv preprint arXiv:2301.00511.

Yin, J., Tang, M., Cao, J., You, M., & Wang, H. (2023). Cybersecurity Applications in Software: Data-Driven Software Vulnerability Assessment and Management. In *Emerging Trends in Cybersecurity Applications* (pp. 371–389). Springer. doi:10.1007/978-3-031-09640-2_17

You, W., Wang, X., Ma, S., Huang, J., Zhang, X., Wang, X., & Liang, B. (2019, May). Profuzzer: On-the-fly input type probing for better zero-day vulnerability discovery. In 2019 IEEE symposium on security and privacy (SP) (pp. 769-786). IEEE.

Zhou, S., Yang, Z., Xiang, J., Cao, Y., Yang, M., & Zhang, Y. (2020, August). An ever-evolving game: Evaluation of real-world attacks and defenses in ethereum ecosystem. In *Proceedings of the 29th USENIX Conference on Security Symposium* (pp. 2793-2809).

# Chapter 7
# Detection of Phishing Websites

**Lakshmipathi Gejjala**
https://orcid.org/0009-0008-5888-1134
*Kalasalingam Academy of Research and Education, India*

**Muthukumar Arunachalam**
https://orcid.org/0000-0001-8070-3475
*Kalasalingam Academy of Research and Education, India*

**Bala Manikanta Eswar Duggisetty**
*Kalasalingam Academy of Research and Education, India*

**Jaswanth Kumar Reddy Vardireddy**
*Kalasalingam Academy of Research and Education, India*

## ABSTRACT

*Phishing attacks are one of the biggest security threats to personal and financial information on the internet. They are a type of cyber-attack where attackers pretend to be a trusted entity in order to trick people into revealing sensitive information, such as passwords and credit card numbers. To address this issue, a web application has been developed for detecting phishing websites. This application utilizes the Beautiful Soup library in Python to extract HTML and XML content and machine learning algorithms for detection. The application was created using the Streamlit software, making it user-friendly and easy to access through a web interface.*

DOI: 10.4018/978-1-6684-7110-4.ch007

# 1. INTRODUCTION

Phishing is a common type of cyber-attack in which an attacker attempts to trick victims into divulging users data containing login credentials or financial data too, by posing as a trustworthy entity (Feng et al., 2018). Phishing attacks are typically carried out through fraudulent emails or websites that mimic legitimate ones (Kiruthiga & Akila, 2019).

Phishing websites are a particularly dangerous form of phishing, as they can be convincing enough to fool even savvy online users. These websites are made to resemble legitimate sites, often using logos and other branding elements to create a false feeling of confidence. As soon as a victim inputs their data on the phishing site, it is captured by the attacker and used for nefarious purposes. Phishing attacks are increasing, making prediction and prevention crucial for online transactions. Data mining tools, machine learning algorithms, and unique features help classify websites into phishing, suspicious, and legitimate categories (Ahmed & Naaz, 2019).

This chapter aims to explore the nature of phishing websites and the various techniques used by attackers to create convincing replicas of legitimate websites. First, the chapter will give a summary of the history and prevalence of phishing attacks and the numerous phishing techniques that exist. The chapter will then delve into the specific tactics used by attackers to create convincing Phishing websites, such as those with similarly related domain names resemble legitimate sites, using SSL certificates to create a false feeling of security, including fabricating login screens that capture user credentials.

The chapter will also discuss the various countermeasures that can be employed to prevent and mitigate initiatives that raise awareness and educate people about phishing attacks, spam filters, and two-factor authentication. authentication. The article will also investigate the legal and ethical implications of Phishing attacks and the effects that they may have attacks on businesses and individuals.

In conclusion, phishing websites are a serious threat to internet users, and it is essential that individuals and businesses take steps to protect themselves from these attacks. By being aware of the attack's strategies and implementing appropriate one can lessen their chance of falling victim to phishing scams, Monitoring by taking precautions.

# 2. LITERATURE REVIEW

The detection of phishing websites is an important task in preventing online fraud and protecting users from identity theft. Here is a brief literature review on the various approaches to detecting phishing websites:

1.  Machine Learning-Based Approaches: Machine learning-based approaches are commonly used to detect phishing websites. These approaches involve training machine learning algorithms on a dataset of known phishing websites, and then using these algorithms to identify new phishing websites. Machine learning algorithms can analyze features such as the URL structure, HTML code, and content of a webpage to determine whether it is a phishing site. Several studies have shown the effectiveness of machine learning algorithms in detecting phishing websites. The internet's strength increases cyberattacks and identity thefts, targeting end-users. Machine learning technology detects and prevents these intrusions using a dataset of phishing websites. Experimental results show high accuracy levels in detecting these attacks (Geyik et al., 2021).

2.  Blacklist-Based Approaches: Blacklist-based approaches involve maintaining a list of known phishing websites and blocking access to these sites. This approach can be effective in blocking known phishing sites, but it may not be effective against newly created phishing websites that are not yet on the blacklist.

3.  Whitelist-Based Approaches: Whitelist-based approaches involve maintaining a list of trusted websites and blocking access to all other sites. This approach can be effective in preventing users from accessing phishing websites, but it may not be practical for all use cases as it can restrict access to legitimate sites.

4.  Hybrid Approaches: Hybrid approaches involve combining multiple detection methods, such as machine learning, blacklisting, and whitelisting, to improve detection accuracy. Hybrid approaches can be more effective than individual methods alone in detecting phishing websites.

5.  User-Based Approaches: User-based approaches involve analyzing user behavior and providing warnings or alerts to users when they visit suspicious websites. These approaches can be effective in preventing users from falling victim to phishing attacks, but they require the user to take action and may not be practical for all use cases.

6. The study conducted by Asiri, Xiao, Alzahrani, Li, and Li in 2023 (Asiri et al., 2023) is focused on exploring different intelligent detection designs for HTML URL phishing attacks. Phishing attacks are cybercrimes were malicious actors attempt to deceive users into revealing sensitive information, such as login credentials or financial details, by posing as legitimate entities.

7. The study (Catal et al., 2022) addressed nine research questions and analyzed 43 journal articles from electronic databases. Results indicate that supervised deep learning algorithms were commonly employed, with widely used data sources including URL-related data, third-party website information, website content data, and emails. Additionally, most studies did not apply feature selection algorithms when building prediction models.

8. Chrome extension to address phishing by combining Blacklisting, semantic analysis, and pattern recognition, ensuring a substantial solution for phishing attacks (Razaque et al., 2020).

9. In the study by Kiran, S., Guru, J., Kumar, R., Kumar, N., Katariya, D., & Sharma, M. (2018) presents the Naïve Bayes improved K-Nearest Neighbor method (NBKNN) for Fraud Detection of Credit Card Fraud. Experimental results show that both classifiers work differently for the same dataset, aiming to improve accuracy and flexibility (Kiran et al., 2018).

In conclusion, the detection of phishing websites is a complex task that requires a combination of approaches, including machine learning-based, blacklist-based, whitelist-based, hybrid, and user-based approaches (Odeh et al., 2021). Each approach has its strengths and weaknesses, and the most effective approach may depend on the specific use case and context. Future research may focus on improving the accuracy of detection methods and developing new approaches that can adapt to the evolving threat of phishing.

## 3. EXISTING SYSTEM

There are several existing phishing website detection frameworks that use a variety of approaches to protect against phishing attacks. As of 2022, there are several existing phishing website detection frameworks that are widely used to protect against phishing attacks. Here are some examples:

1.  Google Safe Browsing
2.  PhishTank
3.  PhishNet
4.  PhishDetect
5.  OpenPhish

These approaches include blacklist-based, machine learning-based, user-based, and hybrid approaches. While these systems can be effective in detecting known phishing sites, the evolving nature of phishing attacks means that new approaches and improvements to existing systems will be necessary to keep users and businesses protected (Tiwari & Singh, 2015)

Phishing involves mimicking a legitimate website to steal user information. Data mining techniques, including Random Forest, are used to detect phishing attacks, with the highest accuracy of 97.36% (Subasi et al., 2017).

# 4. PROPOSED SYSTEM

The proposed system for detecting phishing websites using Streamlit software involves building a web application that is trained with multiple machine learning models to identify phishing websites. The system focuses on the content of the webpage to detect any improper login and redirecting to other pages in order to gain access to the user's login credentials.

The system uses the Gaussian Naive Bayes model, which is a machine learning algorithm that is commonly used in text classification tasks. The model is trained on a dataset of known phishing websites and non-phishing websites, and uses statistical analysis to classify new websites as either phishing or non-phishing.

The system analyses the content of a webpage to identify any suspicious activity, such as a webpage that asks for login credentials without proper encryption or redirects the user to another page that asks for login credentials. The system then provides a warning to the user and blocks access to the suspicious webpage.

Figure 1 shows the flowchart of the proposing system that refer to outlines the process for developing a detection framework for identifying phishing websites. Here's a brief explanation of each step in the process:

*Figure 1. Flowchart for detection of phishing websites*

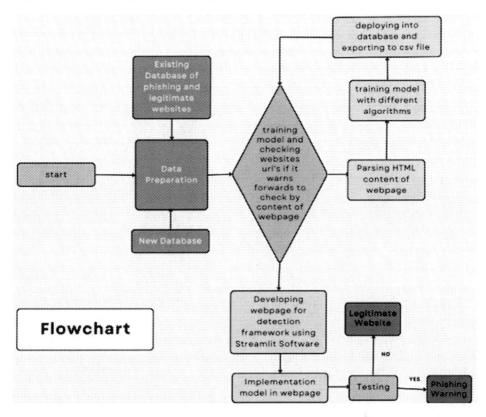

1. Data preparation: The process starts with collecting and preparing a dataset of websites to train the detection framework. This dataset consists of both new websites and an existing database of known phishing and legitimate websites.
2. Training the model: Different machine learning models are trained on the prepared dataset to identify patterns and features that distinguish phishing websites from legitimate ones. If a URL is flagged as potentially phishing, it is forwarded to the content checking step.
3. Content checking: The framework then checks the content of the webpage associated with the URL to determine if it is a phishing attempt or not.
4. Parsing HTML content: The HTML content of the webpage is parsed to extract relevant features, such as links and text content.
5. Training model: The machine learning models are trained on the extracted features to improve their accuracy in detecting phishing websites.

6.  Deploying into database: The trained models are then deployed into a database for use in real-time website scanning.
7.  Developing webpage: A webpage is developed using the Streamlit software to create a user interface for the detection framework.
8.  Implementing models: The machine learning models are integrated into the detection framework to classify URLs as phishing or legitimate.
9.  Testing: The framework is then tested to ensure it performs accurately and efficiently in detecting phishing websites.
10. Detecting legitimate or phishing website: Finally, the detection framework is capable of identifying whether a given website is legitimate or a phishing attempt based on the models trained on the extracted features of the website.

The use of machine learning models, such as the Gaussian Naive Bayes model, can help to improve the accuracy of phishing website detection by analyzing patterns in the content of the webpage. By focusing on the content of the webpage, the proposed system can detect phishing attacks that use social engineering techniques to trick users into divulging their login credentials.

Overall, the proposed system can be a useful tool in preventing users from falling victim to phishing attacks. By detecting suspicious activity in the content of the webpage, the system can provide a warning to the user and prevent them from accessing the phishing website.

# 5. METHODOLOGY

Here is a methodology with flow diagrams for the proposed system for detecting phishing websites using Streamlit software:

1.  *Data Collection:* Gather a dataset of known phishing websites and non-phishing websites.
2.  *Data Pre-processing:* Clean and prepare the dataset for training.

The Pie Chart 1 shows the proportion of phishing websites and legitimate websites in a given dataset or sample. The pie chart is a visual representation of this proportion, with two segments that show the percentage of each type of website in the dataset. The 39% segment of the pie chart represents the proportion of phishing websites in the dataset, while the 61% segment represents the proportion of legitimate websites. This means that out of the total websites in the dataset, 39% are identified as phishing websites, and the remaining 61% are legitimate websites.

Phishing websites are typically designed to look like legitimate websites in order to trick users into sharing sensitive information, such as login credentials or credit card numbers. They are often used in online scams, and can pose a serious threat to users' security and privacy.

Legitimate websites, on the other hand, are those that are trustworthy and have been verified to be safe and secure. They are typically run by reputable organizations and are designed to provide users with useful and accurate information or services.

In this particular dataset, it appears that there are more legitimate websites than phishing websites, with legitimate websites making up the majority (61%) of the sample. However, it's important to note that this proportion may vary depending on the specific dataset or sample being analyzed.

3. *Feature Extraction:* Extract features from the content of the webpage, such as the URL structure, HTML tags, text content, and other relevant information.

*Figure 2. Pie chart*

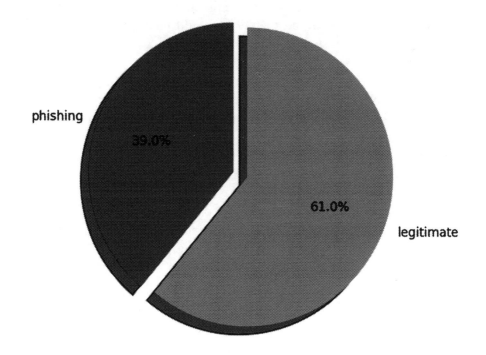

*Table 1. Features extracted from the content of webpage*

| Has Title | Has Input | Has Button | Has Image | Has Submit | Has Link | Has Password |
|---|---|---|---|---|---|---|
| 1 | 1 | 0 | 0 | 1 | 0 | 0 |
| 1 | 1 | 0 | 0 | 0 | 1 | 0 |
| 1 | 1 | 1 | 0 | 0 | 1 | 1 |
| 1 | 1 | 1 | 0 | 0 | 1 | 0 |
| 1 | 1 | 1 | 0 | 0 | 1 | 0 |
| 1 | 1 | 0 | 0 | 0 | 1 | 0 |
| 0 | 1 | 0 | 0 | 1 | 1 | 0 |
| 1 | 0 | 0 | 0 | 0 | 1 | 0 |
| 0 | 0 | 0 | 0 | 0 | 0 | 0 |

As shown in Table 1, a representation of a dataset that contains features extracted from webpages, including titles, inputs, buttons, and images. These features can be used to train machine learning models to distinguish between legitimate and phishing websites. In the table, each row represents a single webpage, and the columns contain the extracted features along with a binary label indicating whether the webpage is classified as phishing (1) or legitimate (0). By analyzing this data, machine learning models can learn to identify patterns and characteristics that distinguish phishing websites from legitimate ones, which can ultimately be used to detect and prevent online scams and protect user security.

4. *Model Training:* Train multiple machine learning models, such as Gaussian Naive Bayes, Super Vector Machine, Decision Tree, Random Forest, AdaBoost, Neural Network, K-Neighbours by using the pre-processed data.
5. *Model Evaluation:* Evaluate the performance of each model using metrics such as accuracy, precision, recall, and F1-score.

Table 2 represents the performance of machine learning models that have been trained and tested to distinguish between phishing and legitimate websites. The table includes three key performance metrics: accuracy, precision, and recall.

Accuracy refers to the percentage of correctly classified websites out of the total number of websites in the dataset. It is a measure of overall model performance.

*Table 2. Performance of each model and their evaluation*

| Machine Learning Models | Accuracy | Precision | Recall |
|---|---|---|---|
| Gaussian Naive Bayes | 0.9779 | 0.9601 | 0.9963 |
| Support Vector Machine | 0.9779 | 0.7496 | 0.6851 |
| Decision Tree | 0.9779 | 0.2893 | 0.5076 |
| Random Forest | 0.9779 | 0.1559 | 0.3028 |
| AdaBoost | 0.9779 | 0.4686 | 0.1793 |
| MLP Classifier | 0.9779 | <NA> | 0.0581 |
| K-Neighbours | 0.9779 | 0.5101 | 0.1547 |

Precision refers to the percentage of true positive classifications (i.e., correctly identified phishing websites) out of all websites that were classified as phishing. It is a measure of the model's ability to correctly identify phishing websites without falsely labeling legitimate websites as phishing.

Recall refers to the percentage of true positive classifications out of all actual phishing websites in the dataset. It is a measure of the model's ability to correctly identify all instances of phishing websites, without missing any.

The table shows the performance of each machine learning model in terms of these three metrics, as well as their overall evaluation. Models with higher accuracy, precision, and recall values are generally considered to be better performers.

By analyzing this data, developers can choose the most effective machine learning model for identifying phishing websites based on their specific needs and requirements.

6. *Model Selection:* Select the best-performing model, which in this case is the Gaussian Naive Bayes model, based on the evaluation results. The performance of different machine learning models for detecting phishing websites were evaluated using the same dataset and the same evaluation metrics.

Looking at the evaluation results, we can conclude that all the models achieved the same accuracy of 0.9779, which means they correctly classified 97.79% of the phishing websites. However, the precision and recall values for each model are different.

Precision refers to the proportion of true positives (correctly classified phishing websites) among all positive predictions made by the model. Recall, on the other hand, refers to the proportion of true positives identified by the model out of all actual positive cases in the dataset.

The Gaussian Naive Bayes model (NB) achieved the highest precision (0.9605) and recall (0.9962) among all the models evaluated. This means that out of all the phishing websites predicted by the model, 96.05% were actually phishing websites, and the model correctly identified 99.62% of all the phishing websites in the dataset.

In comparison, the other models had lower precision and recall values, with SVM achieving the second-highest precision (0.9697) and K-Nearest Neighbors achieving the second-highest recall (0.1700).

Overall, based on the evaluation results, the Gaussian Naive Bayes model appears to be the best-performing model for detecting phishing websites.

7. *Model Deployment:* Build a web application using Streamlit software that utilizes the selected model for real-time phishing website detection.
8. *User Input:* Users enter the URL of a website they wish to check for phishing activity into the web application.
9. *Content Analysis:* The system analyzes the content of the webpage using the selected model to identify any suspicious activity, such as an improper login form or redirects to another page for login credentials.
10. *Result Display:* The system provides a warning to the user if a phishing website is detected and blocks access to the suspicious webpage.

In summary, the proposed system involves collecting and pre-processing data, extracting features from the content of the webpage, training and evaluating multiple machine learning models, selecting the best-performing model, building a web application for real-time phishing website detection, analyzing the content of the webpage using the selected model, and providing a warning to the user if a phishing website is detected.

## 6. EXPERIMENTAL RESULT

To evaluate the performance of the system, a dataset of known phishing websites and non-phishing websites could be used. The dataset would be split into training and testing sets, where the training set would be used to train the machine learning models, and the testing set would be used to evaluate the performance of the models.

Several performance metrics could be used to evaluate the system, such as accuracy, precision, recall, and F1 score. These metrics would provide a measure of how well the system is able to correctly classify websites as phishing or non-phishing.

In addition to the performance metrics, the system could also be evaluated on its ability to detect new and unknown phishing attacks. This would involve testing the system on a set of phishing websites that were not included in the training set, to see how well the system is able to detect new and unknown attacks.

Streamlit is an open-source Python library that enables developers to create interactive web applications for machine learning, data analysis, and visualization. It simplifies the process of building and sharing data-driven applications by providing an intuitive user interface and making it easy to deploy and iterate on applications.

Streamlit allows developers to create web applications using Python, which is a popular programming language used in data analysis and machine learning. The library provides a simple, declarative syntax that enables developers to create complex applications quickly and easily. Streamlit is designed to be easy to use and requires minimal code, which makes it a popular choice for data scientists and developers who want to build applications quickly.

*Figure 3. Phishing website detection*

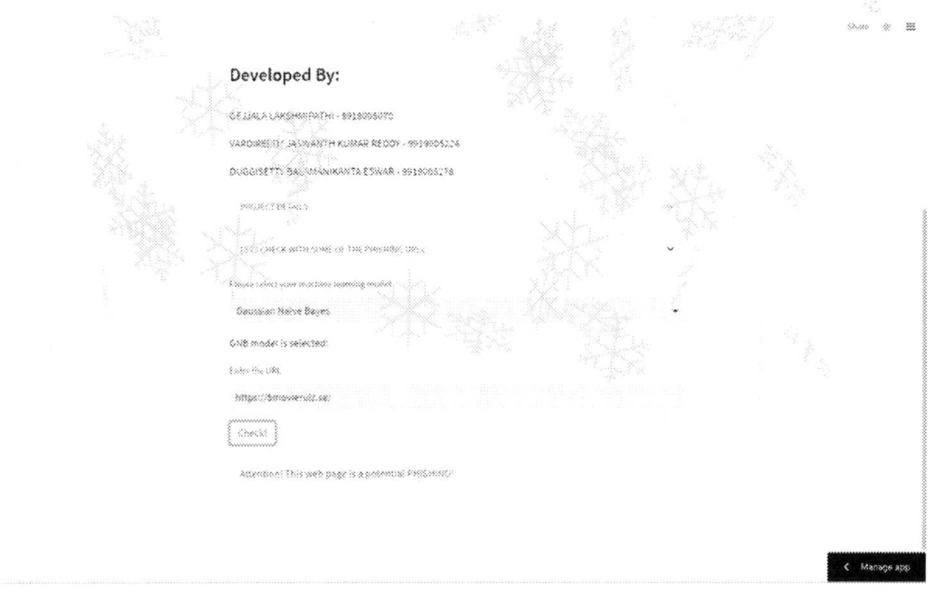

One of the key features of Streamlit is its ability to automatically update the application's user interface as the developer makes changes to the underlying code. This allows developers to iterate quickly and see the impact of their changes in real-time. Streamlit also provides a range of built-in widgets and components that enable developers to create interactive charts, tables, and other data visualizations.

*Figure 4. Legitimate website detection*

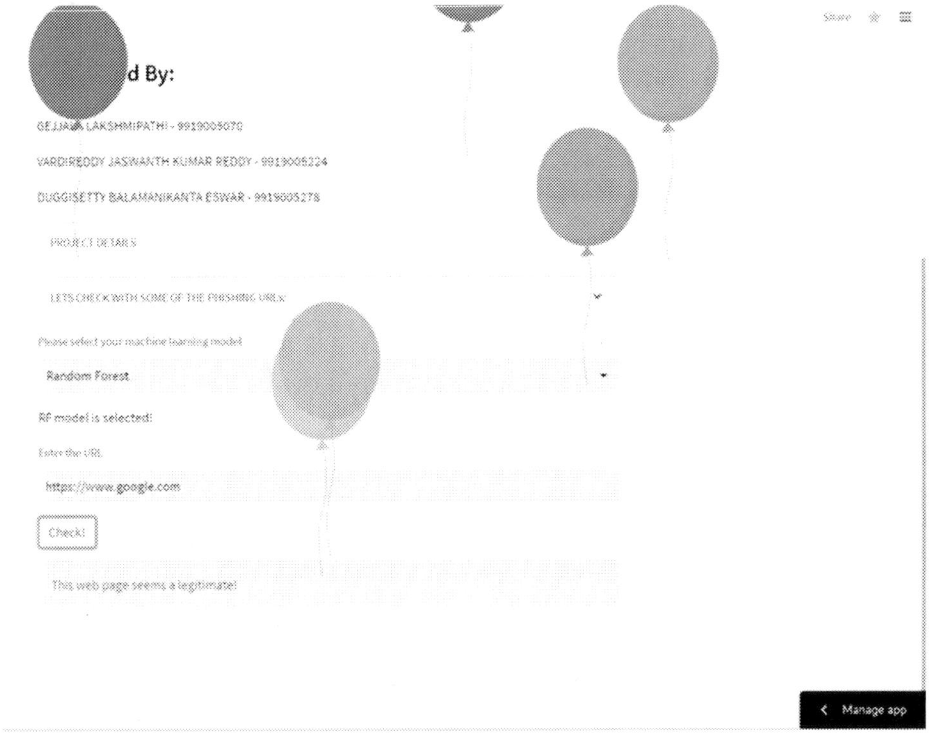

The webpage is designed to detect whether a given URL is a phishing website or a legitimate one. It accepts user input in the form of a URL and allows the user to select a machine learning model to use for the detection process.

If the machine learning model determines that the website is a phishing attempt, the webpage will display a warning message, such as "Attention: This webpage is potential PHISHING". To draw attention to the warning, a freezing effect is added to the detection webpage as shown in the Figure 2, which can indicate to the user that they should avoid visiting the website.

On the other hand, if the machine learning model determines that the website is legitimate, the webpage will display a confirmation message, such as "This webpage seems legitimate." To draw attention to the confirmation, balloons are raised from the bottom to the top of the detection webpage as shown in the Figure 3, which can indicate to the user that the website is safe to visit.

*Dataset limitations*: The performance of the models evaluated in this study may be limited by the dataset used. It is possible that the models would perform differently on a different dataset.

*Generalizability:* The models evaluated in this study were trained and evaluated using a specific set of features and parameters. It is possible that these models may not generalize well to other datasets or scenarios.

*Model complexity:* The models evaluated in this study may be relatively simple compared to more advanced machine learning algorithms. It is possible that more complex models could achieve even better performance, but may be more difficult to interpret and implement.

Overall, the experimental results would provide insights into the performance of the system in detecting phishing websites, and would help to identify areas for improvement in the system's design and implementation. The detection webpage is designed to provide a clear and concise indication of whether a website is safe or unsafe to visit, which can help users avoid online scams and protect their personal information.

# 7. CONCLUSION

In conclusion, the proposed system for detecting phishing websites by using streamlit software provides a powerful and effective tool for protecting users from phishing attacks. By analyzing the content of webpages and using machine learning models to classify them as either phishing or legitimate, the system is able to identify and block phishing websites, preventing users from falling victim to phishing attacks.

The system's focus on the content of webpages, and specifically on the presence of improper login forms and redirections to suspicious websites, makes it well-suited for detecting many different types of phishing attacks. The use of the Gaussian Naive Bayes model has also been shown to provide high accuracy in detecting phishing websites.

The system's web application interface built using Streamlit software provides a user-friendly and accessible way for users to access the system's protection, making it easy to use for a wide range of users. The continuous updating of the machine learning models with the latest phishing patterns and user feedback also ensures that the system is always up-to-date and effective in detecting the latest phishing attacks.

Overall, the proposed system provides a robust and reliable solution for detecting phishing websites and protecting users from falling victim to phishing attacks. Its focus on the content of webpages, machine learning-based classification, and user-friendly web application interface make it a valuable addition to the field of cybersecurity.

# 8. FUTURE RESEARCH

As the accuracy of current models is better with the result of **97.78%** and we will try to improve the accuracy of the models by considering the new features and we will try with the new machine learning models to improve the accuracy.

Creating a system that can detect the phishing websites as users browse the internet. This can include designing a mobile app or browser extension that can alert users when they are about to visit a known phishing website.

Creating an open-source toolkit that other programmers can use to make their own phishing website detection programmes. This could provide a set of previously trained machine learning models, code examples for feature engineering, and instructions for spotting phishing websites.

In addition to phishing websites, there are additional online dangers to be aware of, including malware, ransomware, and denial-of-service attacks. extending our study to find similar approaches to other cyber threats.

There are several promising directions for future research on detecting phishing websites using machine learning models. These include:

*Exploring the use of deep learning models:* While the machine learning models evaluated in this study achieved high accuracy, precision, and recall values, deep learning models have shown promising results in other related tasks such as malware detection. Future research can explore the use of deep learning models for detecting phishing websites and compare their performance with the models used in this study.

*Improving the accuracy of detection methods:* While the models used in this study achieved high accuracy, there is always room for improvement. Future research could explore ways to improve the accuracy of detection methods, such as by using more advanced machine learning algorithms or incorporating more features into the models.

*Investigating the impact of feature selection:* The performance of machine learning models is highly dependent on the features used for training the model. Future research can investigate the impact of different feature selection methods on the performance of the models for detecting phishing websites.

*Improving the robustness of the models:* One limitation of the models evaluated in this study is that they may not perform as well on new, previously unseen phishing websites. Future research can explore methods for improving the robustness of the models and ensuring that they can accurately detect new phishing websites.

*Evaluating the models on different datasets:* The models evaluated in this study were trained and evaluated on a specific dataset. Future research can evaluate the performance of these models on different datasets to ensure that their performance is consistent across different contexts.

*Developing new approaches:* As phishing attacks continue to evolve, it may be necessary to develop new approaches to detecting them. For example, researchers could explore the use of deep learning techniques, which have been shown to be effective in other areas of cybersecurity.

*Evaluating the effectiveness of detection methods in real-world scenarios:* While the models evaluated in this study achieved high accuracy, it is important to evaluate their effectiveness in real-world scenarios. Future research could explore how well these models perform in practice and whether they can detect new and emerging types of phishing attacks.

It would be important to address this issue and ensure that the system is able to continue detecting new phishing websites as they emerge. This could involve regularly updating the dataset used to train the models, and potentially incorporating more advanced machine learning algorithms that are able to adapt to new types of attacks.

In terms of the relevance of the topic to the value of the dollar ($), it is possible that phishing attacks targeting financial websites could have a significant impact on the value of the dollar and other financial markets. For example, if a large-scale phishing attack were to successfully steal sensitive financial information, this could lead to a loss of confidence in the financial system and potentially impact the value of the dollar.

However, there are still opportunities for future research to improve the accuracy of detection methods and develop new approaches for detecting phishing attacks. It is important to consider the limitations of this work, such as dataset limitations and generalizability, when interpreting the results.

# REFERENCES

Ahmed, K., & Naaz, S. (2019, February). Detection of phishing websites using machine learning approach. *Proceedings of International Conference on Sustainable Computing in Science, Technology and Management (SUSCOM), Amity University Rajasthan, Jaipur-India*. 10.2139srn.3357736

Asiri, S., Xiao, Y., Alzahrani, S., Li, S., & Li, T. (2023). A Survey of Intelligent Detection Designs of HTML URL Phishing Attacks. *IEEE Access : Practical Innovations, Open Solutions*, *11*, 6421–6443. doi:10.1109/ACCESS.2023.3237798

Catal, C., Giray, G., Tekinerdogan, B., Kumar, S., & Shukla, S. (2022). Applications of deep learning for phishing detection: A systematic literature review. *Knowledge and Information Systems*, *64*(6), 1457–1500. doi:10.100710115-022-01672-x PMID:35645443

Feng, F., Zhou, Q., Shen, Z., Yang, X., Han, L., & Wang, J. (2018). The application of a novel neural network in the detection of phishing websites. *Journal of Ambient Intelligence and Humanized Computing*, ●●●, 1–15. doi:10.100712652-018-0786-3

Geyik, B., Erensoy, K., & Kocyigit, E. (2021, January). Detection of phishing websites from URLs by using classification techniques on WEKA. In *2021 6th International Conference on Inventive Computation Technologies (ICICT)* (pp. 120-125). IEEE. 10.1109/ICICT50816.2021.9358642

JainS. (2019). Phishing websites detection using machine learning. *Available at* SSRN 4121102.

Kiran, S., Guru, J., Kumar, R., Kumar, N., Katariya, D., & Sharma, M. (2018). Credit card fraud detection using Naïve Bayes model based and KNN classifier. *International Journal of Advance Research. Ideas and Innovations in Technoloy*, *4*(3), 44.

Kiruthiga, R., & Akila, D. (2019). Phishing websites detection using machine learning. *International Journal of Recent Technology and Engineering*, *8*(2), 111–114.

Odeh, A., Keshta, I., & Abdelfattah, E. (2021, January). Machine learningtechniquesfor detection of website phishing: A review for promises and challenges. In *2021 IEEE 11th Annual Computing and Communication Workshop and Conference (CCWC)* (pp. 0813-0818). IEEE. 10.1109/CCWC51732.2021.9375997

Razaque, A., Frej, M. B. H., Sabyrov, D., Shaikhyn, A., Amsaad, F., & Oun, A. (2020, October). *Detection of phishing websites using machine learning. In 2020 IEEE Cloud Summit*. IEEE.

Subasi, A., Molah, E., Almkallawi, F., & Chaudhery, T. J. (2017, November). Intelligent phishing website detection using random forest classifier. In *2017 International conference on electrical and computing technologies and applications (ICECTA)* (pp. 1-5). IEEE. 10.1109/ICECTA.2017.8252051

Tiwari, P., & Singh, R. R. (2015). Machine learning based phishing website detection system. *International Journal of Engine Research, 4*(12), 172–174.

# Chapter 8
# Real–Time Object Detection in Video for Traffic Monitoring

**Sai Deepak Alapati**

https://orcid.org/0009-0004-1029-8629

*Kalasalingam Academy of Research and Education, India*

**Muthukumar Arunachalam**

https://orcid.org/0000-0001-8070-3475

*Kalasalingam Academy of Research and Education, India*

**Chandana Chennamsetty**

*Kalasalingam Academy of Research and Education, India*

**Pujitha Dantam**

*Kalasalingam Academy of Research and Education, India*

**Anusha Dabbara**

*Kalasalingam Academy of Research and Education, India*

## ABSTRACT

*This chapter presents the application of YOLO, a deep learning-based object detection algorithm, for traffic monitoring. The algorithm was applied to real-time video streams from roadway cameras to detect and track vehicles. The results were compared with traditional computer vision methods and showed superior accuracy and processing speed. This study highlights the potential of YOLO for traffic monitoring and the significance of incorporating deep learning into intelligent transportation systems. YOLO V7 outperforms all other real-time object detectors on the GPU V100 in terms of speed and*

DOI: 10.4018/978-1-6684-7110-4.ch008

*accuracy in the range of 5 to 160 frames per second and has the highest accuracy of 56.8% AP. YOLO V7 also introduces a new training methodology that improves the convergence rate and the generalization capabilities of the model. Experimental results show that YOLO V7 outperforms existing methods in terms of accuracy, speed, and efficiency, making it an attractive solution for real-world applications.*

# INTRODUCTION

Traffic monitoring is a crucial aspect of road safety and transportation efficiency. The increasing number of vehicles on the roads has created a demand for efficient and reliable methods for monitoring traffic flow and detecting abnormal events. The traditional methods for traffic monitoring, such as background subtraction and object tracking, often fall short in terms of accuracy and processing speed. This has led to the search for more advanced techniques that can provide a better solution to the challenges faced in traffic monitoring.

In recent years, the field of computer vision has made significant progress with the advent of deep learning algorithms. These algorithms have been applied to various computer vision tasks, including object detection, classification, and segmentation. One such algorithm that has shown promising results in object detection is YOLO (You Only Look Once). YOLO is a fast and accurate object detection algorithm based on deep neural networks (Egodawela et al., 2020). It has been applied to a wide range of applications, including autonomous vehicles, security, and surveillance.

This study aims to evaluate the performance of YOLO in detecting and tracking vehicles in real-time video streams from cameras mounted on roadways for traffic monitoring purposes. The results of the study will be compared with traditional computer vision techniques to assess the advantages of using YOLO for traffic monitoring. The findings of this study will provide insights into the potential of using deep learning algorithms for traffic monitoring applications and highlight the significance of incorporating these algorithms into intelligent transportation systems.

**Background:** Real-time object detection in video for traffic monitoring is a computer vision application that involves detecting and tracking vehicles, pedestrians, and other objects in live video feeds captured by cameras installed on roads and highways. This technology is used to monitor traffic flow, detect incidents such as accidents or congestion, and provide real-time information to traffic management systems. Object detection algorithms such as YOLO,

167

Faster R-CNN, and SSD are commonly used for this application, and deep learning models trained on large datasets are often employed to improve accuracy and robustness (Jiangzhou, 2021). Other techniques such as optical flow and background subtraction may also be used in combination with object detection to improve performance in challenging conditions.

**Focus of the Article:** The focus of an article related to real-time object detection in video for traffic monitoring. The focus of such an article would likely be on discussing the various object detection algorithms and techniques used in this application, their performance, and any challenges or limitations associated with them. The applications and benefits of real-time object detection in traffic monitoring, including improving road safety, reducing congestion, and enhancing traffic management systems. Additionally, the current trends and future directions in this field, including new algorithms, hardware and software advancements, and emerging applications.

## EXISTING SYSTEM

One of the most significant advancements in recent history has been image/video processing, which has applications in the industries of agriculture, military, medical, and road safety. A universal method for multiple object detection in densely populated settings still needs to be developed due to its complexity. In image processing and video processing literature, the conventional techniques of optical flow, connected component analysis, and picture segmentation have been thoroughly researched. Deep neural networks are increasingly being used in image processing applications as a result of recent advancements in machine learning and numerical optimization approaches. These deep learning-based techniques frequently applied in this setting include RCNN variations, Mask RCNN, and YOLOv3 (Redmon, 2018). A comprehensive comparison of deep learning-based methods versus conventional methods.

## PROPOSED SYSTEM

In the proposed system the MS COCO instance segmentation dataset was used to refine the YOLO V7 object detection model, which was trained across 30 epochs. It achieves state-of-the-art real-time instance segmentation outcomes. An improved object detection performance, a more reliable loss function, and improved label assignment and model training efficiency are all provided by a quicker and more robust network design. The YOLO algorithm divides the image into N grids, each with an equal-sized S X S region.

And in the video each frame is divided, and it shows the objects detected in the video each frame. In this the architecture is improved for 56.8% in YOLO V7. And in this it will take less usage of GPU for better efficiency for the device. Figure 1 shows algorithm of object detection.

*Figure 1. Shows the object detection using YOLO V7 algorithm*

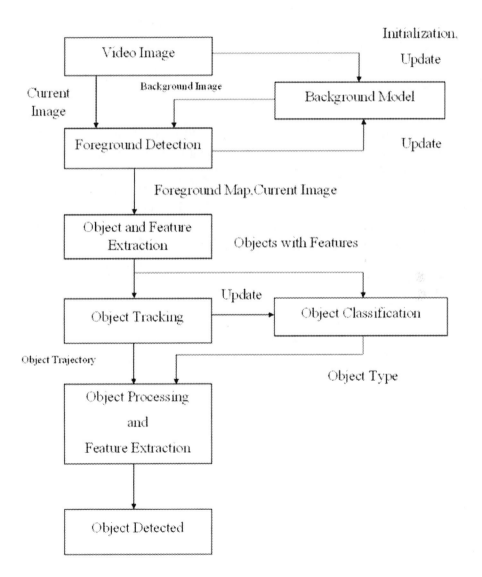

*Table 1. Average processing time of proposed system in frames per second (fps) for video of various resolutions*

| Average Frame and Pixel Rate | | Resolution | | |
|---|---|---|---|---|
| | | 1920 X 1080 | 1280 X 720 | 854 X 480 |
| FpS | Frames per Second | 13.7 | 33 | 67.4 |
| N | No. of Megapixels | 2.1 | 1.2 | 0.62 |
| N x FpS | No. of Megapixels per Second | 29.4 | 28.7 | 28.2 |

Table 1 shows the Average processing time of proposed system in frames per second in video.

# METHODOLOGY

YOLO (You Only Look Once) is an object detection algorithm that is designed to detect multiple objects in an image or a video in real-time. YOLOv7 is one of the latest versions of the algorithm.

The YOLOv7 algorithm works by dividing the input image into a grid of cells, and each cell predicts a fixed number of bounding boxes along with the class probabilities. Each bounding box consists of four coordinates (x, y, w, h) representing the center point of the box and its width and height. The class probabilities represent the likelihood of the object belonging to a particular class.

The YOLOv7 algorithm uses a deep neural network to perform object detection. The network is trained on a large dataset of images that have been labeled with object annotations. During training, the network learns to predict the bounding boxes and class probabilities for each cell in the grid.

During inference, the YOLOv7 algorithm uses the network to predict the bounding boxes and class probabilities for each cell in the grid. It then applies a threshold to filter out low-confidence predictions, and uses non-maximum suppression to merge overlapping bounding boxes and eliminate duplicates (Xiaomeng, 2022).

One of the advantages of the YOLOv7 algorithm is that it is designed to be fast and efficient, allowing it to perform real-time object detection on video streams. It is also able to detect objects at different scales and aspect ratios, making it well-suited for a wide range of object detection applications. And Table 2 explains about the features in the YOLO algorithm.

*Table 2. YOLO features and description for object detection*

| Feature | Description |
| --- | --- |
| Input Image | The image or video frame to be processed |
| Grid | The image is divided into a grid of cells |
| Bounding Boxes | Each cell predicts a fixed number of bounding boxes |
| Coordinates | Each bounding box consists of four coordinates (x, y, w, h) |
| Class Probabilities | Each cell predicts class probabilities for each bounding box |
| Non-maximum Suppression | Merging overlapping bounding boxes and eliminating duplicates |
| Threshold | Filter out low-confidence predictions |
| Deep Neural Network | Used to perform object detection |
| Training Dataset | Large dataset of labeled images used to train the network |
| Real-time | Designed to perform object detection in real-time |
| Object Scales | Able to detect objects at different scales and aspect ratios |

The YOLO framework on the other hand, deals with object detection in a different way. It takes the entire image in a single instance and predicts the bounding box coordinates and class probabilities for these boxes (Chan, 2021).

1. *Data Collection:* The first step is to collect the video data from traffic cameras installed on roads and highways. The data can be stored in a central database or streamed in real-time.
2. *Pre-processing:* The video data needs to be pre-processed before it can be used for object detection. This step may involve tasks such as video stabilization, frame extraction, and resizing to a standardized resolution.
3. *Object Detection:* The YOLO V7 model can be used for real-time object detection in the pre-processed video data. The YOLO V7 model has been shown to achieve high accuracy and speed, making it suitable for real-time applications.
4. *Object Tracking:* Once objects are detected in the video, the next step is to track them over time using a tracking algorithm. Bayesian tracking can be used to track objects even when they are partially or fully occluded.
5. *Visualization:* The final step is to visualize the results of the object detection and tracking.
6. *Architecture:* The integration of a Convolution Neural Network into visual tracking techniques may lead to an acceptable result. Now a day's use of imaging sensors (cameras) with increased resolution and increased fps are widely for different applications such security, traffic monitoring and for other applications. This has increased demand or

need for high performance implementation of an algorithms for real-time object tracking in high-resolution videos. The processing time for target tracking is quite great challenge for researchers to track the object in a high-definition/Full HD videos in real time. As the resolution of video increases, the number of pixels per frame increases and hence this needs fast computational/processing algorithm for tracking the object in high resolution video. Figure 2 shows the YOLO and CNN architecture for object detection.

*Figure 2. Object detection YOLO and CNN architecture*

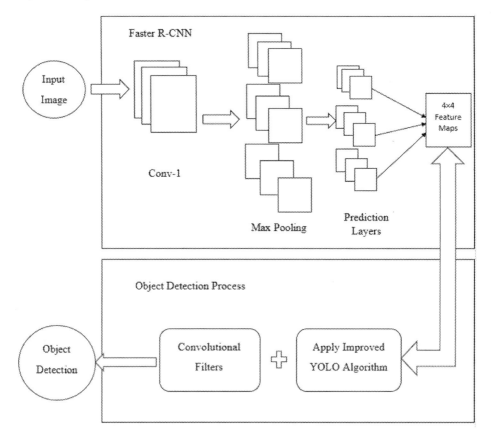

7. *Bounding Boxes:* From picture pixels to bounding box coordinates and class probabilities, reframe object detection as a single regression problem. System splits the input image into a S × S grid. A grid cell is in charge of detecting an object if its centre falls within that grid cell (Shubho, 2021).

In object detection, the confidence score associated with a bounding box is calculated as C = Pr(object) * IoU, where Pr(object) is the probability that an object is present inside the bounding box, and IoU is the Intersection over Union metric.

IoU measures the overlap between the ground truth bounding box (i.e., the actual position of the object in the image) and the predicted bounding box generated by the object detection algorithm. IoU is calculated as the ratio of the area of the intersection of the two bounding boxes to the area of their union. In other words, IoU measures the extent to which the predicted bounding box aligns with the ground truth bounding box (Wu, 2006).

The value of IoU ranges from 0 (no overlap) to 1 (perfect overlap). The higher the IoU, the more accurate the predicted bounding box is. A low IoU suggests that the predicted bounding box is inaccurate or imprecise.

Pr(object) is the probability that an object is present inside the predicted bounding box. It is calculated by the object detection algorithm based on the features extracted from the region inside the bounding box. Pr(object) is a measure of how likely it is that the object detection algorithm has accurately identified an object within the region of the bounding box (Muthukumar, 2019).

The confidence score C is the product of Pr(object) and IoU. A high-confidence bounding box indicates that the object detection algorithm is accurate and reliable, whereas a low-confidence bounding box may require additional analysis or follow-up to confirm the presence of an object.

In summary, the confidence score associated with a bounding box in object detection is calculated as the product of the probability that an object is present inside the bounding box and the Intersection over Union metric, which measures the overlap between the predicted bounding box and the ground truth bounding box. And the process of Bounding boxes and confidence as shown in Figure 3.

**Confidence:**

C= Pr(object)*IoU

IoU = Area of the Intersection / Area of the Union

*Figure 3. Process of input image to final detection*

*Solutions and Recommendations* - In the context of real-time object detection in video for traffic monitoring, some potential solutions and recommendations may include:

1.  Using deep learning models for object detection, as they have been shown to be effective in achieving high accuracy and robustness (Sun, 2019).
2.  Employing multiple cameras to cover a larger area and increase the accuracy and reliability of object detection.
3.  Using object tracking algorithms to improve the efficiency of object detection and reduce false positives.
4.  Incorporating other techniques such as optical flow and background subtraction to improve performance in challenging conditions (Liu, 2016).
5.  Integrating real-time object detection with other traffic monitoring systems such as intelligent transportation systems (ITS) and traffic management centers (TMCs).
6.  Ensuring that the system is designed to be scalable, flexible, and easily maintainable, with sufficient processing power and storage to handle large amounts of data.

7.  Ensuring that the system is designed with privacy and security in mind, including using encryption and access control mechanisms to protect sensitive data (Zhang, 2014).

8.  Regularly testing and validating the system to ensure that it meets performance and accuracy requirements and to identify and address any issues or limitations.

9.  Continuously monitoring and evaluating the system to identify areas for improvement and to adapt to changing traffic conditions and requirements.

*Future Research Directions* - Some potential future research directions in the field of real-time object detection in video for traffic monitoring may include:

1.  Developing more efficient and accurate object detection algorithms that can handle complex scenarios such as occlusions, partial visibility, and crowded scenes. Table 3 shows the accuracy evaluation of custom images.

2.  Exploring the use of new technologies such as LiDAR and radar for object detection in addition to cameras, to enhance accuracy and robustness.

3.  Investigating the use of real-time object detection for other applications such as monitoring pedestrian traffic, monitoring public transportation, and detecting traffic violations.

4.  Developing new techniques for combining object detection with other forms of data such as weather and traffic flow data, to enhance the accuracy and usefulness of traffic monitoring systems.

*Table 3. Accuracy evaluation of custom images*

| Sl. No. | No. of Objects Detected | | First Detected Accuracy | | Second Detected Accuracy | | Motion Tracking Accuracy | |
|---------|------|------|------|------|------|------|------|------|
| Side | L | R | L | R | L | R | L | R |
| 1 | 10 | 13 | 95% | 92% | 92% | 89% | 95% | 91% |
| 2 | 12 | 5 | 95% | 96% | 92% | 88% | 97% | 96% |
| 3 | 11 | 3 | 94% | 96% | 89% | 83% | 92% | 88% |
| 4 | 4 | 6 | 98% | 97% | 98% | 98% | 98% | 97% |
| 5 | 11 | 10 | 92% | 91% | 92% | 91% | 92% | 91% |
| 6 | 20 | 14 | 90% | 94% | 90% | 94% | 90% | 94% |

5. Improving the scalability and efficiency of real-time object detection systems by developing new hardware and software architectures (Ren, 2015).

6. Addressing privacy and security concerns associated with real-time object detection, and developing new methods for preserving privacy while still providing useful traffic monitoring data.

7. Developing more accurate and reliable object tracking algorithms to enhance the efficiency and usefulness of traffic monitoring systems.

8. Exploring the use of real-time object detection in autonomous vehicles and other emerging transportation technologies.

9. Investigating the potential of real-time object detection for improving road safety and reducing traffic-related fatalities and injuries.

## EXPERIMENTAL RESULT

Experimental results in object detection typically involve evaluating the accuracy and performance of the detection system on a set of test images or videos. The results are usually reported in terms of various metrics, such as precision, recall, F1-score, and mean average precision (mAP).

Precision is the ratio of true positives (i.e., correctly identified objects) to the total number of objects detected, while recall is the ratio of true positives to the total number of objects in the image. F1-score is the harmonic mean of precision and recall and provides a combined measure of accuracy.

MAP is a popular metric for object detection that measures the average precision across different levels of confidence scores. mAP is calculated by averaging the precision values at various recall levels for all classes in the dataset. A higher mAP score indicates better accuracy and performance of the object detection system.

In addition, experimental results may include a qualitative analysis of the detected objects, such as their sizes, positions, and orientations, to evaluate the robustness and reliability of the detection system under different conditions, such as varying lighting and weather conditions. Figure 4 gives the object detected in real time environment.

*Figure 4. Object detection in real time environment*

# CONCLUSION

Real-time object detection in video for traffic monitoring is a rapidly evolving field with many potential applications and benefits. It involves the use of computer vision algorithms and techniques to detect and track vehicles, pedestrians, and other objects in live video feeds captured by cameras installed on roads and highways. Object detection algorithms such as YOLO, Faster R-CNN, and SSD are commonly used for this application, and deep learning models trained on large datasets are often employed to improve accuracy and robustness. Other techniques such as optical flow and background subtraction may also be used in combination with object detection to improve performance in challenging conditions.

In the future, there are many potential research directions for real-time object detection in traffic monitoring, including developing more efficient and accurate algorithms, exploring the use of new technologies such as LiDAR and radar, and investigating the potential for real-time object detection in autonomous vehicles and emerging transportation technologies. The development of these new technologies and research directions will likely lead to more accurate and reliable traffic monitoring systems, with potential benefits including improved road safety, reduced congestion, and enhanced traffic management systems.

# REFERENCES

Chan, M. N., & Tint, T. (2021). A Review on Advanced Detection Methods in Vehicle Traffic Scenes. *2021 6th International Conference on Inventive Computation Technologies (ICICT),* 642-649. 10.1109/ICICT50816.2021.9358791

Egodawela, S. M. K. C. S. B. (2020). Vehicle Detection and Localization for Autonomous Traffic Monitoring Systems in Unstructured Crowded Scenes. *2020 IEEE 15th International Conference on Industrial and Information Systems (ICIIS),* 192-197. 10.1109/ICIIS51140.2020.9342663

Jiangzhou, Z., Yingying, Z., Shuai, W., & Zhenxiao, L. (2021). Research on Real-time Object Detection Algorithm in Traffic Monitoring Scene. *2021 IEEE International Conference on Power Electronics, Computer Applications (ICPECA),* 513-519. 10.1109/ICPECA51329.2021.9362684

Li, J., Li, Y., Liu, Z., Chen, Y., & He, Y. (2020). Real-time vehicle detection and tracking in UAV-based intelligent transportation systems. *Sensors (Basel),* *20*(11), 3118. PMID:32486430

Liu, W., Anguelov, D., Erhan, D., Szegedy, C., Reed, S., Fu, C. Y., & Berg, A. C. (2016). SSD: Single shot multibox detector. In *European conference on computer vision* (pp. 21-37). Springer.

Muthukumar, A., & Kavipriya, A. (2019). A biometric system based on Gabor feature extraction with SVM classifier for Finger-Knuckle-Print. *Pattern Recognition Letters.* 10.1016/j.patrec.2019.04.007

Redmon, J., & Farhadi, A. (2018). YOLOv3: An Incremental Improvement. arXiv preprint arXiv:1804.02767.

Ren, S., He, K., Girshick, R., & Sun, J. (2015). Faster R-CNN: Towards real-time object detection with region proposal networks. In Advances in neural information processing systems (pp. 91-99). Academic Press.

Shubho, F. H., Iftekhar, F., Hossain, E., & Siddique, S. (2021). *Real-time traffic monitoring and traffic offense detection using YOLOv4 and OpenCV DNN. In TENCON 2021 - 2021 IEEE Region 10 Conference.* TENCON. doi:10.1109/TENCON54134.2021.9707406

Sun, Z., Li, X., Zhang, L., & Han, J. (2019). Deep learning for real-time traffic signal control. *Transportation Research Part C, Emerging Technologies, 99,* 30–45.

Wu, B., & Nevatia, R. (2006). Detection and tracking of multiple, partially occluded humans by Bayesian combination of edgelet based part detectors. *International Journal of Computer Vision*, *72*(1), 53–77.

Xiaomeng, L., Jun, F., & Peng, C. (2022). Vehicle Detection in Traffic Monitoring Scenes Based on Improved YOLOV5s. *2022 International Conference on Computer Engineering and Artificial Intelligence (ICCEAI),* 467-471. 10.1109/ICCEAI55464.2022.00103

Zhang, K., Zhang, L., & Yang, M. H. (2014). Real-time compressive tracking. In *Proceedings of the IEEE conference on computer vision and pattern recognition* (pp. 1357-1364). IEEE.

# KEY TERMS AND DEFINITIONS

**Convolutional Neural Network (CNN):** A type of deep neural network that is commonly used for image and video processing tasks, including object detection.

**Deep Learning:** A type of machine learning that uses neural networks to model and solve complex problems.

**Faster R-CNN:** A real-time object detection system that uses a region proposal network to identify regions of interest in an image or video.

**Object Detection:** A computer vision task that involves identifying and localizing objects in an image or video.

**Real-Time:** Refers to systems that process data in near-real-time or with very low latency, such that the system can respond to new data quickly.

**Single-Shot Detector (SSD):** A type of object detection algorithm that uses a single neural network to detect objects in an image or video.

**Traffic Monitoring:** The use of sensors and other technologies to monitor the flow of traffic on roads and highways.

**Video:** A sequence of images that are played back in rapid succession to create the illusion of motion.

**You Only Look Once (YOLO):** A real-time object detection system that uses a single neural network to detect objects in an image or video.

# Conclusion

We are in the third millennium and new era of AI driven Cyberspace has just begun. The Big Data, Massive Data Storage and Ubiquitous access to high speed Internet 24/7 is a reality. The future for Applied AI in support of secure and safe Cyberspace is at the very beginning of new discoveries to provide the most effective and robust cyber security worldwide.

There are already a number of applications of AI that enhance cybersecurity and prevent most common cyber-attacks. Despite making significant investments in AI and Cyber Security, business, industry, government and others continue to struggle with security breaches. The new generation of very sophisticated cyber-attacks, continue to evolve and to adapt every day which presents new challenges to existing Cyber Security Technology.

Due to current political and economic factor apart from technology including, hardware & software, there is a Human Factor that is very difficult to identify and control, and yet it ultimately contributes to new generation of cyber-attacks that are very sophisticated and posse important difficulties of detecting cyberattacks.

There are many challenges to effectively analyze, monitor and prevent malicious data flowing into and out of the Data Centers all across the Cyber Security Technical Stack. In addition, the information communicated from organization's internal networks, application data, and data transmitted across the broader technology stack are often targets of sophisticated cyber-attacks, such as ransomware and malware. The organizations continue to invest heavily in new Cyber Security Technologies to protect the company's Asset and the Internet Communication Infrastructures.

The book discusses the current and future dynamic trends in research, innovation and developments of Applied AI in Cyber Security in support of more Safe and Secure Cyberspace for today and tomorrow.

# Compilation of References

Abadi, M., & Fournet, C. (2001). Mobile values, new names, and secure communication. In C. Hankin & D. Schmidt (Eds.), *Conference Record of POPL 2001: The 28th ACM SIGPLAN-SIGACT Symposium on Principles of Programming Languages*. ACM. doi:10.1145/360204.360213

Abadi, M., & Gordon, A. D. (1997). A calculus for cryptographic protocols: The Spi calculus, In *CCS '97, Proceedings of the 4th ACM Conference on Computer and Communications Security*. ACM. doi:10.1145/266420.266432

Abri, F., Siami-Namini, S., Khanghah, M. A., Soltani, F. M., & Namin, A. S. (2019, December). Can machine/deep learning classifiers detect zero-day malware with high accuracy? In 2019 IEEE international conference on big data (Big Data) (pp. 3252-3259). IEEE.

Afianian, A., Niksefat, S., Sadeghiyan, B., & Baptiste, D. (2019). Malware dynamic analysis evasion techniques: A survey. *ACM Computing Surveys*, *52*(6), 1–28. doi:10.1145/3365001

Aggarwal, K., Mijwil, M. M., Al-Mistarehi, A. H., Alomari, S., Gök, M., Alaabdin, A. M. Z., & Abdulrhman, S. H. (2022). Has the future started? The current growth of artificial intelligence, machine learning, and deep learning. *Iraqi Journal for Computer Science and Mathematics*, *3*(1), 115–123. Retrieved January 27, 2023, from https://journal.esj.edu.iq/index.php/IJCM/article/view/100/139

Aghajani, G., & Ghadimi, N. (2018). *Multi-objective energy management in a micro-grid Energy Rep*. Academic Press.

Ahmed, O. (2022). *Behaviour Anomaly on Linux Systems to Detect Zero-day Malware Attacks* (Doctoral dissertation, Auckland University of Technology).

Ahmed, K., & Naaz, S. (2019, February). Detection of phishing websites using machine learning approach. *Proceedings of International Conference on Sustainable Computing in Science, Technology and Management (SUSCOM), Amity University Rajasthan, Jaipur-India*. 10.2139srn.3357736

Ahmed, S., Lee, Y., Hyun, S., & Koo, I. (2018). Feature Selection – Based Detection of Covert Cyber Deception Assaults in Smart Grid Communications Networks Using Machine Learning. *IEEE Access : Practical Innovations, Open Solutions*, *6*, 27518–27529. doi:10.1109/ACCESS.2018.2835527

*AI in cyber security: predicting and quantifying the threat*. (n.d.). Retrieved November 29, 2022, from https://www.information-age.com/ai-in-cyber-security-predicting-quantifying-13818/

*AI in Cybersecurity: Incident Response Automation Opportunities*. (n.d.). Retrieved November 29, 2022, from https://www.sisainfosec.com/blogs/ai-in-cybersecurity-incident-response-automation-opportunities/

Aissa, N. B., & Guerroumi, M. (2015). A genetic clustering technique for Anomaly-based Intrusion Detection Systems. *2015 IEEE/ACIS 16th International Conference on Software Engineering, Artificial Intelligence, Networking and Parallel/Distributed Computing, SNPD 2015 - Proceedings*, 1–6. 10.1109/SNPD.2015.7176182

Akhtar, N., & Mian, A. (2018). Threat of adversarial attacks on deep learning in computer vision: A survey. *IEEE Access : Practical Innovations, Open Solutions*, 6, 14410–14430. doi:10.1109/ACCESS.2018.2807385

Al-Ajlan, A. (2015). The comparison between forward and backward chaining. *International Journal of Machine Learning and Computing*, 5(2), 106–113. doi:10.7763/IJMLC.2015.V5.492

Alauthman, M., Aslam, N., Al-kasassbeh, M., Khan, S., Al-Qerem, A., & Choo, K.-K. R. (2020). An efficient reinforcement learning based botnet detection approach. *Journal of Network and Computer Applications*, 150(102479). doi:10.1016/j.jnca.2019.102479

Alazab, M., Venkatraman, S., Watters, P., & Alazab, M. (2010). *Zero-day malware detection based on supervised learning algorithms of api call signatures*. Academic Press.

Alazab, A., Hobbs, M., Abawajy, J., & Alazab, M. (2012). Using feature selection for intrusion detection system. In *2012 International symposium on communications and information technologies (ISCIT)*. IEEE. 10.1109/ISCIT.2012.6380910

Alexandron, G., Armoni, M., Gordon, M., & Harel, D. (2012). The effect of previous programming experience on the learning of scenario-based programming. In Proceedings of the 12th KOLI Calling International Conference on Computing Education Research. ACM. https://doi.org/10.1145/2401796.2401821.

Al-Ghazawi, D. (2022). *How is artificial intelligence exploited in the offensive side of cybersecurity?* Information Security Association Protection. Extracted from: https://www.youtube.com/watch?v=2ER4P-yOiw4

Allodi, L., Cremonini, M., Massacci, F., & Shim, W. (2018). *The Effect of Security Education and Expertise on Security Assessments: the Case of Software Vulnerabilities*. Academic Press.

Almi'Ani, Ghazleh, Al-Rahayfeh, & Razaque. (2018). Intelligent intrusion detection system using clustered self organized map. *5th International Conference on Software Defined Systems, SDS 2018, 1*, 138–144.

Ambusaidi, M. A., He, X., Nanda, P., & Tan, Z. (2016). Building an intrusion detection system using a fifilter-based feature selection algorithm. *IEEE Transactions on Computers*, 65(10), 2986–2998. doi:10.1109/TC.2016.2519914

Amin, A. (2018). Distinguishing Between Cyber Injection and Faults Using Machine Learning Algorithms. *2018 IEEE Region Ten Symposium (Tensymp),* 19-24. https://ieeexplore.ieee.org/document/8691899 doi:10.1109/TENCONSpring.2018.8691899

Amir, M., & Givargis, T. (2020). Pareto optimal design space exploration of cyber–physical systems. *Internet Things, 12.*

Anand, P., Singh, Y., & Selwal, A. (2022). Learning-Based Techniques for Assessing Zero-Day Attacks and Vulnerabilities in IoT. In *Recent Innovations in Computing* (pp. 497–504). Springer. doi:10.1007/978-981-16-8248-3_41

Ankireddy. (2019). A Novel Approach to the Diagnosis of Heart Disease using Machine Learning and Deep Neural Networks. *2019 IEEE MIT Undergraduate Research Technology Conference (URTC),* 1-4. https://ieeexplore.ieee.org/document/9660581 doi:10.1109/URTC49097.2019.9660581

Aoudni, Y., Donald, C., Farouk, A., Sahay, K. B., Babu, D. V., Tripathi, V., & Dhabliya, D. (2022). Cloud security based attack detection using transductive learning integrated with Hidden Markov Model. *Pattern Recognition Letters, 157,* 16–26. doi:10.1016/j.patrec.2022.02.012

Armstrong, M. E., Jones, K. S., Namin, A. S., & Newton, D. C. (2018, September). The knowledge, skills, and abilities used by penetration testers: Results of interviews with cybersecurity professionals in vulnerability assessment and management. In *Proceedings of the Human Factors and Ergonomics Society Annual Meeting* (Vol. 62, No. 1, pp. 709-713). SAGE Publications. Extracted from: https://search.ebscohost.com/login.aspx?direct=true&profile=ehost&scope=site&authtype=crawler&jrnl=17881919&AN=132742665&h=NFF%2BpGs8uZcYYqZqqxCHH7bySrXe2wmxGfS2hdcME1i2303nm3AyUlXrKRIikSE1Ij96Uq9dTBFDyUy60Mv3EQ%3D%3D&crl=c

Aryal, K., Gupta, M., & Abdelsalam, M. *(2023). Analysis of Label-Flip Poisoning Attack on Machine Learning Based Malware Detector.* arXiv preprint arXiv:2301.01044.

Asiri, S., Xiao, Y., Alzahrani, S., Li, S., & Li, T. (2023). A Survey of Intelligent Detection Designs of HTML URL Phishing Attacks. *IEEE Access : Practical Innovations, Open Solutions, 11,* 6421–6443. doi:10.1109/ACCESS.2023.3237798

Belani, G. (2021). *The Use of Artificial Intelligence in Cybersecurity: A Review.* Https://Www. Computer. Org/Publications/Tech-News/Trends/the-Use-Ofartificial-Intelligence-in-Cybersecurity

Ben Neria, M., Yacovzada, N.-S., & Ben-Gal, I. (2017). A Risk-Scoring Feedback Model for Webpages and Web Users Based on Browsing Behavior. *ACM Transactions on Intelligent Systems and Technology, 8*(4), 1–21. doi:10.1145/2928274

Ben-Ari, M. (2001). Constructivism in computer science education. *Journal of Computers in Mathematics and Science Teaching, 20*(1), 45–74.

Ben-Ari, M., & Yeshno, T. (2006). Conceptual models of software artifacts. *Interacting with Computers, 18*(6), 1336–1350.

Benko, A., & Lányi, C. S. (2009). History of artificial intelligence. In *Encyclopedia of Information Science and Technology* (2nd ed., pp. 1759–1762). IGI Global. doi:10.4018/978-1-60566-026-4.ch276

Berman, D. S., Buczak, A. L., Chavis, J. S., & Corbett, C. L. (2019). A survey of deep learning methods for cyber security. *Information (Basel)*, *10*(4), 1–35. doi:10.3390/info10040122

Bhamare, D., Salman, T., Samaka, M., Erbad, A., & Jain, R. (2016). Feasibility of supervised machine learning for cloud security. *2016 International Conference on Information Science and Security (ICISS)*, 1–5. 10.1109/ICISSEC.2016.7885853

Bikeev, K. (2019). *Criminological risks and legal aspects of artificial intelligence implementation*. https://www.researchgate.net/profile/Pavel-Kabanov-3/publication/337883901_Criminological_risks_and_legal_aspects_of_artificial_intelligence_implementation/links/5e04ec92a6fdcc28374010af/Criminological-risks-and-legal-aspects-of-artificial-intelligence-implementation.pdf doi:10.1145/3371425.3371476

Bilge, L., & Dumitraş, T. (2012, October). Before we knew it: an empirical study of zero-day attacks in the real world. In *Proceedings of the 2012 ACM conference on Computer and communications security* (pp. 833-844). 10.1145/2382196.2382284

Bishop, M. (2000). Education in information security. *IEEE Concurrency*, *8*(4), 4–8.

Bishop, M. (2002). Computer security education: Training, scholarship, and research. *Computer*, *35*(4), 31.

Bishop, M., & Frincke, D. A. (2005). Teaching secure programming. *IEEE Security and Privacy*, *3*(5), 54–56.

Blaise, A., Bouet, M., Conan, V., & Secci, S. (2020). Detection of zero-day attacks: An unsupervised port-based approach. *Computer Networks*, *180*, 107391. doi:10.1016/j.comnet.2020.107391

Blanchet, B. (2012). Security protocol verification: Symbolic and computational models. In *Proceedings of the First International Conference on Principles of Security and Trust*. Springer-Verlag.

Blumbergs, B., Dobelis, E., & Paikens, P. (2023). WearSec: Towards Automated Security Evaluation of Wireless Wearable Devices. In *Secure IT Systems: 27th Nordic Conference, NordSec 2022, Reykjavic, Iceland, November 30–December 2, 2022* []. Springer Nature.]. *Proceedings*, *13700*, 311.

Bowen, J. P., Trickett, T., Green, J., & Lomas, A. (2018). Turing's Genius–Defining an apt microcosm. *Proceedings of EVA London 2018*. https://research.gold.ac.uk/id/eprint/24886/1/ewic_eva18_ha_paper4.pdf

Breck, P. (2019). *Data Validation for Machine Learning*. MLSYS. https://proceedings.mlsys.org/book/2019/file/5878a7ab84fb43402106c575658472fa-Paper.pdf

Breiman, L. (2001). Random forests. *Machine Learning*, *45*(1), 5–32. doi:10.1023/A:1010933404324

**Compilation of References**

Brian, P. (2015). *Kime Threat Intelligence: Planning and Direction.* SANS Institute.

Brundage. (2018). *The malicious use of artificial intelligence: forecasting, prevention, and mitigation.* https://www.eff.org/files/2018/02/20/malicious_ai_report_final.pdf

Buczak, A. L., & Guven, E. (2015). A survey of data mining and machine learning methods for cyber security intrusion detection. *IEEE Communications Surveys and Tutorials, 18*(2), 1153–1176. doi:10.1109/COMST.2015.2494502

Business, A. (2022). *Resecurity drives AI-powered cybersecurity in Saudi Arabia with new R&D centre.* https://www.arabianbusiness.com/industries/technology/resecurity-drives-ai-powered-cybersecurity-in-saudi-arabia-with-new-rd-centre

Cadwalladr, C., & Graham-Harrison, E. (2018). Revealed: 50 million Facebook profiles harvested for Cambridge Analytica in major data breach. *The Guardian.*

Cai, F. (2021). Sequential Detection of Cyber-attacks Using a Classification Filter. *2021 IEEE Intl Conf on Dependable, Autonomic and Secure Computing, Intl Conf on Pervasive Intelligence and Computing, Intl Conf on Cloud and Big Data Computing, Intl Conf on Cyber Science and Technology Congress (DASC/PiCom/CBDCom/CyberSciTech),* 659-666. 10.1109/DASC-PICom-CBDCom-CyberSciTech52372.2021.00111

Catal, C., Giray, G., Tekinerdogan, B., Kumar, S., & Shukla, S. (2022). Applications of deep learning for phishing detection: A systematic literature review. *Knowledge and Information Systems, 64*(6), 1457–1500. doi:10.100710115-022-01672-x PMID:35645443

Center for Strategic and International Studies. (2016). *Hacking the skills shortage. A study of the international shortage in cybersecurity skills.* Author.

Chan, L., Morgan, I., Simon, H., Alshabanat, F., Ober, D., Gentry, J., Min, D., & Cao, R. (2019). Survey of AI in Cybersecurity for Information Technology Management. *2019 IEEE Technology & Engineering Management Conference (TEMSCON),* 1–8. doi:10.1109/TEMSCON.2019.8813605

Chan, M. N., & Tint, T. (2021). A Review on Advanced Detection Methods in Vehicle Traffic Scenes. *2021 6th International Conference on Inventive Computation Technologies (ICICT),* 642-649. 10.1109/ICICT50816.2021.9358791

Chen, C., Cui, B., Ma, J., Wu, R., Guo, J., & Liu, W. (2018). A systematic review of fuzzing techniques. *Computers & Security, 75,* 118–137. doi:10.1016/j.cose.2018.02.002

Choi, M. K., Yeun, C. Y., & Seong, P. H. (2020). A novel monitoring system for the data integrity of reactor protection system using blockchain technology. *IEEE Access, 8,* 118732-118740. https://ieeexplore.ieee.org/stamp/stamp.jsp?arnumber=9126779

Cho, L. (2020). *Detecting C&C Server in the APT Attack based on Network Traffic using Machine Learning. International Journal of Advanced Computer Science and Applications, 11(5).* doi:10.14569/IJACSA.2020.0110504

Chuan-long, Y., Yue-fei, Z., Jin-long, F., & Xin-zheng, H. (2017). A Deep Learning Approach for Intrusion Detection using Recurrent Neural Networks. *IEEE Access : Practical Innovations, Open Solutions*, *5*, 21954–21961. doi:10.1109/ACCESS.2017.2762418

CIO. (2022). *Capitalizing on Artificial Intelligence. Opportunities. The Journey to Building a World-Class Artificial Intelligence Practice.* Sponsored by SBM. Extracted from: https://www.cio.com/article/405700/capitalizing-on-artificial-intelligence-opportunities.html

CNBC. (2022). *Artificial intelligence is playing a bigger role in cybersecurity, but the bad guys may benefit the most.* Extracted from: https://www.cnbc.com/2022/09/13/ai-has-bigger-role-in-cybersecurity-but-hackers-may-benefit-the-most.html

Coelho, I. M., Coelho, V. N., Luz, E. J. S., Ochi, L. S., Guimarães, F. G., & Rios, E. (2017). A gpu deep learning metaheuristic based model for time series forecasting. *Applied Energy*, *201*, 412–418. doi:10.1016/j.apenergy.2017.01.003

CompTIA. (2022). *Ethical Issues in Cybersecurity.* Extracted from: https://www.futureoftech.org/cybersecurity/4-ethical-issues-in-cybersecurity/

Cosmodium CyberSecurity. (2022). *The Story of Rockyou.* Extracted from: https://www.cosmodiumcs.com/post/the-story-of-rockyou

Craigen, D., Diakun-Thibault, N., & Purse, R. (2014). Defining Cybersecurity. *Technology Innovation Management Review*, *4*(10), 13–21. doi:10.22215/timreview/835

Curphey, M., & Arawo, R. (2006). Web application security assessment tools. *IEEE Security and Privacy*, *4*(4), 32–41. doi:10.1109/MSP.2006.108

CyberTalk. (2022). *Top 15 phishing attack statistics (and they might scare you).* Extracted from: https://www.cybertalk.org/2022/03/30/top-15-phishing-attack-statistics-and-they-might-scare-you/

Dada, E. G., Bassi, J. S., Chiroma, H., Abdulhamid, S. M., Adetunmbi, A. O., & Ajibuwa, O. E. (2019). Machine learning for email spam filtering: Review, approaches and open research problems. *Heliyon*, *5*(6), e01802. Advance online publication. doi:10.1016/j.heliyon.2019.e01802 PMID:31211254

Dark, M., Belcher, S., Bishop, M., & Ngambeki, I. (2015). Practice, practice, practice... secure programmer! *Proceeding of the 19th Colloquium for Information System Security Education.*

Das, R., & Sandhane, R. (1964). Artificial Intelligence in Cyber Security. *Journal of Physics: Conference Series*, *042072*(4). doi:10.1088/1742-6596/1964/4/042072

Deng, L., & Yu, D. (2014). Deep learning: methods and applications. *Found Trend Sig Process*, *7*(3-4), 197-387. doi:10.1561/2000000039

Deng, P. S., Wang, J.-H., Shieh, W.-G., Yen, C.-P., & Tung, C.-T. (2003). Intelligent automatic malicious code signatures extraction. *IEEE 37th Annual 2003 International Carnahan Conference on Security Technology*, 600–603. 10.1109/CCST.2003.1297626

Dijk. (2021). Detection of Advanced Persistent Threats using Artificial Intelligence for Deep Packet Inspection. *IEEE International Conference on Big Data (Big Data)*, 2092-2097. https://ieeexplore.ieee.org/document/9671464 doi:10.1109/BigData52589.2021.9671464

Dionísio, N., Alves, F., Ferreira, P. M., & Bessani, A. (2019, July). Cyberthreat detection from twitter using deep neural networks. In 2019 international joint conference on neural networks (IJCNN) (pp. 1-8). IEEE. doi:10.1109/IJCNN.2019.8852475

Djenouri, Y., Belhadi, A., Lin, J. C.-W., Djenouri, D., & Cano, A. (2019). A survey on urban traffic anomalies detection algorithms. *IEEE Access : Practical Innovations, Open Solutions, 7*, 12192–12205. doi:10.1109/ACCESS.2019.2893124

Dolev, D., & Yao, A. (1983). On the security of public-key protocols. *IEEE Transactions on Information Theory, 2*(29).

Dougherty, C., Sayre, K., Seacord, R. C., Svoboda, D., & Togashi, K. (2009). *Secure design patterns*. Carnegie-Mellon Univ Pittsburgh Pa Software Engineering Inst.

Duc, H. N. (2021, May 7). *Eyeballer - A convolutional neural network for analyzing pentest screenshots by bishop fox*. Hakin9. Retrieved January 27, 2023, from https://hakin9.org/eyeballer-a-convolutional-neural-network-for-analyzing-pentest-screenshots/

Dutt, Borah, Maitra, Bhowmik, Maity, & Das. (2018). Real-time hybrid intrusion detection system using machine learning techniques. *Advances in Communication, Devices and Networking*, 885–94.

EasyDmarc. (2022). *The Use of Artificial Intelligence in Cybersecurity*. Extracted from: https://easydmarc.com/blog/the-use-of-artificial-intelligence-in-cybersecurity/

Efe, A., & Abacı, İ. N. (2022). Comparison of the host based intrusion detection systems and network based intrusion detection systems. *Celal Bayar University Journal of Science, 18*(1), 23–32. doi:10.18466/cbayarfbe.832533

Efstathopoulos, G., Grammatikis, P. R., Sarigiannidis, P., Argyriou, V., Sarigiannidis, A., Stamatakis, K., . . . Athanasopoulos, S. K. (2019, September). Operational data based intrusion detection system for smart grid. In *2019 IEEE 24th International Workshop on Computer Aided Modeling and Design of Communication Links and Networks (CAMAD)* (pp. 1-6). IEEE. 10.1109/CAMAD.2019.8858503

Egodawela, S. M. K. C. S. B. (2020). Vehicle Detection and Localization for Autonomous Traffic Monitoring Systems in Unstructured Crowded Scenes. *2020 IEEE 15th International Conference on Industrial and Information Systems (ICIIS)*, 192-197. 10.1109/ICIIS51140.2020.9342663

Elbasiony, R. M., Sallam, E. A., Eltobely, T. E., & Fahmy, M. M. (2013). A hybrid network intrusion detection framework based on random forests and weighted k-means. *Ain Shams Engineering Journal, 4*(4), 753–762. doi:10.1016/j.asej.2013.01.003

Enck, W., Octeau, D., McDaniel, P. D., & Chaudhuri, S. (2011). A study of android application security. *USENIX Security Symposium, 2*(2).

Erma, Inc. (2022). *Artificial Intelligence and Its Ethical Challenges*. ERMA | Enterprise Risk Management Academy. https://www2.erm-academy.org/publication/risk-management-article/artificial-intelligence-and-its-ethical-challenges/

Farid, D. M., Harbi, N., & Rahman, M. Z. (2010). Combining naive bayes and decision tree for adaptive intrusion detection. *International Journal of Network Security & its Applications*, *2*(2), 12–25. doi:10.5121/ijnsa.2010.2202

Feng, F., Zhou, Q., Shen, Z., Yang, X., Han, L., & Wang, J. (2018). The application of a novel neural network in the detection of phishing websites. *Journal of Ambient Intelligence and Humanized Computing*, ●●●, 1–15. doi:10.100712652-018-0786-3

Fischer, E. A. (2014). *Cybersecurity issues and challenges: In brief*. Congressional Research Service.

Fox, B. (2019). *BishopFox/Eyeballer: Convolutional neural network for analyzing pentest screenshots*. GitHub. Retrieved November 6, 2022, extracted from: https://github.com/bishopfox/eyeballer

Fox, B. (2022). *Bishop Fox Tool Eyeballer - Explained*. YouTube. Retrieved November 6, 2022, extracted from: https://www.youtube.com/watch?v=5Utfy8SuWeg

Frost & Sullivan. (2017). *2017 Global information security workforce study. Benchmarking workforce capacity and response to cyber risk*. Academic Press.

Garg, S., & Baliyan, N. (2019). A novel parallel classifier scheme for vulnerability detection in android. *Computers & Electrical Engineering*, *77*, 12–26. doi:10.1016/j.compeleceng.2019.04.019

Garre, J. T. M., Pérez, M. G., & Ruiz-Martínez, A. (2021). A novel Machine Learning-based approach for the detection of SSH botnet infection. *Future Generation Computer Systems*, *115*, 387–396. doi:10.1016/j.future.2020.09.004

*GAVS Technologies | IT Process and Digital Transformation Solutions Powered by AIOps*. (n.d.). Retrieved November 29, 2022, from https://www.gavstech.com/

Geetha, R., & Thilagam, T. (2021). A review on the effectiveness of machine learning and deep learning algorithms for cyber security. *Archives of Computational Methods in Engineering*, *28*(4), 2861–2879. doi:10.100711831-020-09478-2

Geyik, B., Erensoy, K., & Kocyigit, E. (2021, January). Detection of phishing websites from URLs by using classification techniques on WEKA. In *2021 6th International Conference on Inventive Computation Technologies (ICICT)* (pp. 120-125). IEEE. 10.1109/ICICT50816.2021.9358642

Goh, J., Adepu, S., Tan, M., & Lee, Z. S. (2017). Anomaly detection in cyber physical systems using recurrent neural networks. *Proceedings of IEEE International Symposium on High Assurance Systems Engineering*, 140–145. 10.1109/HASE.2017.36

Golovko, V. A. (2017). Deep learning: An overview and main paradigms. *Optical Memory and Neural Networks (Information Optics)*, *26*(1), 1–17. doi:10.3103/S1060992X16040081

Govanguard. (2020, January 17). *Gowitness – a Golang, web screenshot utility using chrome headless*. GoVanguard Threat Center. Retrieved January 27, 2023, from https://govanguard.com/threat-center/2020/01/17/gowitness-a-golang-web-screenshot-utility-using-chrome-headless/

Griffiths, R. (2004). Knowledge production and the research-teaching nexus: The case of the built environment disciplines. *Studies in Higher Education*, *29*(6), 709–726.

Gu, J., Wang, L., Wang, H., & Wang, S. (2019). A novel approach to intrusion detection using SVM ensemble with feature augmentation. *Computers & Security*, *86*, 53–62. doi:10.1016/j.cose.2019.05.022

Gümüşbaş, D., Yıldırım, T., Genovese, A., & Scotti, F. (2021). A comprehensive survey of databases and deep learning methods for cybersecurity and intrusion detection systems. *IEEE Systems Journal*, *15*(2), 1717–1731. doi:10.1109/JSYST.2020.2992966

Gupta, B. B., Tewari, A., Jain, A. K., & Agrawal, D. P. (2017). Fighting against phishing attacks: State of the art and future challenges. *Neural Computing & Applications*, *28*(12), 3629–3654. doi:10.100700521-016-2275-y

Gupta, C., Johri, I., Srinivasan, K., Hu, Y. C., Qaisar, S. M., & Huang, K. (2022). A systematic review on machine learning and deep learning models for electronic information security in mobile networks. *Sensors (Basel)*, *22*(5), 2017. doi:10.339022052017 PMID:35271163

Hadjerrouit, S. (1998). A constructivist framework for integrating the java paradigm into the undergraduate curriculum. In *ACM SIGCSE Bulletin*. ACM.

Hadjerrouit, S. (1999). A constructivist approach to object-oriented design and programming. In *ACM SIGCSE Bulletin*. ACM.

Hadjerrouit, S. (2005). Constructivism as guiding philosophy for software engineering education. *ACM SIGCSE Bulletin*, *37*(4), 45–49.

Haenlein, M., & Kaplan, A. (2019). A brief history of artificial intelligence: On the past, present, and future of artificial intelligence. *California Management Review*, *61*(4), 5–14. doi:10.1177/0008125619864925

Halbouni, A., Gunawan, T. S., Habaebi, M. H., Halbouni, M., Kartiwi, M., & Ahmad, R. (2022a). CNN-LSTM: Hybrid deep neural network for network intrusion detection system. *IEEE Access : Practical Innovations, Open Solutions*, *10*, 99837–99849. doi:10.1109/ACCESS.2022.3206425

Halbouni, A., Gunawan, T. S., Habaebi, M. H., Halbouni, M., Kartiwi, M., & Ahmad, R. (2022b). Machine learning and deep learning approaches for cybersecurity: A review. *IEEE Access : Practical Innovations, Open Solutions*, *10*, 19572–19585. doi:10.1109/ACCESS.2022.3151248

Hamra, S. (2020). *Ethical hacking: Threat modeling and penetration testing a remote terminal unit*. Extracted from https://www.diva-portal.org/smash/get/diva2:1517798/FULLTEXT01.pdf

Hatcher, W. G., & Yu, W. (2018). *A Survey of Deep Learning: Platforms, Applications and Emerging Research Trends* (Vol. 6). doi:10.1109/ACCESS.2018.2830661

Hitaj. (2019). PassGAN: A Deep Learning Approach for Password Guessing. *International Conference on Applied Cryptography and Network Security*, 217–237. Extracted from: https://arxiv.org/pdf/1709.00440.pdf

*How AI Can Improve Fraud Detection & Prevention in 2022 ?* (n.d.). Retrieved November 29, 2022, from https://research.aimultiple.com/ai-fraud-detection/

*How Does Artificial Intelligence Work? | CSU Global.* (n.d.). Retrieved November 28, 2022, from https://csuglobal.edu/blog/how-does-ai-actually-work

*How is AI used in Fraud Detection? | Analytics Steps.* (n.d.). Retrieved November 29, 2022, from https://analyticssteps.com/blogs/how-ai-used-fraud-detection

Huang, C., Zheng, L., Wang, S., Leung, V. C. M., Lin, T., & Peng, K. (2018). Intrusion Detection System Based on Decision Tree over Big Data inFog Environment. *Wireless Communications and Mobile Computing*, *2018*, 1–10.

IBM, Inc. (2020). *Unsupervised Learning*. IBM Cloud Education. Extracted from: https://www.ibm.com/cloud/learn/unsupervised-learning

Ienca, M., & Vayena, E. (2018). *Cambridge Analytica and Online Manipulation*. Scientific American Blog Network.

Inoue, J., Yamagata, Y., Chen, Y., Poskitt, C. M., & Sun, J. (2017). Anomaly detection for a water treatment system using unsupervised machine learning. *IEEE International Conference on Data Mining Workshops, ICDMW*, 1058–1065. 10.1109/ICDMW.2017.149

*Is AI-Based Vulnerability Management Really that Efficient ?* (n.d.). Retrieved November 29, 2022, from https://aithority.com/machine-learning/is-ai-based-vulnerability-management-really-that-efficient/

Issquared, Inc. (2021). ISSQUARED. *Pros and Cons of Artificial Intelligence in Cybersecurity.* Extracted from: https://www.issquaredinc.com/insights/resources/blogs/pros-and-cons-of-artificial-intelligence-in-cybersecurity

Jaber, A., & Fritsch, L. (2023). Towards AI-powered Cybersecurity Attack Modeling with Simulation Tools: Review of Attack Simulators. In *International Conference on P2P, Parallel, Grid, Cloud and Internet Computing* (pp. 249-257). Springer, Cham.

Jacobs, J., Romanosky, S., Adjerid, I., & Baker, W. (2020). Improving vulnerability remediation through better exploit prediction. *Journal of Cybersecurity*, *6*(1), tyaa015. doi:10.1093/cybsec/tyaa015

JainS. (2019). Phishing websites detection using machine learning. *Available at* SSRN 4121102.

Jiang, T., Gradus, J. L., & Rosellini, A. J. (2020). *Supervised Machine Learning: A Brief Primer.* Behavior Therapy, U.S. National Library of Medicine. Extracted from: https://www.ncbi.nlm.nih.gov/pmc/articles/PMC7431677/

Jiangzhou, Z., Yingying, Z., Shuai, W., & Zhenxiao, L. (2021). Research on Real-time Object Detection Algorithm in Traffic Monitoring Scene. *2021 IEEE International Conference on Power Electronics, Computer Applications (ICPECA),* 513-519. 10.1109/ICPECA51329.2021.9362684

Johnstone, M. N. (2013). Embedding secure programming in the curriculum: Some lessons learned. *IACSIT International Journal of Engineering and Technology, 5*(2), 287.

Jordan, M. I., & Mitchell, T. M. (2015). Machine learning: Trends, perspectives, and prospects. *Science, 349*(6245), 255–260. doi:10.1126cience.aaa8415 PMID:26185243

Jøsang, A., Ødegaard, M., & Oftedal, E. (2015). Cybersecurity through secure software development. In *IFIP World Conference on Information Security Education.* Springer.

Jose, S., Malathi, D., Reddy, B., & Jayaseeli, D. (2018). A Survey on Anomaly Based Host Intrusion Detection System. *Journal of Physics: Conference Series, 1000*(1), 012049. doi:10.1088/1742-6596/1000/1/012049

Jouini, M., Rabai, L. B. A., & Aissa, A. (2014). Classification of security threats in information systems. *Procedia Computer Science, 32,* 489–496. doi:10.1016/j.procs.2014.05.452

Juniper Research. (n.d.). https://www.juniperresearch.com/

Karacan, H., & Sevri, M. (2021). A novel data augmentation technique and deep learning model for web application security. *IEEE Access : Practical Innovations, Open Solutions, 9,* 150781–150797. doi:10.1109/ACCESS.2021.3125785

Karjalainen, M., Sarker, S., & Siponen, M. (2019). Toward a Theory of Information Systems Security Behaviors of Organizational Employees: A Dialectical Process Perspective. *Information Systems Research, 30*(2), 351–710. doi:10.1287/isre.2018.0827

Kavak, H. (2021). Simulation for cybersecurity: state of the art and future directions. *Journal of Cybersecurity, 7*(1). doi:10.1093/cybsec/tyab005

Kayes, A. S. M., Rahayu, W., & Dillon, T. (2018). An ontology-based approach to dynamic contextual role for pervasive access control. In *AINA 2018.* IEEE Computer Society. doi:10.1109/AINA.2018.00093

Kayid, A. (2020). *The role of Artificial intelligence in future technology.* Retrieved January 25, 2023, from https://www.researchgate.net/profile/Amr-Kayid/publication/342106972_The_role_of_Artificial_Intelligence_in_future_technology/links/5ee257bd92851ce9e7d97e90/The-role-of-Artificial-Intelligence-in-future-technology.pdf

Khandelwal, Y., & Bhargava, R. (2021). Spam Filtering Using AI. *Artificial Intelligence and Data Mining Approaches in Security Frameworks,* 87–99.

Khan, H. A., Sehatbakhsh, N., Nguyen, L. N., Prvulovic, M., & Zajić, A. (2019). Malware detection in embedded systems using neural network model for electromagnetic side-channel signals. *Journal of Hardware and Systems Security, 3*(4), 305–318. doi:10.100741635-019-00074-w

Khan, S., & Mailewa, A. B. (2023). Discover Botnets in IoT Sensor Networks: A Lightweight Deep Learning Framework with Hybrid Self-Organizing Maps. *Microprocessors and Microsystems*, *97*, 104753. doi:10.1016/j.micpro.2022.104753

Khisamova, B. (2019). *Artificial Intelligence and Problems of Ensuring Cyber Security - ProQuest*. Extracted from: https://www.proquest.com/openview/a0f125d3f2115d338e180961818a409d/1?pq-origsite=gscholar&cbl=55114

Kim, T. (2021). A study on the influence of artificial intelligence research on the development of information security research. *Asia-Pacific Journal of Convergent Research Interchange*, *7*(12), 41–53. doi:10.47116/apjcri.2021.12.05

Kim, T., Kim, C. H., Rhee, J., Fei, F., Tu, Z., Walkup, G., ... Xu, D. (2019). {RVFuzzer}: Finding Input Validation Bugs in Robotic Vehicles through {Control-Guided} Testing. In *28th USENIX Security Symposium (USENIX Security 19)* (pp. 425-442).

Kiran, S., Guru, J., Kumar, R., Kumar, N., Katariya, D., & Sharma, M. (2018). Credit card fraud detection using Naïve Bayes model based and KNN classifier. *International Journal of Advance Research. Ideas and Innovations in Technoloy*, *4*(3), 44.

Kirat. (2018). *DeepLocker - Concealing Targeted Attacks with AI Locksmithing*. Black Hat. Retrieved on November 6, 2022, from: https://i.blackhat.com/us-18/Thu-August-9/us-18-Kirat-DeepLocker-Concealing-Targeted-Attacks-with-AI-Locksmithing.pdf

Kiruthiga, R., & Akila, D. (2019). Phishing websites detection using machine learning. *International Journal of Recent Technology and Engineering*, *8*(2), 111–114.

Konstantinov, L. (2019). *Robust Learning from Untrusted Sources*. PMLR. https://proceedings.mlr.press/v97/konstantinov19a.html

Kshetri, N. (2021). Economics of Artificial Intelligence in Cybersecurity. *IT Professional*, *23*(5), 73-77. Extracted from: https://ieeexplore.ieee.org/document/9568267 doi:10.1109/MITP.2021.3100177

Kumar, R., & Subbiah, G. (2022). Zero-Day Malware Detection and Effective Malware Analysis Using Shapley Ensemble Boosting and Bagging Approach. *Sensors (Basel)*, *22*(7), 2798. doi:10.339022072798 PMID:35408413

Lansky, J., Ali, S., Mohammadi, M., Majeed, M. K., Karim, S. H. T., Rashidi, S., Hosseinzadeh, M., & Rahmani, A. M. (2021). Deep learning-based intrusion detection systems: A systematic review. *IEEE Access : Practical Innovations, Open Solutions*, *9*, 101574–101599. doi:10.1109/ACCESS.2021.3097247

Lei, Y. (2017). Network Anomaly Traffific Detection Algorithm Based on SVM. *Proceedings - 2017 International Conference on Robots and Intelligent System, ICRIS 2017*, 217–220.

Lei, Y. (2017). Network Anomaly Traffic Detection Algorithm Based on SVM. *Proceedings of International Conference on Robots and Intelligent System*, 217–220. 10.1109/ICRIS.2017.61

Le, T. H., Chen, H., & Babar, M. A. (2022). A survey on data-driven software vulnerability assessment and prioritization. *ACM Computing Surveys*, *55*(5), 1–39. doi:10.1145/3529757

Li, H. (2010). Research and implementation of an anomaly detection model based on clustering analysis. *Proceedings - 2010 International Symposium on Intelligence Information Processing and Trusted Computing, IPTC 2010*, 458–462. 10.1109/IPTC.2010.94

Li, J. H. (2018). Cyber security meets artificial intelligence: A survey. *Frontiers of Information Technology & Electronic Engineering*, *19*(12), 1462-1474. Extracted from: https://jzus.zju.edu.cn/oldversion/article.php?doi=10.1631/FITEE.1800573&refdsp=ALL&comnowpage=0

Liao, H.-J., Lin, C.-H. R., Lin, Y.-C., & Tung, K.-Y. (2013). Intrusion detection system: A comprehensive review. *Journal of Network and Computer Applications*, *36*(1), 16–24. doi:10.1016/j.jnca.2012.09.004

Li, J., Li, Y., Liu, Z., Chen, Y., & He, Y. (2020). Real-time vehicle detection and tracking in UAV-based intelligent transportation systems. *Sensors (Basel)*, *20*(11), 3118. PMID:32486430

Lippmann, R. P., Fried, D. J., Graf, I., Haines, J. W., Kendall, K. R., McClung, D., Weber, D., Webster, S. E., Wyschogrod, D., Cunningham, R. K., & Zissman, M. A. (2002). Evaluating intrusion detection systems: the 1998 DARPA off-line intrusion detection evaluation. In *Proceedings DARPA Information Survivability Conference and Exposition (DISCEX'00)* (pp. 12–26). IEEE. 10.1109/DISCEX.2000.821506

Li, R., Tian, B., Li, Y., & Qu, Y. (2019). Information security evaluation based on artificial neural network. *International Journal of Performability Engineering*, *15*(11), 2908–2915. doi:10.23940/ijpe.19.11.p9.29082915

Li, S., Da Xu, L., & Zhao, S. (2015). The internet of things: A survey. *Information Systems Frontiers*, *17*(2), 243–259. doi:10.100710796-014-9492-7

Liu, W., Anguelov, D., Erhan, D., Szegedy, C., Reed, S., Fu, C. Y., & Berg, A. C. (2016). SSD: Single shot multibox detector. In *European conference on computer vision* (pp. 21-37). Springer.

Liu, C., Gu, Z., & Wang, J. (2021). A hybrid intrusion detection system based on scalable K-means+ random forest and deep learning. *IEEE Access: Practical Innovations, Open Solutions*, *9*, 75729–75740. doi:10.1109/ACCESS.2021.3082147

Liu, X., Lin, Y., Li, H., & Zhang, J. (2020). A novel method for malware detection on ML-based visualization technique. *Computers & Security*, *89*, 101682. doi:10.1016/j.cose.2019.101682

Lopez-Martin, Carro, & Sanchez-Esguevillas. (2020). Application of deep reinforcement learning to intrusion detection for supervised problems. *Exp Syst Appl, 141*(112963).

Macnish, K., & van der Ham, J. (2019). Ethics and Cybersecurity Research. *Journal of Science and Engineering Ethics*.

Macnish, K. (2018). Government Surveillance and Why Defining Privacy Matters in a Post-Snowden World. *Journal of Applied Philosophy*, *35*(2), 417–432. doi:10.1111/japp.12219

Malhotra, P., Singh, Y., Anand, P., Bangotra, D. K., Singh, P. K., & Hong, W. C. (2021). Internet of things: Evolution, concerns and security challenges. *Sensors (Basel)*, *21*(5), 1809. doi:10.339021051809 PMID:33807724

Manjikian, M. (2017). *Cybersecurity Ethics* (1st ed.). Routledge. doi:10.4324/9781315196275

Maraju, K. (2018). *Applying AI in Application Security*. https://www.isaca.org/resources/isaca-journal/issues/2018/volume-1/applying-ai-in-application-security

Markets and Markets Research. (2022). *Artificial Intelligence Market by Offering – Global forecast to 2027.* Extracted from: https://www.marketsandmarkets.com/Market-Reports/artificial-intelligence-market-74851580.html

Martins, I., Resende, J. S., Sousa, P. R., Silva, S., Antunes, L., & Gama, J. (2022). Host-based IDS: A review and open issues of an anomaly detection system in IoT. *Future Generation Computer Systems*, *133*, 95–113. doi:10.1016/j.future.2022.03.001

Masood, L. (2011). *Data Mining Applications in Malware Detection*. CRC Press.

Masud, M. M., Gao, J., Khan, L., Han, J., & Thuraisingham, B. M. (2011). Classification and Novel Class Detection in Concept-Drifting Data Streams under Time Constraints. *IEEE Transactions on Knowledge and Data Engineering*, *23*(6), 859–874. doi:10.1109/TKDE.2010.61

MATLAB. (n.d.). *What Is Reinforcement Learning?* MathWorks. Retrieved on November 6, 2022, from: https://www.mathworks.com/discovery/reinforcement-learning.html

Mavrona, K., & Csernatoni, R. (2022). *The Artificial Intelligence and Cybersecurity Nexus: Taking stock of the European Union's approach.* Carnegie Europe. Accessed: November 23, 2022. Extracted from: https://carnegieeurope.eu/2022/09/15/artificial-intelligence-and-cybersecurity-nexus-taking-stock-of-european-union-s-approach-pub-87886

Mccarthy, J. (2007). *What is artificial intelligence?* http://www-formal.stanford.edu/jmc/

McCorduck, P., Minsky, M., Selfridge, O. G., & Simon, H. A. (1977). History of artificial intelligence. *IJCAI (United States)*, 951–954.

McIntosh, T., Jang-Jaccard, J., Watters, P., & Susnjak, T. (2019). The inadequacy of entropy-based ransomware detection. In *International conference on neural information processing*. New York: Springer.

Meira, J., Andrade, R., Praça, I., Carneiro, J., Bolón-Canedo, V., Alonso-Betanzos, A., & Marreiros, G. (2020). Performance evaluation of unsupervised techniques in cyber-attack anomaly detection. *Journal of Ambient Intelligence and Humanized Computing*, *11*(11), 4477–4489. doi:10.100712652-019-01417-9

Mercaldo, F., & Santone, A. (2020). Deep learning for image-based mobile malware detection. *Journal of Computer Virology and Hacking Techniques*, *16*(2), 157–171. doi:10.100711416-019-00346-7

Miao, Y., Chen, C., Pan, L., Han, Q., Zhang, J., & Xiang, Y. (2022). Machine learning-based cyber attacks targeting on controlled information: A Survey. *ACM Computing Surveys, 54*(7), 1–36. doi:10.1145/3465171

Mikalauskas, E. (2022). *RockYou2021: Largest Ever Password Compilation Leaked online with 8.4 billion entries.* Cybernews. Extracted from: https://cybernews.com/security/rockyou2021-alltime-largest-password-compilation-leaked/

Mitre. (2020). *Reconnaissance, Tactic TA0043 - Enterprise.* MITRE ATT&CK®. Retrieved on November 6, 2022, from: https://attack.mitre.org/tactics/TA0043/

Mödersheim, S. (2009). Algebraic properties in Alice and Bob notation. *International Conference on Availability, Reliability and Security (ARES 2009).* doi:10.1109/ARES.2009.95

Moore. (2015). *Privacy, Security and Accountability: Ethics, Law and Policy.* Rowman & Littlefield.

Morovat, K., & Panda, B. (2020). A Survey of Artificial Intelligence in Cybersecurity. *2020 International Conference on Computational Science and Computational Intelligence (CSCI),* 109–115. 10.1109/CSCI51800.2020.00026

Moustafa, N., Creech, G., Sitnikova, E., & Keshk, M. (2017). Collaborative anomaly detection framework for handling big data of cloud computing. https://arxiv.org/abs/1711.02829

Moustafa, N., & Slay, J. (2015). UNSW-NB15: a comprehensive data set for network intrusion detection systems (UNSW-NB15 network data set). In *Proceedings of 2015 Military Communications and Information Systems Conference (MilCIS).* IEEE. 10.1109/MilCIS.2015.7348942

Mughaid. (2022). An intelligent cyber security phishing detection system using deep learning techniques. *Cluster Comput, 25,* 3819–3828. doi:10.1007/s10586-022-03604-4

Muthukumar, A., & Kavipriya, A. (2019). A biometric system based on Gabor feature extraction with SVM classifier for Finger-Knuckle-Print. *Pattern Recognition Letters.* 10.1016/j.patrec.2019.04.007

Nafees, T., Coull, N., Ferguson, I., & Sampson, A. (2018, November). Vulnerability anti-patterns: a timeless way to capture poor software practices (vulnerabilities). In *24th Conference on Pattern Languages of Programs* (p. 23). The Hillside Group.

Nagendran, K., Adithyan, A., Chethana, R., Camillus, P., & Varshini, K. B. S. (2019). Web application penetration testing. *International Journal of Innovative Technology and Exploring Engineering, 8*(10), 1029–1035. doi:10.35940/ijitee.J9173.0881019

Naoum, R. S., Abid, N. A., & Al-Sultani, Z. N. (2013). An Enhanced Resilient Backpropagation Artificial Neural Network for Intrusion Detection System. *International Journal of Computer Science and Network Security, 13*(3), 98–104. Available: http://paper.ijcsns.org/07{\ } book/201203/20120302.pdf

Nasir, R., Afzal, M., Latif, R., & Iqbal, W. (2021). Behavioral based insider threat detection using deep learning. *IEEE Access : Practical Innovations, Open Solutions*, *9*, 143266–143274. doi:10.1109/ACCESS.2021.3118297

Nichols, S. (2016). *St Jude sues short-selling MedSec over pacemaker "hack" report*. The Register. https://www.theregister.co.uk/2016/09/07/st_jude_sues_over_hacking_claim/

Nielsen, M. A. (2015). Neural networks and deep learning (Vol. 25). Determination Press.

O'Brien, N. (2018). *Machine learning for detection of fake news* [MS Thesis]. MIT.

Odeh, A., Keshta, I., & Abdelfattah, E. (2021, January). Machine learning techniques for detection of website phishing: A review for promises and challenges. In *2021 IEEE 11th Annual Computing and Communication Workshop and Conference (CCWC)* (pp. 0813-0818). IEEE. 10.1109/CCWC51732.2021.9375997

Onyango, O. (2021). Artificial intelligence and its application to information security management. doi:10.13140/RG.2.2.12066.09921

Operational Cyber Intelligence. (2014). INSA.

Ovchinsky, V. S. (2018). *Criminology of the digital world*. Extracted from: https://www.cybercrimejournal.com/pdf/KhisamovaetalVol13Issue2IJCC2019.pdf

Park, N. E., Lee, Y. R., Joo, S., Kim, S. Y., Kim, S. H., Park, J. Y., Kim, S.-Y., & Lee, I. G. (2023). Performance evaluation of a fast and efficient intrusion detection framework for advanced persistent threat-based cyberattacks. *Computers & Electrical Engineering*, *105*, 108548. doi:10.1016/j.compeleceng.2022.108548

Patil, P. (2016). Artificial intelligence in cybersecurity. *Int. J. Res. Comput. Appl. Robot*, *4*(5), 1–5.

Pérez-Díaz, N. W., Chinchay-Maldonado, J. O., Mejía-Cabrera, H. I., Bances-Saavedra, D. E., & Bravo-Ruiz, J. A. (2023). Ransomware Identification Through Sandbox Environment. In *Proceedings of the Future Technologies Conference* (pp. 326-335). Springer, Cham.

Podder, P., Bharati, S., Mondal, M. R. H., Paul, P. K., & Kose, U. (2021). Artificial neural network for cybersecurity: A comprehensive review. *Journal of Information Assurance and Security*, *16*(1), 10–23. doi:10.48550/arXiv.2107.01185

Pothamsetty, V. (2005). Where security education is lacking. In *Proceedings of the 2nd Annual Conference on Information Security Curriculum Development*. ACM. https://doi.org/10.1145/1107622.1107635

Pretorius, B., & van Niekerk, B. (2020). Cyber-security for ICS/SCADA. *Cyber Warfare and Terrorism*, 613–630. doi:10.4018/978-1-7998-2466-4.ch038

Pupillo. (2021). *Artificial intelligence and cybersecurity*. Centre for European Policy Studies (CEPS). Extracted from: https://www.ceps.eu/wp-content/uploads/2021/05/CEPS-TFR-Artificial-Intelligence-and-Cybersecurity.pdf

Qiao, L.-B., Zhang, B.-F., Lai, Z.-Q., & Su, J.-S. (2012). Mining of attack models in ids alerts from network backbone by a two-stage clustering method. In *2012 IEEE 26th international parallel and distributed processing symposium workshops & PhD Forum*. IEEE. 10.1109/IPDPSW.2012.146

Quadri, A., & Khan, M. K. (2019). *The G-War: Race for Technological Supremacy in 5G and 6G The G-War: Race for Technological Supremacy in 5G and 6G. Policy.* Extracted from https://www.abacademies.org/articles/Advanced-persistent-threats-apt-an-awareness-review-1533-3604-21-6-202.pdf

Razaque, A., Frej, M. B. H., Sabyrov, D., Shaikhyn, A., Amsaad, F., & Oun, A. (2020, October). *Detection of phishing websites using machine learning. In 2020 IEEE Cloud Summit.* IEEE.

Redini, N., Machiry, A., Wang, R., Spensky, C., Continella, A., Shoshitaishvili, Y., ... Vigna, G. (2020, May). Karonte: Detecting insecure multi-binary interactions in embedded firmware. In *2020 IEEE Symposium on Security and Privacy (SP)* (pp. 1544-1561). IEEE. 10.1109/SP40000.2020.00036

Redino, C., Nandakumar, D., Schiller, R., Choi, K., Rahman, A., Bowen, E., . . . Nehila, J. *(2022). Zero Day Threat Detection Using Graph and Flow Based Security Telemetry.* arXiv preprint arXiv:2205.02298. doi:10.1109/ICCCIS56430.2022.10037596

Redmon, J., & Farhadi, A. (2018). YOLOv3: An Incremental Improvement. arXiv preprint arXiv:1804.02767.

Ren, S., He, K., Girshick, R., & Sun, J. (2015). Faster R-CNN: Towards real-time object detection with region proposal networks. In Advances in neural information processing systems (pp. 91-99). Academic Press.

Reporter. (2022). *Hackers leveraging AI to launch phishing scams.* Cybersecurity Connect. Extracted from: https://www.cybersecurityconnect.com.au/commercial/8261-hackers-leveraging-ai-to-launch-phishing-scams#:~:text=Adding%20to%20cyber%20threats&text=%22For%20instance%2C%20AI%20can%20be,weaknesses%2C%22%20Finch%20further%20explained

Republic of Bulgaria. (2016). *National Cyber Security Strategy "Cyber Resilient Bulgaria 2020", 2016- 03 NCSS Bulgaria final draft v 5 3.* Bulgarian Government.

Richard, S. (2020). *John McCarthy's Definition of Intelligence.* Extracted from: http://www.incompleteideas.net/papers/Sutton-JAGI-2020.pdf

Rodriguez, M., & Buyya, R. (2020). Container orchestration with cost-efficient autoscaling in cloud computing environments. *Handbook of Research on Multimedia Cyber Security*, 190–213. doi:10.4018/978-1-7998-2701-6.ch010

Rokach, L. (2010). A survey of clustering algorithms. In *Data Mining and Knowledge Discovery Handbook* (pp. 269–298). Springer.

Roponena, E., Kampars, J., Gailitis, A., & Strods, J. (2021). A literature review of machine learning techniques for cybersecurity in data centers. In *2021 62nd International Scientific Conference on Information Technology and Management Science of Riga Technical University, Proceedings (ITMS)* (pp. 1–6). IEEE. 10.1109/ITMS52826.2021.9615321

Sarker, I. H. (2019). A machine learning based robust prediction model for real-life mobile phone data. *Internet of Things*, *5*, 180–193. doi:10.1016/j.iot.2019.01.007

Sarker, I. H. (2019). Context-aware rule learning from smartphone data: Survey, challenges and future directions. *Journal of Big Data*, *6*(95), 95. Advance online publication. doi:10.118640537-019-0258-4

Sarker, I. H. (2021). Deep cybersecurity: A comprehensive overview from neural network and deep learning perspective. *SN Computer Science*, *2*(3), 154. Advance online publication. doi:10.100742979-021-00535-6 PMID:33778771

Sarker, I. H., Colman, A., & Han, J. (2019). Mining recency-based personalized behavior from contextual smartphone data. *Journal of Big Data*, *6*(49), 49. doi:10.118640537-019-0211-6

Sarker, I. H., Kayes, A., & Watters, P. (2019). Effectiveness analysis of machine learning classification models for predicting personalized context-aware smartphone usage. *Journal of Big Data*, *6*(1), 1–28. doi:10.118640537-019-0219-y

Schneider, F. B. (2013). Cybersecurity education in universities. *IEEE Security and Privacy*, *11*(4), 3–4.

Schwarz, M., Lackner, F., & Gruss, D. (2019, February). JavaScript Template Attacks: Automatically Inferring Host Information for Targeted Exploits. In NDSS.

Schwarz, M., Weiser, S., & Gruss, D. (2019, June). Practical enclave malware with Intel SGX. In *International Conference on Detection of Intrusions and Malware, and Vulnerability Assessment* (pp. 177-196). Springer, Cham.

Scientific American. (n.d.). https://blogs.scientificamerican.com/observations/cambridge-analytica-and-onlinemanipulation/

Shabtai, A., Kanonov, U., Elovici, Y., Glezer, C., & Weiss, Y. (2012). Andromaly: A behavioral malware detection framework for android devices. *Journal of Intelligent Information Systems*, *38*(1), 161–190. doi:10.100710844-010-0148-x

Sharafaldin, I., Lashkari, A. H., & Ghorbani, A. A. (2018). Toward generating a new intrusion detection dataset and intrusion traffic characterization. In *Proceedings of the 4th International Conference on Information Systems Security and Privacy (ICISSP 2018)* (pp. 108–116). SCITEPRESS. 10.5220/0006639801080116

Shaukat, K. (2020). Performance comparison and current challenges of using machine learning techniques in cybersecurity. *Energies, 13*(10), 2509. Extracted from: https://www.mdpi.com/1996-1073/13/10/2509/pdf?version=1589770863

Shaukat, K., Luo, S., Varadharajan, V., Hameed, I. A., & Xu, M. (2020). A survey on machine learning techniques for cyber security in the last decade. *IEEE Access : Practical Innovations, Open Solutions*, 8, 222310–222354. doi:10.1109/ACCESS.2020.3041951

Shaw, A. (2009). Data breach: From notifcation to prevention using pci dss. *Colum Soc Probs.*, 43, 517.

Shiravi, A., Shiravi, H., Tavallaee, M., & Ghorbani, A. A. (2012). Toward developing a systematic approach to generate benchmark datasets for intrusion detection. *Computers & Security*, 31(3), 357–374. doi:10.1016/j.cose.2011.12.012

Shon, T., Kim, Y., Lee, C., & Moon, J. (2005). A machine learning framework for network anomaly detection using svm and ga. In *Proceedings from the sixth annual IEEE SMC information assurance workshop*. IEEE. 10.1109/IAW.2005.1495950

Shubho, F. H., Iftekhar, F., Hossain, E., & Siddique, S. (2021). *Real-time traffic monitoring and traffic offense detection using YOLOv4 and OpenCV DNN. In TENCON 2021 - 2021 IEEE Region 10 Conference*. TENCON. doi:10.1109/TENCON54134.2021.9707406

Singer & Friedman. (2014). *Review - Cybersecurity and Cyberwar*. https://www.e-ir. info/2014/01/06/review-cybersecurity-and-cyberwar/

Singh, U. K., Joshi, C., & Kanellopoulos, D. (2019). A framework for zero-day vulnerabilities detection and prioritization. *Journal of Information Security and Applications*, 46, 164–172. doi:10.1016/j.jisa.2019.03.011

Sivilotti, P. A., & Lang, M. (2010). Interfaces first (and foremost) with Java. In Proceedings of the 41st ACM Technical Symposium on Computer Science Education. ACM. https://doi. org/10.1145/1734263.1734436.

Spring, T. (2016). *Researchers: MedSec, Muddy Waters Set Bad Precedent With St. Jude Medical Short*. https://threatpost.com/researchers- medsec-muddy-waters-set-bad-precedent-with-st-judemedical-short/120266/

Squicciarini, A., Caragea, C., & Balakavi, R. (2017). Toward Automated Online Photo Privacy. *ACM Transactions on the Web*, 11(1), 1–29. doi:10.1145/2983644

Sriraghavan, R. G., & Lucchese, L. (2008). Data processing and anomaly detection in web-based applications. In *2008 IEEE Workshop on Machine Learning for Signal Processing* (pp. 187–192). IEEE. 10.1109/MLSP.2008.4685477

Stahl. (2021). *Ethical Issues of AI*. Extracted from: https://link.springer.com/chapter/10.1007/978-3-030-69978-9_4?error=cookies_not_supported&code=09313d7e-2c23-4bbd-9ffc-4d1ce6eac90b

Subasi, A., Molah, E., Almkallawi, F., & Chaudhery, T. J. (2017, November). Intelligent phishing website detection using random forest classifier. In *2017 International conference on electrical and computing technologies and applications (ICECTA)* (pp. 1-5). IEEE. 10.1109/ICECTA.2017.8252051

Suciu, O., Nelson, C., Lyu, Z., Bao, T., & Dumitraş, T. (2022). Expected exploitability: Predicting the development of functional vulnerability exploits. In *31st USENIX Security Symposium (USENIX Security 22)* (pp. 377-394).

Sun, N., Zhang, J., Rimba, P., Gao, S., Zhang, L. Y., & Xiang, Y. (2018). Data-driven cybersecurity incident prediction: A survey. *IEEE Communications Surveys and Tutorials*, *21*(2), 1744–1772. doi:10.1109/COMST.2018.2885561

Sun, Z., Li, X., Zhang, L., & Han, J. (2019). Deep learning for real-time traffic signal control. *Transportation Research Part C, Emerging Technologies*, *99*, 30–45.

Taddeo. (2019). *Three Ethical Challenges of Applications of Artificial Intelligence in Cybersecurity. Minds and Machines*. Extracted from: https://www.researchgate.net/publication/333580685_Three_Ethical_Challenges_of_Applications_of_Artificial_Intelligence_in_Cybersecurity doi:10.1007/s11023-019-09504-8

Takaesu, I. (2018). *DeepExploit*. GitHub. https://github.com/13o-bbr-bbq/machine_learning_security/tree/master/DeepExploit

Tan, S. (2021). Attack detection design for dc microgrid using eigenvalue assignment approach. *Energy Rep., 7*, 469-476.

Taylor, V. F., Spolaor, R., Conti, M., & Martinovic, I. (2017). Robust smartphone app identification via encrypted network traffic analysis. *IEEE Transactions on Information Forensics and Security*, *13*(1), 63–78. doi:10.1109/TIFS.2017.2737970

Tehranipoor, M. M., & Koushanfar, F. (2010). A Survey of Hardware Trojan Taxonomy and Detection. *IEEE Design & Test of Computers*, 27.

*The Importance of AI Spam Filtering - Cii Technology Solutions*. (n.d.). Retrieved November 29, 2022, from https://ciinc.com/the-importance-of-ai-spam-filtering/

Thirumalairaj, A., & Jeyakarthic, M. (2020). Perimeter intrusion detection with multi layer perception using quantum classifier. In *2020 Fourth International Conference on Inventive Systems and Control (ICISC)* (pp. 348–352). IEEE. 10.1109/ICISC47916.2020.9171159

Thuraisingham. (2020). The Role of Artificial Intelligence and Cyber Security for Social Media. *IEEE International Parallel and Distributed Processing Symposium Workshops (IPDPSW)*, 1116-1118.

Thuraisingham, B. M., Cadenhead, T., & Kantarcioglu, M. (2014). *Access Control and Inference with Semantic Web*. CRC Press.

Thuraisingham, B. M., Kantarcioglu, M., Khan, L., Carminati, B., Ferrari, E., & Bahri, L. (2016). *Emergency-Driven Assured Information Sharing in Secure Online Social Networks: A Position Paper*. IPDPS Workshops. doi:10.1109/IPDPSW.2016.201

Thuraisingham, B., Pallabi, P., Masud, M., & Khan, L. (2017). *Big Data Analytics with Applications in Insider Threat Detection*. CRC Press. doi:10.1201/9781315119458

## Compilation of References

Tian, Q., Han, D., Li, K.-C., Liu, X., Duan, L., & Castiglione, A. (2020). An intrusion detection approach based on improved deep belief network. *Applied Intelligence*, *50*(10), 3162–3178. doi:10.100710489-020-01694-4

Tiwari, P., & Singh, R. R. (2015). Machine learning based phishing website detection system. *International Journal of Engine Research*, *4*(12), 172–174.

Toosi, A., Bottino, A. G., Saboury, B., Siegel, E., & Rahmim, A. (2021). A brief history of AI: How to prevent another winter (a critical review). *PET Clinics*, *16*(4), 449–469. doi:10.1016/j.cpet.2021.07.001 PMID:34537126

Torrance, R., & James, D. (2009). *The State-of-the-Art in IC Reverse Engineering.*. doi:10.1007/978-3-642-04138-9_26

Trifonov, R., Nakov, O., & Mladenov, V. (2018). Artificial Intelligence in Cyber Threats Intelligence. IEEE European Union, 2018 International Conference on Intelligent and Innovative Computing Applications (ICONIC). doi:10.1109/ICONIC.2018.8601235

Truong, T. C., Zelinka, I., Plucar, J., Čandík, M., & Šulc, V. (2020). Artificial intelligence and cybersecurity: Past, presence, and future. In *Artificial intelligence and evolutionary computations in engineering systems* (pp. 351–363). Springer. doi:10.1007/978-981-15-0199-9_30

Tsai, C.-F., & Lin, C.-Y. (2010). A triangle area based nearest neighbors approach to intrusion detection. *Pattern Recognition*, *43*(1), 222–229. doi:10.1016/j.patcog.2009.05.017

Tucker, E. (2018). *Cyber security – why you're doing it all wrong.* https://www.computerweekly.com/opinion/Cyber-securitywhy-youre-doing-it-all-wrong

Ullah, F., Naeem, H., Jabbar, S., Khalid, S., Latif, M. A., Al-Turjman, F., & Mostarda, L. (2019). Cyber security threats detection in internet of things using deep learning approach. *IEEE Access : Practical Innovations, Open Solutions*, *7*, 124379–124389. doi:10.1109/ACCESS.2019.2937347

Veiga, A. P. (2018). *Applications of artificial intelligence to network security.* ArXiv Preprint ArXiv:1803.09992.

Vetterl, A., & Clayton, R. (2019, November). Honware: A virtual honeypot framework for capturing CPE and IoT zero days. In *2019 APWG Symposium on Electronic Crime Research (eCrime)* (pp. 1-13). IEEE. 10.1109/eCrime47957.2019.9037501

Vigderman, A., & Turner, G. (2022, October 17). *How does antivirus software work?* Security.org. Retrieved January 27, 2023, from https://www.security.org/antivirus/how-does-antivirus-work/

Vigna, G. (2020). *How AI will help in the fight against malware.* Retrieved from TechBeacon.

Vishwakarma, R., & Jain, A. K. (2019, April). A honeypot with machine learning based detection framework for defending IoT based botnet DDoS attacks. In *2019 3rd International Conference on Trends in Electronics and Informatics (ICOEI)* (pp. 1019-1024). IEEE. 10.1109/ICOEI.2019.8862720

*Vulnerability Management and Remediation: Leveraging AI to Modernize your Program?* | *Secureworks*. (n.d.). Retrieved November 29, 2022, from https://www.secureworks.com/resources/wp-the-role-of-ai-in-modernizing-vulnerability-management

Walden, J., & Frank, C. E. (2006). Secure software engineering teaching modules. In *Proceedings of the 3rd Annual Conference on Information Security Curriculum Development*. ACM. https://doi.org/10.1145/1231047.1231052.

Wang, Y., Jia, X., Liu, Y., Zeng, K., Bao, T., Wu, D., & Su, P. (2020, February). Not All Coverage Measurements Are Equal: Fuzzing by Coverage Accounting for Input Prioritization. In NDSS.

Wang, C., Zhao, Z., Gong, L., Zhu, L., Liu, Z., & Cheng, X. (2018). A Distributed Anomaly Detection System for In-Vehicle Network Using HTM. *IEEE Access : Practical Innovations, Open Solutions*, 6, 9091–9098. doi:10.1109/ACCESS.2018.2799210

Wang, R., & Ji, W. (2020). Computational intelligence for information security: A survey. *IEEE Transactions on Emerging Topics in Computational Intelligence*, 4(5), 616–629. doi:10.1109/TETCI.2019.2923426

Watters, P. A., McCombie, S., Layton, R., & Pieprzyk, J. (2012). *Characterising and predicting cyber attacks using the cyber attacker model profile (camp)*. J Money Launder Control. doi:10.1108/13685201211266015

Webb, G. I., Pazzani, M. J., & Billsus, D. (2001). Machine learning for user modeling. *User Modeling and User-Adapted Interaction*, 11(1/2), 19–29. doi:10.1023/A:1011117102175

*What is a Data Breach & How to Prevent One*. (n.d.). Retrieved November 29, 2022, from https://www.kaspersky.com/resource-center/definitions/data-breach

*What is Endpoint Protection? - Check Point Software*. (n.d.). Retrieved November 29, 2022, from https://www.checkpoint.com/cyber-hub/threat-prevention/what-is-endpoint-security/

*What Is Next-Generation Endpoint Security?* | *Trellix*. (n.d.). Retrieved November 29, 2022, from https://www.trellix.com/en-us/security-awareness/endpoint/what-is-next-gen-endpoint-protection.html

WhiteBlueOcean. (2021, July 6). *Is rockyou2021 really a password leak?* Retrieved January 27, 2023, from https://www.whiteblueocean.com/newsroom/is-rockyou2021-really-a-password-leak/

Wiafe, Koranteng, Obeng, Assyne, Wiafe, & Gulliver. (2017). Artificial Intelligence for Cybersecurity: A Systematic Mapping of Literature. *IEEE Access*. doi:10.1109/ACCESS.2017

Williams, K. A., Yuan, X., Yu, H., & Bryant, K. (2014). Teaching secure coding for beginning programmers. *Journal of Computing Sciences in Colleges*, 29(5), 91–99.

Wilner, A. (2018). Cybersecurity and its discontinuities: Artificial intelligence, the Internet of things, and digital misinformation. *International Journal*, 73(2), 308-316. Extracted from: https://journals.sagepub.com/doi/abs/10.1177/0020702018782496

**Compilation of References**

Wirkuttis, N., & Klein, H. (2017). Artificial intelligence in cybersecurity. *Cyber, Intelligence, and Security, 1*(1), 103–119.

Wu, B., & Nevatia, R. (2006). Detection and tracking of multiple, partially occluded humans by Bayesian combination of edgelet based part detectors. *International Journal of Computer Vision, 72*(1), 53–77.

Xiaomeng, L., Jun, F., & Peng, C. (2022). Vehicle Detection in Traffic Monitoring Scenes Based on Improved YOLOV5s. *2022 International Conference on Computer Engineering and Artificial Intelligence (ICCEAI)*, 467-471. 10.1109/ICCEAI55464.2022.00103

Xin, Y., Kong, L., Liu, Z., Chen, Y., Li, Y., Zhu, H., Gao, M., Hou, H., & Wang, C. (2018). Machine learning and deep learning methods for cybersecurity. *IEEE Access : Practical Innovations, Open Solutions, 6*, 35365–35381. doi:10.1109/ACCESS.2018.2836950

Yang, S., Dong, C., Xiao, Y., Cheng, Y., Shi, Z., Li, Z., & Sun, L. *(2023). Asteria-Pro: Enhancing Deep-Learning Based Binary Code Similarity Detection by Incorporating Domain Knowledge.* arXiv preprint arXiv:2301.00511.

Yan, X., Cui, B., Xu, Y., Shi, P., & Wang, Z. (2021). A method of information protection for collaborative deep learning under GAN model attack. *IEEE/ACM Transactions on Computational Biology and Bioinformatics, 18*(3), 871–881. doi:10.1109/TCBB.2019.2940583 PMID:31514150

Yavanoglu, O., & Aydos, M. (2017). A review on cyber security datasets for machine learning algorithms. In *IEEE International Conference on Big Data (Big Data)* (pp. 2186–2193). IEEE. 10.1109/BigData.2017.8258167

Yin, J., Tang, M., Cao, J., You, M., & Wang, H. (2023). Cybersecurity Applications in Software: Data-Driven Software Vulnerability Assessment and Management. In *Emerging Trends in Cybersecurity Applications* (pp. 371–389). Springer. doi:10.1007/978-3-031-09640-2_17

You, W., Wang, X., Ma, S., Huang, J., Zhang, X., Wang, X., & Liang, B. (2019, May). Profuzzer: On-the-fly input type probing for better zero-day vulnerability discovery. In *2019 IEEE symposium on security and privacy (SP)* (pp. 769-786). IEEE.

Yuan, X. Y. (2017). *PhD forum: Deep learning-based real-time malware detection with multi-stage analysis.* IEEE Int Conf on Smart Computing. doi:10.1109/SMARTCOMP.2017.7946997

Yu, J., Zhang, B., Kuang, Z., Lin, D., & Fan, J. (2017). iPrivacy : Image Privacy Protection by Identifying Sensitive Objects via Deep Multi-Task Learning. *IEEE Transactions on Information Forensics and Security, 12*(5), 1005–1016. doi:10.1109/TIFS.2016.2636090

Zanaty. (2018). An empirical study of design discussions in code review. In *Proceedings of the 12th ACM/IEEE International Symposium on Empirical Software Engineering and Measurement (ESEM '18).* Association for Computing Machinery.

Zeadally, A. (2020). *Harnessing Artificial Intelligence Capabilities to Improve Cybersecurity* (Vol. 8). doi:10.1109/ACCESS.2020.2968045

Zeng, H., Liu, Z., & Cai, H. (2020). Research on the application of deep learning in computer network information security. *Journal of Physics: Conference Series*, *1650*(3), 032117. doi:10.1088/1742-6596/1650/3/032117

Zhang, H. (2012). User intention-based traffic dependence analysis for anomaly detection. In *2012 IEEE Symposium on Security and Privacy Workshops*. IEEE. 10.1109/SPW.2012.15

Zhang, K., Zhang, L., & Yang, M. H. (2014). Real-time compressive tracking. In *Proceedings of the IEEE conference on computer vision and pattern recognition* (pp. 1357-1364). IEEE.

Zhong, W., Yu, N., & Ai, C. (2020). Applying big data based deep learning system to intrusion detection. *Big Data Mining and Analytics*, *3*(3), 181–195. doi:10.26599/BDMA.2020.9020003

Zhou, Y., & Feng, D. (2005). Side-Channel Attacks: Ten Years After Its Publication and the Impacts on Cryptographic Module Security Testing. *IACR Cryptology ePrint Archive, 388.*

Zhou, S., Yang, Z., Xiang, J., Cao, Y., Yang, M., & Zhang, Y. (2020, August). An ever-evolving game: Evaluation of real-world attacks and defenses in ethereum ecosystem. In *Proceedings of the 29th USENIX Conference on Security Symposium* (pp. 2793-2809).

Zhou, Y., Kantarcioglu, M., Thuraisingham, B. M., & Xi, B. (2012). Adversarial support vector machine learning. *KDD : Proceedings / International Conference on Knowledge Discovery & Data Mining. International Conference on Knowledge Discovery & Data Mining*, 1059–1067.

# Related References

To continue our tradition of advancing information science and technology research, we have compiled a list of recommended IGI Global readings. These references will provide additional information and guidance to further enrich your knowledge and assist you with your own research and future publications.

Abbas, R., Michael, K., & Michael, M. G. (2017). What Can People Do with Your Spatial Data?: Socio-Ethical Scenarios. In A. Marrington, D. Kerr, & J. Gammack (Eds.), *Managing Security Issues and the Hidden Dangers of Wearable Technologies* (pp. 206–237). Hershey, PA: IGI Global. doi:10.4018/978-1-5225-1016-1.ch009

Abulaish, M., & Haldar, N. A. (2018). Advances in Digital Forensics Frameworks and Tools: A Comparative Insight and Ranking. *International Journal of Digital Crime and Forensics*, *10*(2), 95–119. doi:10.4018/IJDCF.2018040106

Ahmad, F. A., Kumar, P., Shrivastava, G., & Bouhlel, M. S. (2018). Bitcoin: Digital Decentralized Cryptocurrency. In G. Shrivastava, P. Kumar, B. Gupta, S. Bala, & N. Dey (Eds.), *Handbook of Research on Network Forensics and Analysis Techniques* (pp. 395–415). Hershey, PA: IGI Global. doi:10.4018/978-1-5225-4100-4.ch021

Ahmed, A. A. (2017). Investigation Approach for Network Attack Intention Recognition. *International Journal of Digital Crime and Forensics*, *9*(1), 17–38. doi:10.4018/IJDCF.2017010102

Akhtar, Z. (2017). Biometric Spoofing and Anti-Spoofing. In M. Dawson, D. Kisku, P. Gupta, J. Sing, & W. Li (Eds.), Developing Next-Generation Countermeasures for Homeland Security Threat Prevention (pp. 121-139). Hershey, PA: IGI Global. doi:10.4018/978-1-5225-0703-1.ch007

Akowuah, F. E., Land, J., Yuan, X., Yang, L., Xu, J., & Wang, H. (2018). Standards and Guides for Implementing Security and Privacy for Health Information Technology. In Y. Maleh (Ed.), *Security and Privacy Management, Techniques, and Protocols* (pp. 214–236). Hershey, PA: IGI Global. doi:10.4018/978-1-5225-5583-4.ch008

Akremi, A., Sallay, H., & Rouached, M. (2018). Intrusion Detection Systems Alerts Reduction: New Approach for Forensics Readiness. In Y. Maleh (Ed.), *Security and Privacy Management, Techniques, and Protocols* (pp. 255–275). Hershey, PA: IGI Global. doi:10.4018/978-1-5225-5583-4.ch010

Aldwairi, M., Hasan, M., & Balbahaith, Z. (2017). Detection of Drive-by Download Attacks Using Machine Learning Approach. *International Journal of Information Security and Privacy*, *11*(4), 16–28. doi:10.4018/IJISP.2017100102

Alohali, B. (2017). Detection Protocol of Possible Crime Scenes Using Internet of Things (IoT). In M. Moore (Ed.), *Cybersecurity Breaches and Issues Surrounding Online Threat Protection* (pp. 175–196). Hershey, PA: IGI Global. doi:10.4018/978-1-5225-1941-6.ch008

AlShahrani, A. M., Al-Abadi, M. A., Al-Malki, A. S., Ashour, A. S., & Dey, N. (2017). Automated System for Crops Recognition and Classification. In N. Dey, A. Ashour, & S. Acharjee (Eds.), *Applied Video Processing in Surveillance and Monitoring Systems* (pp. 54–69). Hershey, PA: IGI Global. doi:10.4018/978-1-5225-1022-2.ch003

Anand, R., Shrivastava, G., Gupta, S., Peng, S., & Sindhwani, N. (2018). Audio Watermarking With Reduced Number of Random Samples. In G. Shrivastava, P. Kumar, B. Gupta, S. Bala, & N. Dey (Eds.), *Handbook of Research on Network Forensics and Analysis Techniques* (pp. 372–394). Hershey, PA: IGI Global. doi:10.4018/978-1-5225-4100-4.ch020

Anand, R., Sinha, A., Bhardwaj, A., & Sreeraj, A. (2018). Flawed Security of Social Network of Things. In G. Shrivastava, P. Kumar, B. Gupta, S. Bala, & N. Dey (Eds.), *Handbook of Research on Network Forensics and Analysis Techniques* (pp. 65–86). Hershey, PA: IGI Global. doi:10.4018/978-1-5225-4100-4.ch005

Aneja, M. J., Bhatia, T., Sharma, G., & Shrivastava, G. (2018). Artificial Intelligence Based Intrusion Detection System to Detect Flooding Attack in VANETs. In G. Shrivastava, P. Kumar, B. Gupta, S. Bala, & N. Dey (Eds.), *Handbook of Research on Network Forensics and Analysis Techniques* (pp. 87–100). Hershey, PA: IGI Global. doi:10.4018/978-1-5225-4100-4.ch006

Antunes, F., Freire, M., & Costa, J. P. (2018). From Motivation and Self-Structure to a Decision-Support Framework for Online Social Networks. In V. Ahuja & S. Rathore (Eds.), *Multidisciplinary Perspectives on Human Capital and Information Technology Professionals* (pp. 116–136). Hershey, PA: IGI Global. doi:10.4018/978-1-5225-5297-0.ch007

Atli, D. (2017). Cybercrimes via Virtual Currencies in International Business. In M. Moore (Ed.), *Cybersecurity Breaches and Issues Surrounding Online Threat Protection* (pp. 121–143). Hershey, PA: IGI Global. doi:10.4018/978-1-5225-1941-6.ch006

Baazeem, R. M. (2018). The Role of Religiosity in Technology Acceptance: The Case of Privacy in Saudi Arabia. In J. McAlaney, L. Frumkin, & V. Benson (Eds.), *Psychological and Behavioral Examinations in Cyber Security* (pp. 172–193). Hershey, PA: IGI Global. doi:10.4018/978-1-5225-4053-3.ch010

Bailey, W. J. (2017). Protection of Critical Homeland Assets: Using a Proactive, Adaptive Security Management Driven Process. In M. Dawson, D. Kisku, P. Gupta, J. Sing, & W. Li (Eds.), Developing Next-Generation Countermeasures for Homeland Security Threat Prevention (pp. 17-50). Hershey, PA: IGI Global. https://doi.org/doi:10.4018/978-1-5225-0703-1.ch002

Bajaj, S. (2018). Current Drift in Energy Efficiency Cloud Computing: New Provocations, Workload Prediction, Consolidation, and Resource Over Commitment. In S. Aljawarneh & M. Malhotra (Eds.), *Critical Research on Scalability and Security Issues in Virtual Cloud Environments* (pp. 283–303). Hershey, PA: IGI Global. doi:10.4018/978-1-5225-3029-9.ch014

Balasubramanian, K. (2018). Hash Functions and Their Applications. In K. Balasubramanian & M. Rajakani (Eds.), *Algorithmic Strategies for Solving Complex Problems in Cryptography* (pp. 66–77). Hershey, PA: IGI Global. doi:10.4018/978-1-5225-2915-6.ch005

Balasubramanian, K. (2018). Recent Developments in Cryptography: A Survey. In K. Balasubramanian & M. Rajakani (Eds.), *Algorithmic Strategies for Solving Complex Problems in Cryptography* (pp. 1–22). Hershey, PA: IGI Global. doi:10.4018/978-1-5225-2915-6.ch001

Balasubramanian, K. (2018). Secure Two Party Computation. In K. Balasubramanian & M. Rajakani (Eds.), *Algorithmic Strategies for Solving Complex Problems in Cryptography* (pp. 145–153). Hershey, PA: IGI Global. doi:10.4018/978-1-5225-2915-6.ch012

Balasubramanian, K. (2018). Securing Public Key Encryption Against Adaptive Chosen Ciphertext Attacks. In K. Balasubramanian & M. Rajakani (Eds.), *Algorithmic Strategies for Solving Complex Problems in Cryptography* (pp. 134–144). Hershey, PA: IGI Global. doi:10.4018/978-1-5225-2915-6.ch011

Balasubramanian, K. (2018). Variants of the Diffie-Hellman Problem. In K. Balasubramanian & M. Rajakani (Eds.), *Algorithmic Strategies for Solving Complex Problems in Cryptography* (pp. 40–54). Hershey, PA: IGI Global. doi:10.4018/978-1-5225-2915-6.ch003

Balasubramanian, K., & K., M. (2018). Secure Group Key Agreement Protocols. In K. Balasubramanian, & M. Rajakani (Eds.), *Algorithmic Strategies for Solving Complex Problems in Cryptography* (pp. 55-65). Hershey, PA: IGI Global. https://doi.org/ doi:10.4018/978-1-5225-2915-6.ch004

Balasubramanian, K., & M., R. (2018). Problems in Cryptography and Cryptanalysis. In K. Balasubramanian, & M. Rajakani (Eds.), *Algorithmic Strategies for Solving Complex Problems in Cryptography* (pp. 23-39). Hershey, PA: IGI Global. https://doi.org/ doi:10.4018/978-1-5225-2915-6.ch002

Balasubramanian, K., & Abbas, A. M. (2018). Integer Factoring Algorithms. In K. Balasubramanian & M. Rajakani (Eds.), *Algorithmic Strategies for Solving Complex Problems in Cryptography* (pp. 228–240). Hershey, PA: IGI Global. doi:10.4018/978-1-5225-2915-6.ch017

Balasubramanian, K., & Abbas, A. M. (2018). Secure Bootstrapping Using the Trusted Platform Module. In K. Balasubramanian & M. Rajakani (Eds.), *Algorithmic Strategies for Solving Complex Problems in Cryptography* (pp. 167–185). Hershey, PA: IGI Global. doi:10.4018/978-1-5225-2915-6.ch014

Balasubramanian, K., & Mathanan, J. (2018). Cryptographic Voting Protocols. In K. Balasubramanian & M. Rajakani (Eds.), *Algorithmic Strategies for Solving Complex Problems in Cryptography* (pp. 124–133). Hershey, PA: IGI Global. doi:10.4018/978-1-5225-2915-6.ch010

Balasubramanian, K., & Rajakani, M. (2018). Secure Multiparty Computation. In K. Balasubramanian & M. Rajakani (Eds.), *Algorithmic Strategies for Solving Complex Problems in Cryptography* (pp. 154–166). Hershey, PA: IGI Global. doi:10.4018/978-1-5225-2915-6.ch013

Balasubramanian, K., & Rajakani, M. (2018). The Quadratic Sieve Algorithm for Integer Factoring. In K. Balasubramanian & M. Rajakani (Eds.), *Algorithmic Strategies for Solving Complex Problems in Cryptography* (pp. 241–252). Hershey, PA: IGI Global. doi:10.4018/978-1-5225-2915-6.ch018

Barone, P. A. (2017). Defining and Understanding the Development of Juvenile Delinquency from an Environmental, Sociological, and Theoretical Perspective. In S. Egharevba (Ed.), *Police Brutality, Racial Profiling, and Discrimination in the Criminal Justice System* (pp. 215–238). Hershey, PA: IGI Global. doi:10.4018/978-1-5225-1088-8.ch010

Beauchere, J. F. (2018). Encouraging Digital Civility: What Companies and Others Can Do. In R. Luppicini (Ed.), *The Changing Scope of Technoethics in Contemporary Society* (pp. 262–274). Hershey, PA: IGI Global. doi:10.4018/978-1-5225-5094-5. ch014

Behera, C. K., & Bhaskari, D. L. (2017). Malware Methodologies and Its Future: A Survey. *International Journal of Information Security and Privacy*, *11*(4), 47–64. doi:10.4018/IJISP.2017100104

Benson, V., McAlaney, J., & Frumkin, L. A. (2018). Emerging Threats for the Human Element and Countermeasures in Current Cyber Security Landscape. In J. McAlaney, L. Frumkin, & V. Benson (Eds.), *Psychological and Behavioral Examinations in Cyber Security* (pp. 266–271). Hershey, PA: IGI Global. doi:10.4018/978-1-5225-4053-3.ch016

Berbecaru, D. (2018). On Creating Digital Evidence in IP Networks With NetTrack. In G. Shrivastava, P. Kumar, B. Gupta, S. Bala, & N. Dey (Eds.), *Handbook of Research on Network Forensics and Analysis Techniques* (pp. 225–245). Hershey, PA: IGI Global. doi:10.4018/978-1-5225-4100-4.ch012

Berki, E., Valtanen, J., Chaudhary, S., & Li, L. (2018). The Need for Multi-Disciplinary Approaches and Multi-Level Knowledge for Cybersecurity Professionals. In V. Ahuja & S. Rathore (Eds.), *Multidisciplinary Perspectives on Human Capital and Information Technology Professionals* (pp. 72–94). Hershey, PA: IGI Global. doi:10.4018/978-1-5225-5297-0.ch005

Bhardwaj, A. (2017). Ransomware: A Rising Threat of new age Digital Extortion. In S. Aljawarneh (Ed.), *Online Banking Security Measures and Data Protection* (pp. 189–221). Hershey, PA: IGI Global. doi:10.4018/978-1-5225-0864-9.ch012

Bhattacharjee, J., Sengupta, A., Barik, M. S., & Mazumdar, C. (2018). An Analytical Study of Methodologies and Tools for Enterprise Information Security Risk Management. In M. Gupta, R. Sharman, J. Walp, & P. Mulgund (Eds.), *Information Technology Risk Management and Compliance in Modern Organizations* (pp. 1–20). Hershey, PA: IGI Global. doi:10.4018/978-1-5225-2604-9.ch001

Bruno, G. (2018). Handling the Dataflow in Business Process Models. In V. Ahuja & S. Rathore (Eds.), *Multidisciplinary Perspectives on Human Capital and Information Technology Professionals* (pp. 137–151). Hershey, PA: IGI Global. doi:10.4018/978-1-5225-5297-0.ch008

Bush, C. L. (2021). Policing Strategies and Approaches to Improving Community Relations: Black Citizens' Perceptions of Law Enforcement Efforts to Intentionally Strengthen Relationships. In M. Pittaro (Ed.), *Global Perspectives on Reforming the Criminal Justice System* (pp. 56–75). IGI Global. https://doi.org/10.4018/978-1-7998-6884-2.ch004

Carneiro, A. D. (2017). Defending Information Networks in Cyberspace: Some Notes on Security Needs. In M. Dawson, D. Kisku, P. Gupta, J. Sing, & W. Li (Eds.), Developing Next-Generation Countermeasures for Homeland Security Threat Prevention (pp. 354-375). Hershey, PA: IGI Global. https://doi.org/ doi:10.4018/978-1-5225-0703-1.ch016

Chakraborty, S., Patra, P. K., Maji, P., Ashour, A. S., & Dey, N. (2017). Image Registration Techniques and Frameworks: A Review. In N. Dey, A. Ashour, & S. Acharjee (Eds.), *Applied Video Processing in Surveillance and Monitoring Systems* (pp. 102–114). Hershey, PA: IGI Global. doi:10.4018/978-1-5225-1022-2.ch005

Chaudhari, G., & Mulgund, P. (2018). Strengthening IT Governance With COBIT 5. In M. Gupta, R. Sharman, J. Walp, & P. Mulgund (Eds.), *Information Technology Risk Management and Compliance in Modern Organizations* (pp. 48–69). Hershey, PA: IGI Global. doi:10.4018/978-1-5225-2604-9.ch003

Cheikh, M., Hacini, S., & Boufaida, Z. (2018). Visualization Technique for Intrusion Detection. In Y. Maleh (Ed.), *Security and Privacy Management, Techniques, and Protocols* (pp. 276–290). Hershey, PA: IGI Global. doi:10.4018/978-1-5225-5583-4.ch011

Chen, G., Ding, L., Du, J., Zhou, G., Qin, P., Chen, G., & Liu, Q. (2018). Trust Evaluation Strategy for Single Sign-on Solution in Cloud. *International Journal of Digital Crime and Forensics*, *10*(1), 1–11. doi:10.4018/IJDCF.2018010101

Chen, J., & Peng, F. (2018). A Perceptual Encryption Scheme for HEVC Video with Lossless Compression. *International Journal of Digital Crime and Forensics*, *10*(1), 67–78. doi:10.4018/IJDCF.2018010106

Chen, K., & Xu, D. (2018). An Efficient Reversible Data Hiding Scheme for Encrypted Images. *International Journal of Digital Crime and Forensics*, *10*(2), 1–22. doi:10.4018/IJDCF.2018040101

Chen, Z., Lu, J., Yang, P., & Luo, X. (2017). Recognizing Substitution Steganography of Spatial Domain Based on the Characteristics of Pixels Correlation. *International Journal of Digital Crime and Forensics, 9*(4), 48–61. doi:10.4018/IJDCF.2017100105

Cherkaoui, R., Zbakh, M., Braeken, A., & Touhafi, A. (2018). Anomaly Detection in Cloud Computing and Internet of Things Environments: Latest Technologies. In K. Munir (Ed.), *Cloud Computing Technologies for Green Enterprises* (pp. 251–265). Hershey, PA: IGI Global. doi:10.4018/978-1-5225-3038-1.ch010

Chowdhury, A., Karmakar, G., & Kamruzzaman, J. (2017). Survey of Recent Cyber Security Attacks on Robotic Systems and Their Mitigation Approaches. In R. Kumar, P. Pattnaik, & P. Pandey (Eds.), *Detecting and Mitigating Robotic Cyber Security Risks* (pp. 284–299). Hershey, PA: IGI Global. doi:10.4018/978-1-5225-2154-9.ch019

Cortese, F. A. (2018). The Techoethical Ethos of Technic Self-Determination: Technological Determinism as the Ontic Fundament of Freewill. In R. Luppicini (Ed.), *The Changing Scope of Technoethics in Contemporary Society* (pp. 74–104). Hershey, PA: IGI Global. doi:10.4018/978-1-5225-5094-5.ch005

Crosston, M. D. (2017). The Fight for Cyber Thoreau: Distinguishing Virtual Disobedience from Digital Destruction. In M. Korstanje (Ed.), *Threat Mitigation and Detection of Cyber Warfare and Terrorism Activities* (pp. 198–219). Hershey, PA: IGI Global. doi:10.4018/978-1-5225-1938-6.ch009

da Costa, F., & de Sá-Soares, F. (2017). Authenticity Challenges of Wearable Technologies. In A. Marrington, D. Kerr, & J. Gammack (Eds.), *Managing Security Issues and the Hidden Dangers of Wearable Technologies* (pp. 98–130). Hershey, PA: IGI Global. doi:10.4018/978-1-5225-1016-1.ch005

Dafflon, B., Guériau, M., & Gechter, F. (2017). Using Physics Inspired Wave Agents in a Virtual Environment: Longitudinal Distance Control in Robots Platoon. *International Journal of Monitoring and Surveillance Technologies Research, 5*(2), 15–28. doi:10.4018/IJMSTR.2017040102

Dash, S. R., Sheeraz, A. S., & Samantaray, A. (2018). Filtration and Classification of ECG Signals. In C. Pradhan, H. Das, B. Naik, & N. Dey (Eds.), *Handbook of Research on Information Security in Biomedical Signal Processing* (pp. 72–94). Hershey, PA: IGI Global. doi:10.4018/978-1-5225-5152-2.ch005

Dhavale, S. V. (2018). Insider Attack Analysis in Building Effective Cyber Security for an Organization. In J. McAlaney, L. Frumkin, & V. Benson (Eds.), *Psychological and Behavioral Examinations in Cyber Security* (pp. 222–238). Hershey, PA: IGI Global. doi:10.4018/978-1-5225-4053-3.ch013

Dixit, P. (2018). Security Issues in Web Services. In G. Shrivastava, P. Kumar, B. Gupta, S. Bala, & N. Dey (Eds.), *Handbook of Research on Network Forensics and Analysis Techniques* (pp. 57–64). Hershey, PA: IGI Global. doi:10.4018/978-1-5225-4100-4.ch004

Doraikannan, S. (2018). Efficient Implementation of Digital Signature Algorithms. In K. Balasubramanian & M. Rajakani (Eds.), *Algorithmic Strategies for Solving Complex Problems in Cryptography* (pp. 78–86). Hershey, PA: IGI Global. doi:10.4018/978-1-5225-2915-6.ch006

E., J. V., Mohan, J., & K., A. (2018). Automatic Detection of Tumor and Bleed in Magnetic Resonance Brain Images. In C. Pradhan, H. Das, B. Naik, & N. Dey (Eds.), *Handbook of Research on Information Security in Biomedical Signal Processing* (pp. 291-303). Hershey, PA: IGI Global. https://doi.org/ doi:10.4018/978-1-5225-5152-2.ch015

Escamilla, I., Ruíz, M. T., Ibarra, M. M., Soto, V. L., Quintero, R., & Guzmán, G. (2018). Geocoding Tweets Based on Semantic Web and Ontologies. In M. Lytras, N. Aljohani, E. Damiani, & K. Chui (Eds.), *Innovations, Developments, and Applications of Semantic Web and Information Systems* (pp. 372–392). Hershey, PA: IGI Global. doi:10.4018/978-1-5225-5042-6.ch014

Essefi, E. (2022). Advances in Forensic Geophysics: Magnetic Susceptibility as a Tool for Environmental Forensic Geophysics. In C. Chen, W. Yang, & L. Chen (Eds.), *Technologies to Advance Automation in Forensic Science and Criminal Investigation* (pp. 15-36). IGI Global. https://doi.org/10.4018/978-1-7998-8386-9.ch002

Farhadi, M., Haddad, H. M., & Shahriar, H. (2018). Compliance of Electronic Health Record Applications With HIPAA Security and Privacy Requirements. In Y. Maleh (Ed.), *Security and Privacy Management, Techniques, and Protocols* (pp. 199–213). Hershey, PA: IGI Global. doi:10.4018/978-1-5225-5583-4.ch007

Fatma, S. (2018). Use and Misuse of Technology in Marketing: Cases from India. *International Journal of Technoethics*, 9(1), 27–36. doi:10.4018/IJT.2018010103

Fazlali, M., & Khodamoradi, P. (2018). Metamorphic Malware Detection Using Minimal Opcode Statistical Patterns. In Y. Maleh (Ed.), *Security and Privacy Management, Techniques, and Protocols* (pp. 337–359). Hershey, PA: IGI Global. doi:10.4018/978-1-5225-5583-4.ch014

Filiol, É., & Gallais, C. (2017). Optimization of Operational Large-Scale (Cyber) Attacks by a Combinational Approach. *International Journal of Cyber Warfare & Terrorism*, 7(3), 29–43. doi:10.4018/IJCWT.2017070103

Forge, J. (2018). The Case Against Weapons Research. In R. Luppicini (Ed.), *The Changing Scope of Technoethics in Contemporary Society* (pp. 124–134). Hershey, PA: IGI Global. doi:10.4018/978-1-5225-5094-5.ch007

G., S., & Durai, M. S. (2018). Big Data Analytics: An Expedition Through Rapidly Budding Data Exhaustive Era. In D. Lopez, & M. Durai (Eds.), *HCI Challenges and Privacy Preservation in Big Data Security* (pp. 124-138). Hershey, PA: IGI Global. https://doi.org/ doi:10.4018/978-1-5225-2863-0.ch006

Gammack, J., & Marrington, A. (2017). The Promise and Perils of Wearable Technologies. In A. Marrington, D. Kerr, & J. Gammack (Eds.), *Managing Security Issues and the Hidden Dangers of Wearable Technologies* (pp. 1–17). Hershey, PA: IGI Global. doi:10.4018/978-1-5225-1016-1.ch001

Gamoura, S. C. (2018). A Cloud-Based Approach for Cross-Management of Disaster Plans: Managing Risk in Networked Enterprises. In S. Aljawarneh & M. Malhotra (Eds.), *Critical Research on Scalability and Security Issues in Virtual Cloud Environments* (pp. 240–268). Hershey, PA: IGI Global. doi:10.4018/978-1-5225-3029-9.ch012

Gao, L., Gao, T., Zhao, J., & Liu, Y. (2018). Reversible Watermarking in Digital Image Using PVO and RDWT. *International Journal of Digital Crime and Forensics*, *10*(2), 40–55. doi:10.4018/IJDCF.2018040103

Ghany, K. K., & Zawbaa, H. M. (2017). Hybrid Biometrics and Watermarking Authentication. In S. Zoughbi (Ed.), *Securing Government Information and Data in Developing Countries* (pp. 37–61). Hershey, PA: IGI Global. doi:10.4018/978-1-5225-1703-0.ch003

Ghosh, P., Sarkar, D., Sharma, J., & Phadikar, S. (2021). An Intrusion Detection System Using Modified-Firefly Algorithm in Cloud Environment. *International Journal of Digital Crime and Forensics*, *13*(2), 77–93. https://doi.org/10.4018/IJDCF.2021030105

Grant, B. S. (2022). All the World's a Stage: Achieving Deliberate Practice and Performance Improvement Through Story-Based Learning. In *Research Anthology on Advancements in Cybersecurity Education* (pp. 394-413). IGI Global. https://doi.org/10.4018/978-1-6684-3554-0.ch019

Hacini, S., Guessoum, Z., & Cheikh, M. (2018). False Alarm Reduction: A Profiling Mechanism and New Research Directions. In Y. Maleh (Ed.), *Security and Privacy Management, Techniques, and Protocols* (pp. 291–320). Hershey, PA: IGI Global. doi:10.4018/978-1-5225-5583-4.ch012

Hadlington, L. (2018). The "Human Factor" in Cybersecurity: Exploring the Accidental Insider. In J. McAlaney, L. Frumkin, & V. Benson (Eds.), *Psychological and Behavioral Examinations in Cyber Security* (pp. 46-63). Hershey, PA: IGI Global. https://doi.org/ doi:10.4018/978-1-5225-4053-3.ch003

Haldorai, A., & Ramu, A. (2018). The Impact of Big Data Analytics and Challenges to Cyber Security. In G. Shrivastava, P. Kumar, B. Gupta, S. Bala, & N. Dey (Eds.), *Handbook of Research on Network Forensics and Analysis Techniques* (pp. 300–314). Hershey, PA: IGI Global. doi:10.4018/978-1-5225-4100-4.ch016

Hariharan, S., Prasanth, V. S., & Saravanan, P. (2018). Role of Bibliographical Databases in Measuring Information: A Conceptual View. In J. Jeyasekar & P. Saravanan (Eds.), *Innovations in Measuring and Evaluating Scientific Information* (pp. 61–71). Hershey, PA: IGI Global. doi:10.4018/978-1-5225-3457-0.ch005

Hore, S., Chatterjee, S., Chakraborty, S., & Shaw, R. K. (2017). Analysis of Different Feature Description Algorithm in object Recognition. In N. Dey, A. Ashour, & P. Patra (Eds.), *Feature Detectors and Motion Detection in Video Processing* (pp. 66–99). Hershey, PA: IGI Global. doi:10.4018/978-1-5225-1025-3.ch004

Hurley, J. S. (2017). Cyberspace: The New Battlefield - An Approach via the Analytics Hierarchy Process. *International Journal of Cyber Warfare & Terrorism*, 7(3), 1–15. doi:10.4018/IJCWT.2017070101

Hussain, M., & Kaliya, N. (2018). An Improvised Framework for Privacy Preservation in IoT. *International Journal of Information Security and Privacy*, 12(2), 46–63. doi:10.4018/IJISP.2018040104

Ilahi-Amri, M., Cheniti-Belcadhi, L., & Braham, R. (2018). Competence E-Assessment Based on Semantic Web: From Modeling to Validation. In V. Ahuja & S. Rathore (Eds.), *Multidisciplinary Perspectives on Human Capital and Information Technology Professionals* (pp. 246–267). Hershey, PA: IGI Global. doi:10.4018/978-1-5225-5297-0.ch013

Jambhekar, N., & Dhawale, C. A. (2018). Cryptography in Big Data Security. In D. Lopez & M. Durai (Eds.), *HCI Challenges and Privacy Preservation in Big Data Security* (pp. 71–94). Hershey, PA: IGI Global. doi:10.4018/978-1-5225-2863-0.ch004

Jansen van Vuuren, J., Leenen, L., Plint, G., Zaaiman, J., & Phahlamohlaka, J. (2017). Formulating the Building Blocks for National Cyberpower. *International Journal of Cyber Warfare & Terrorism*, 7(3), 16–28. doi:10.4018/IJCWT.2017070102

*Related References*

Jaswal, S., & Malhotra, M. (2018). Identification of Various Privacy and Trust Issues in Cloud Computing Environment. In S. Aljawarneh & M. Malhotra (Eds.), *Critical Research on Scalability and Security Issues in Virtual Cloud Environments* (pp. 95–121). Hershey, PA: IGI Global. doi:10.4018/978-1-5225-3029-9.ch005

Jaswal, S., & Singh, G. (2018). A Comprehensive Survey on Trust Issue and Its Deployed Models in Computing Environment. In S. Aljawarneh & M. Malhotra (Eds.), *Critical Research on Scalability and Security Issues in Virtual Cloud Environments* (pp. 150–166). Hershey, PA: IGI Global. doi:10.4018/978-1-5225-3029-9.ch007

Javid, T. (2018). Secure Access to Biomedical Images. In C. Pradhan, H. Das, B. Naik, & N. Dey (Eds.), *Handbook of Research on Information Security in Biomedical Signal Processing* (pp. 38–53). Hershey, PA: IGI Global. doi:10.4018/978-1-5225-5152-2.ch003

Jeyakumar, B., Durai, M. S., & Lopez, D. (2018). Case Studies in Amalgamation of Deep Learning and Big Data. In D. Lopez & M. Durai (Eds.), *HCI Challenges and Privacy Preservation in Big Data Security* (pp. 159–174). Hershey, PA: IGI Global. doi:10.4018/978-1-5225-2863-0.ch008

Jeyaprakash, H. M. K., K., & S., G. (2018). A Comparative Review of Various Machine Learning Approaches for Improving the Performance of Stego Anomaly Detection. In G. Shrivastava, P. Kumar, B. Gupta, S. Bala, & N. Dey (Eds.), Handbook of Research on Network Forensics and Analysis Techniques (pp. 351-371). Hershey, PA: IGI Global. https://doi.org/ doi:10.4018/978-1-5225-4100-4.ch019

Jeyasekar, J. J. (2018). Dynamics of Indian Forensic Science Research. In J. Jeyasekar & P. Saravanan (Eds.), *Innovations in Measuring and Evaluating Scientific Information* (pp. 125–147). Hershey, PA: IGI Global. doi:10.4018/978-1-5225-3457-0.ch009

Jones, H. S., & Moncur, W. (2018). The Role of Psychology in Understanding Online Trust. In J. McAlaney, L. Frumkin, & V. Benson (Eds.), *Psychological and Behavioral Examinations in Cyber Security* (pp. 109–132). Hershey, PA: IGI Global. doi:10.4018/978-1-5225-4053-3.ch007

Jones, H. S., & Towse, J. (2018). Examinations of Email Fraud Susceptibility: Perspectives From Academic Research and Industry Practice. In J. McAlaney, L. Frumkin, & V. Benson (Eds.), *Psychological and Behavioral Examinations in Cyber Security* (pp. 80–97). Hershey, PA: IGI Global. doi:10.4018/978-1-5225-4053-3.ch005

Joseph, A., & Singh, K. J. (2018). Digital Forensics in Distributed Environment. In G. Shrivastava, P. Kumar, B. Gupta, S. Bala, & N. Dey (Eds.), *Handbook of Research on Network Forensics and Analysis Techniques* (pp. 246–265). Hershey, PA: IGI Global. doi:10.4018/978-1-5225-4100-4.ch013

K., I., & A, V. (2018). Monitoring and Auditing in the Cloud. In K. Munir (Ed.), *Cloud Computing Technologies for Green Enterprises* (pp. 318-350). Hershey, PA: IGI Global. https://doi.org/ doi:10.4018/978-1-5225-3038-1.ch013

Kashyap, R., & Piersson, A. D. (2018). Impact of Big Data on Security. In G. Shrivastava, P. Kumar, B. Gupta, S. Bala, & N. Dey (Eds.), *Handbook of Research on Network Forensics and Analysis Techniques* (pp. 283–299). Hershey, PA: IGI Global. doi:10.4018/978-1-5225-4100-4.ch015

Kastrati, Z., Imran, A. S., & Yayilgan, S. Y. (2018). A Hybrid Concept Learning Approach to Ontology Enrichment. In M. Lytras, N. Aljohani, E. Damiani, & K. Chui (Eds.), *Innovations, Developments, and Applications of Semantic Web and Information Systems* (pp. 85–119). Hershey, PA: IGI Global. doi:10.4018/978-1-5225-5042-6.ch004

Kaur, H., & Saxena, S. (2018). UWDBCSN Analysis During Node Replication Attack in WSN. In C. Pradhan, H. Das, B. Naik, & N. Dey (Eds.), *Handbook of Research on Information Security in Biomedical Signal Processing* (pp. 210–227). Hershey, PA: IGI Global. doi:10.4018/978-1-5225-5152-2.ch011

Kaushal, P. K., & Sobti, R. (2018). Breaching Security of Full Round Tiny Encryption Algorithm. *International Journal of Information Security and Privacy, 12*(1), 89–98. doi:10.4018/IJISP.2018010108

Kavati, I., Prasad, M. V., & Bhagvati, C. (2017). Search Space Reduction in Biometric Databases: A Review. In M. Dawson, D. Kisku, P. Gupta, J. Sing, & W. Li (Eds.), Developing Next-Generation Countermeasures for Homeland Security Threat Prevention (pp. 236-262). Hershey, PA: IGI Global. doi:10.4018/978-1-5225-0703-1.ch011

Kaye, L. K. (2018). Online Research Methods. In J. McAlaney, L. Frumkin, & V. Benson (Eds.), *Psychological and Behavioral Examinations in Cyber Security* (pp. 253–265). Hershey, PA: IGI Global. doi:10.4018/978-1-5225-4053-3.ch015

Kenekar, T. V., & Dani, A. R. (2017). Privacy Preserving Data Mining on Unstructured Data. In S. Tamane, V. Solanki, & N. Dey (Eds.), *Privacy and Security Policies in Big Data* (pp. 167–190). Hershey, PA: IGI Global. doi:10.4018/978-1-5225-2486-1.ch008

*Related References*

Kenny, P., & Leonard, L. J. (2021). Restorative Justice as an "Informal" Alternative to "Formal" Court Processes. In L. Leonard (Ed.), *Global Perspectives on People, Process, and Practice in Criminal Justice* (pp. 226–244). IGI Global. https://doi.org/10.4018/978-1-7998-6646-6.ch014

Khaire, P. A., & Kotkondawar, R. R. (2017). Measures of Image and Video Segmentation. In N. Dey, A. Ashour, & S. Acharjee (Eds.), *Applied Video Processing in Surveillance and Monitoring Systems* (pp. 28–53). Hershey, PA: IGI Global. doi:10.4018/978-1-5225-1022-2.ch002

Knibbs, C., Goss, S., & Anthony, K. (2017). Counsellors' Phenomenological Experiences of Working with Children or Young People who have been Cyberbullied: Using Thematic Analysis of Semi Structured Interviews. *International Journal of Technoethics*, 8(1), 68–86. doi:10.4018/IJT.2017010106

Ko, A., & Gillani, S. (2018). Ontology Maintenance Through Semantic Text Mining: An Application for IT Governance Domain. In M. Lytras, N. Aljohani, E. Damiani, & K. Chui (Eds.), *Innovations, Developments, and Applications of Semantic Web and Information Systems* (pp. 350–371). Hershey, PA: IGI Global. doi:10.4018/978-1-5225-5042-6.ch013

Kohler, J., Lorenz, C. R., Gumbel, M., Specht, T., & Simov, K. (2017). A Security-By-Distribution Approach to Manage Big Data in a Federation of Untrustworthy Clouds. In S. Tamane, V. Solanki, & N. Dey (Eds.), *Privacy and Security Policies in Big Data* (pp. 92–123). Hershey, PA: IGI Global. doi:10.4018/978-1-5225-2486-1.ch005

Korstanje, M. E. (2017). English Speaking Countries and the Culture of Fear: Understanding Technology and Terrorism. In M. Korstanje (Ed.), *Threat Mitigation and Detection of Cyber Warfare and Terrorism Activities* (pp. 92–110). Hershey, PA: IGI Global. doi:10.4018/978-1-5225-1938-6.ch005

Korstanje, M. E. (2018). How Can World Leaders Understand the Perverse Core of Terrorism?: Terror in the Global Village. In C. Akrivopoulou (Ed.), *Global Perspectives on Human Migration, Asylum, and Security* (pp. 48–67). Hershey, PA: IGI Global. doi:10.4018/978-1-5225-2817-3.ch003

Krishnamachariar, P. K., & Gupta, M. (2018). Swimming Upstream in Turbulent Waters: Auditing Agile Development. In M. Gupta, R. Sharman, J. Walp, & P. Mulgund (Eds.), *Information Technology Risk Management and Compliance in Modern Organizations* (pp. 268–300). Hershey, PA: IGI Global. doi:10.4018/978-1-5225-2604-9.ch010

Ksiazak, P., Farrelly, W., & Curran, K. (2018). A Lightweight Authentication and Encryption Protocol for Secure Communications Between Resource-Limited Devices Without Hardware Modification: Resource-Limited Device Authentication. In Y. Maleh (Ed.), *Security and Privacy Management, Techniques, and Protocols* (pp. 1–46). Hershey, PA: IGI Global. doi:10.4018/978-1-5225-5583-4.ch001

Kukkuvada, A., & Basavaraju, P. (2018). Mutual Correlation-Based Anonymization for Privacy Preserving Medical Data Publishing. In C. Pradhan, H. Das, B. Naik, & N. Dey (Eds.), *Handbook of Research on Information Security in Biomedical Signal Processing* (pp. 304–319). Hershey, PA: IGI Global. doi:10.4018/978-1-5225-5152-2.ch016

Kumar, G., & Saini, H. (2018). Secure and Robust Telemedicine using ECC on Radix-8 with Formal Verification. *International Journal of Information Security and Privacy*, *12*(1), 13–28. doi:10.4018/IJISP.2018010102

Kumar, M., & Bhandari, A. (2017). Performance Evaluation of Web Server's Request Queue against AL-DDoS Attacks in NS-2. *International Journal of Information Security and Privacy*, *11*(4), 29–46. doi:10.4018/IJISP.2017100103

Kumar, M., & Vardhan, M. (2018). Privacy Preserving and Efficient Outsourcing Algorithm to Public Cloud: A Case of Statistical Analysis. *International Journal of Information Security and Privacy*, *12*(2), 1–25. doi:10.4018/IJISP.2018040101

Kumar, R. (2018). A Robust Biometrics System Using Finger Knuckle Print. In G. Shrivastava, P. Kumar, B. Gupta, S. Bala, & N. Dey (Eds.), *Handbook of Research on Network Forensics and Analysis Techniques* (pp. 416–446). Hershey, PA: IGI Global. doi:10.4018/978-1-5225-4100-4.ch022

Kumar, R. (2018). DOS Attacks on Cloud Platform: Their Solutions and Implications. In S. Aljawarneh & M. Malhotra (Eds.), *Critical Research on Scalability and Security Issues in Virtual Cloud Environments* (pp. 167–184). Hershey, PA: IGI Global. doi:10.4018/978-1-5225-3029-9.ch008

Kumari, R., & Sharma, K. (2018). Cross-Layer Based Intrusion Detection and Prevention for Network. In G. Shrivastava, P. Kumar, B. Gupta, S. Bala, & N. Dey (Eds.), *Handbook of Research on Network Forensics and Analysis Techniques* (pp. 38–56). Hershey, PA: IGI Global. doi:10.4018/978-1-5225-4100-4.ch003

Lapke, M. (2018). A Semiotic Examination of the Security Policy Lifecycle. In Y. Maleh (Ed.), *Security and Privacy Management, Techniques, and Protocols* (pp. 237–253). Hershey, PA: IGI Global. doi:10.4018/978-1-5225-5583-4.ch009

Liang, Z., Feng, B., Xu, X., Wu, X., & Yang, T. (2018). Geometrically Invariant Image Watermarking Using Histogram Adjustment. *International Journal of Digital Crime and Forensics*, *10*(1), 54–66. doi:10.4018/IJDCF.2018010105

Liu, Z. J. (2017). A Cyber Crime Investigation Model Based on Case Characteristics. *International Journal of Digital Crime and Forensics*, *9*(4), 40–47. doi:10.4018/ IJDCF.2017100104

Loganathan, S. (2018). A Step-by-Step Procedural Methodology for Improving an Organization's IT Risk Management System. In M. Gupta, R. Sharman, J. Walp, & P. Mulgund (Eds.), *Information Technology Risk Management and Compliance in Modern Organizations* (pp. 21–47). Hershey, PA: IGI Global. doi:10.4018/978-1-5225-2604-9.ch002

Long, M., Peng, F., & Gong, X. (2018). A Format-Compliant Encryption for Secure HEVC Video Sharing in Multimedia Social Network. *International Journal of Digital Crime and Forensics*, *10*(2), 23–39. doi:10.4018/IJDCF.2018040102

M., S., & M., J. (2018). Biosignal Denoising Techniques. In C. Pradhan, H. Das, B. Naik, & N. Dey (Eds.), *Handbook of Research on Information Security in Biomedical Signal Processing* (pp. 26-37). Hershey, PA: IGI Global. https://doi. org/ doi:10.4018/978-1-5225-5152-2.ch002

Mahapatra, C. (2017). Pragmatic Solutions to Cyber Security Threat in Indian Context. In R. Kumar, P. Pattnaik, & P. Pandey (Eds.), *Detecting and Mitigating Robotic Cyber Security Risks* (pp. 172–176). Hershey, PA: IGI Global. doi:10.4018/978-1-5225-2154-9.ch012

Majumder, A., Nath, S., & Das, A. (2018). Data Integrity in Mobile Cloud Computing. In K. Munir (Ed.), *Cloud Computing Technologies for Green Enterprises* (pp. 166–199). Hershey, PA: IGI Global. doi:10.4018/978-1-5225-3038-1.ch007

Maleh, Y., Zaydi, M., Sahid, A., & Ezzati, A. (2018). Building a Maturity Framework for Information Security Governance Through an Empirical Study in Organizations. In Y. Maleh (Ed.), *Security and Privacy Management, Techniques, and Protocols* (pp. 96–127). Hershey, PA: IGI Global. doi:10.4018/978-1-5225-5583-4.ch004

Malhotra, M., & Singh, A. (2018). Role of Agents to Enhance the Security and Scalability in Cloud Environment. In S. Aljawarneh & M. Malhotra (Eds.), *Critical Research on Scalability and Security Issues in Virtual Cloud Environments* (pp. 19–47). Hershey, PA: IGI Global. doi:10.4018/978-1-5225-3029-9.ch002

Mali, A. D. (2017). Recent Advances in Minimally-Obtrusive Monitoring of People's Health. *International Journal of Monitoring and Surveillance Technologies Research, 5*(2), 44–56. doi:10.4018/IJMSTR.2017040104

Mali, A. D., & Yang, N. (2017). On Automated Generation of Keyboard Layout to Reduce Finger-Travel Distance. *International Journal of Monitoring and Surveillance Technologies Research, 5*(2), 29–43. doi:10.4018/IJMSTR.2017040103

Mali, P. (2018). Defining Cyber Weapon in Context of Technology and Law. *International Journal of Cyber Warfare & Terrorism, 8*(1), 43–55. doi:10.4018/IJCWT.2018010104

Malik, A., & Pandey, B. (2018). CIAS: A Comprehensive Identity Authentication Scheme for Providing Security in VANET. *International Journal of Information Security and Privacy, 12*(1), 29–41. doi:10.4018/IJISP.2018010103

Manikandakumar, M., & Ramanujam, E. (2018). Security and Privacy Challenges in Big Data Environment. In G. Shrivastava, P. Kumar, B. Gupta, S. Bala, & N. Dey (Eds.), *Handbook of Research on Network Forensics and Analysis Techniques* (pp. 315–325). Hershey, PA: IGI Global. doi:10.4018/978-1-5225-4100-4.ch017

Manogaran, G., Thota, C., & Lopez, D. (2018). Human-Computer Interaction With Big Data Analytics. In D. Lopez & M. Durai (Eds.), *HCI Challenges and Privacy Preservation in Big Data Security* (pp. 1–22). Hershey, PA: IGI Global. doi:10.4018/978-1-5225-2863-0.ch001

Mbale, J. (2018). Computer Centres Resource Cloud Elasticity-Scalability (CRECES): Copperbelt University Case Study. In S. Aljawarneh & M. Malhotra (Eds.), *Critical Research on Scalability and Security Issues in Virtual Cloud Environments* (pp. 48–70). Hershey, PA: IGI Global. doi:10.4018/978-1-5225-3029-9.ch003

McAvoy, D. (2017). Institutional Entrepreneurship in Defence Acquisition: What Don't We Understand? In K. Burgess & P. Antill (Eds.), *Emerging Strategies in Defense Acquisitions and Military Procurement* (pp. 222–241). Hershey, PA: IGI Global. doi:10.4018/978-1-5225-0599-0.ch013

McKeague, J., & Curran, K. (2018). Detecting the Use of Anonymous Proxies. *International Journal of Digital Crime and Forensics, 10*(2), 74–94. doi:10.4018/IJDCF.2018040105

Meitei, T. G., Singh, S. A., & Majumder, S. (2018). PCG-Based Biometrics. In C. Pradhan, H. Das, B. Naik, & N. Dey (Eds.), *Handbook of Research on Information Security in Biomedical Signal Processing* (pp. 1–25). Hershey, PA: IGI Global. doi:10.4018/978-1-5225-5152-2.ch001

*Related References*

Menemencioğlu, O., & Orak, İ. M. (2017). A Simple Solution to Prevent Parameter Tampering in Web Applications. In M. Korstanje (Ed.), *Threat Mitigation and Detection of Cyber Warfare and Terrorism Activities* (pp. 1–20). Hershey, PA: IGI Global. doi:10.4018/978-1-5225-1938-6.ch001

Minto-Coy, I. D., & Henlin, M. G. (2017). The Development of Cybersecurity Policy and Legislative Landscape in Latin America and Caribbean States. In M. Moore (Ed.), *Cybersecurity Breaches and Issues Surrounding Online Threat Protection* (pp. 24–53). Hershey, PA: IGI Global. doi:10.4018/978-1-5225-1941-6.ch002

Mohamed, J. H. (2018). Scientograph-Based Visualization of Computer Forensics Research Literature. In J. Jeyasekar & P. Saravanan (Eds.), *Innovations in Measuring and Evaluating Scientific Information* (pp. 148–162). Hershey, PA: IGI Global. doi:10.4018/978-1-5225-3457-0.ch010

Mohan Murthy, M. K., & Sanjay, H. A. (2018). Scalability for Cloud. In S. Aljawarneh & M. Malhotra (Eds.), *Critical Research on Scalability and Security Issues in Virtual Cloud Environments* (pp. 1–18). Hershey, PA: IGI Global. doi:10.4018/978-1-5225-3029-9.ch001

Moorthy, U., & Gandhi, U. D. (2018). A Survey of Big Data Analytics Using Machine Learning Algorithms. In D. Lopez & M. Durai (Eds.), *HCI Challenges and Privacy Preservation in Big Data Security* (pp. 95–123). Hershey, PA: IGI Global. doi:10.4018/978-1-5225-2863-0.ch005

Mountantonakis, M., Minadakis, N., Marketakis, Y., Fafalios, P., & Tzitzikas, Y. (2018). Connectivity, Value, and Evolution of a Semantic Warehouse. In M. Lytras, N. Aljohani, E. Damiani, & K. Chui (Eds.), *Innovations, Developments, and Applications of Semantic Web and Information Systems* (pp. 1–31). Hershey, PA: IGI Global. doi:10.4018/978-1-5225-5042-6.ch001

Moussa, M., & Demurjian, S. A. (2017). Differential Privacy Approach for Big Data Privacy in Healthcare. In S. Tamane, V. Solanki, & N. Dey (Eds.), *Privacy and Security Policies in Big Data* (pp. 191–213). Hershey, PA: IGI Global. doi:10.4018/978-1-5225-2486-1.ch009

Mugisha, E., Zhang, G., El Abidine, M. Z., & Eugene, M. (2017). A TPM-based Secure Multi-Cloud Storage Architecture grounded on Erasure Codes. *International Journal of Information Security and Privacy*, *11*(1), 52–64. doi:10.4018/IJISP.2017010104

Nachtigall, L. G., Araujo, R. M., & Nachtigall, G. R. (2017). Use of Images of Leaves and Fruits of Apple Trees for Automatic Identification of Symptoms of Diseases and Nutritional Disorders. *International Journal of Monitoring and Surveillance Technologies Research*, *5*(2), 1–14. doi:10.4018/IJMSTR.2017040101

Nagesh, K., Sumathy, R., Devakumar, P., & Sathiyamurthy, K. (2017). A Survey on Denial of Service Attacks and Preclusions. *International Journal of Information Security and Privacy*, *11*(4), 1–15. doi:10.4018/IJISP.2017100101

Nanda, A., Popat, P., & Vimalkumar, D. (2018). Navigating Through Choppy Waters of PCI DSS Compliance. In M. Gupta, R. Sharman, J. Walp, & P. Mulgund (Eds.), *Information Technology Risk Management and Compliance in Modern Organizations* (pp. 99–140). Hershey, PA: IGI Global. doi:10.4018/978-1-5225-2604-9.ch005

Newton, S. (2017). The Determinants of Stock Market Development in Emerging Economies: Examining the Impact of Corporate Governance and Regulatory Reforms (I). In M. Ojo & J. Van Akkeren (Eds.), *Value Relevance of Accounting Information in Capital Markets* (pp. 114–125). Hershey, PA: IGI Global. doi:10.4018/978-1-5225-1900-3.ch008

Nidhyananthan, S. S. A., J. V., & R., S. S. (2018). Wireless Enhanced Security Based on Speech Recognition. In C. Pradhan, H. Das, B. Naik, & N. Dey (Eds.), Handbook of Research on Information Security in Biomedical Signal Processing (pp. 228-253). Hershey, PA: IGI Global. https://doi.org/ doi:10.4018/978-1-5225-5152-2.ch012

Norri-Sederholm, T., Huhtinen, A., & Paakkonen, H. (2018). Ensuring Public Safety Organisations' Information Flow and Situation Picture in Hybrid Environments. *International Journal of Cyber Warfare & Terrorism*, *8*(1), 12–24. doi:10.4018/IJCWT.2018010102

Nunez, S., & Castaño, R. (2017). Building Brands in Emerging Economies: A Consumer-Oriented Approach. In Rajagopal, & R. Behl (Eds.), Business Analytics and Cyber Security Management in Organizations (pp. 183-194). Hershey, PA: IGI Global. doi:10.4018/978-1-5225-0902-8.ch013

Odella, F. (2018). Privacy Awareness and the Networking Generation. *International Journal of Technoethics*, *9*(1), 51–70. doi:10.4018/IJT.2018010105

Ojo, M., & DiGabriele, J. A. (2017). Fundamental or Enhancing Roles?: The Dual Roles of External Auditors and Forensic Accountants. In M. Ojo & J. Van Akkeren (Eds.), *Value Relevance of Accounting Information in Capital Markets* (pp. 59–78). Hershey, PA: IGI Global. doi:10.4018/978-1-5225-1900-3.ch004

Olomojobi, Y., & Omotola, O. T. (2021). Social Media: A Protagonist for Terrorism. *International Journal of Cyber Warfare & Terrorism*, *11*(1), 31–44. https://doi.org/10.4018/IJCWT.2021010103

Pandey, S. (2018). An Empirical Study of the Indian IT Sector on Typologies of Workaholism as Predictors of HR Crisis. In V. Ahuja & S. Rathore (Eds.), *Multidisciplinary Perspectives on Human Capital and Information Technology Professionals* (pp. 202–224). Hershey, PA: IGI Global. doi:10.4018/978-1-5225-5297-0.ch011

Pattabiraman, A., Srinivasan, S., Swaminathan, K., & Gupta, M. (2018). Fortifying Corporate Human Wall: A Literature Review of Security Awareness and Training. In M. Gupta, R. Sharman, J. Walp, & P. Mulgund (Eds.), *Information Technology Risk Management and Compliance in Modern Organizations* (pp. 142–175). Hershey, PA: IGI Global. doi:10.4018/978-1-5225-2604-9.ch006

Prachi. (2018). Detection of Botnet Based Attacks on Network: Using Machine Learning Techniques. In G. Shrivastava, P. Kumar, B. Gupta, S. Bala, & N. Dey (Eds.), *Handbook of Research on Network Forensics and Analysis Techniques* (pp. 101-116). Hershey, PA: IGI Global. https://doi.org/ doi:10.4018/978-1-5225-4100-4.ch007

Pradhan, P. L. (2017). Proposed Round Robin CIA Pattern on RTS for Risk Assessment. *International Journal of Digital Crime and Forensics*, *9*(1), 71–85. doi:10.4018/IJDCF.2017010105

Prentice, S., & Taylor, P. J. (2018). Psychological and Behavioral Examinations of Online Terrorism. In J. McAlaney, L. Frumkin, & V. Benson (Eds.), *Psychological and Behavioral Examinations in Cyber Security* (pp. 151–171). Hershey, PA: IGI Global. doi:10.4018/978-1-5225-4053-3.ch009

Priyadarshini, I. (2017). Cyber Security Risks in Robotics. In R. Kumar, P. Pattnaik, & P. Pandey (Eds.), *Detecting and Mitigating Robotic Cyber Security Risks* (pp. 333–348). Hershey, PA: IGI Global. doi:10.4018/978-1-5225-2154-9.ch022

R., A., & D., E. (2018). Cyber Crime Toolkit Development. In G. Shrivastava, P. Kumar, B. Gupta, S. Bala, & N. Dey (Eds.), *Handbook of Research on Network Forensics and Analysis Techniques* (pp. 184-224). Hershey, PA: IGI Global. https://doi.org/ doi:10.4018/978-1-5225-4100-4.ch011

Raghunath, R. (2018). Research Trends in Forensic Sciences: A Scientometric Approach. In J. Jeyasekar & P. Saravanan (Eds.), *Innovations in Measuring and Evaluating Scientific Information* (pp. 108–124). Hershey, PA: IGI Global. doi:10.4018/978-1-5225-3457-0.ch008

Ramadhas, G., Sankar, A. S., & Sugathan, N. (2018). The Scientific Communication Process in Homoeopathic Toxicology: An Evaluative Study. In J. Jeyasekar & P. Saravanan (Eds.), *Innovations in Measuring and Evaluating Scientific Information* (pp. 163–179). Hershey, PA: IGI Global. doi:10.4018/978-1-5225-3457-0.ch011

Ramani, K. (2018). Impact of Big Data on Security: Big Data Security Issues and Defense Schemes. In G. Shrivastava, P. Kumar, B. Gupta, S. Bala, & N. Dey (Eds.), *Handbook of Research on Network Forensics and Analysis Techniques* (pp. 326–350). Hershey, PA: IGI Global. doi:10.4018/978-1-5225-4100-4.ch018

Ramos, P., Funderburk, P., & Gebelein, J. (2018). Social Media and Online Gaming: A Masquerading Funding Source. *International Journal of Cyber Warfare & Terrorism*, *8*(1), 25–42. doi:10.4018/IJCWT.2018010103

Rao, N., & Srivastava, S., & K.S., S. (2017). PKI Deployment Challenges and Recommendations for ICS Networks. *International Journal of Information Security and Privacy*, *11*(2), 38–48. doi:10.4018/IJISP.2017040104

Rath, M., Swain, J., Pati, B., & Pattanayak, B. K. (2018). Network Security: Attacks and Control in MANET. In G. Shrivastava, P. Kumar, B. Gupta, S. Bala, & N. Dey (Eds.), *Handbook of Research on Network Forensics and Analysis Techniques* (pp. 19–37). Hershey, PA: IGI Global. doi:10.4018/978-1-5225-4100-4.ch002

Ricci, J., Baggili, I., & Breitinger, F. (2017). Watch What You Wear: Smartwatches and Sluggish Security. In A. Marrington, D. Kerr, & J. Gammack (Eds.), *Managing Security Issues and the Hidden Dangers of Wearable Technologies* (pp. 47–73). Hershey, PA: IGI Global. doi:10.4018/978-1-5225-1016-1.ch003

Rossi, J. A. (2017). Revisiting the Value Relevance of Accounting Information in the Italian and UK Stock Markets. In M. Ojo & J. Van Akkeren (Eds.), *Value Relevance of Accounting Information in Capital Markets* (pp. 102–113). Hershey, PA: IGI Global. doi:10.4018/978-1-5225-1900-3.ch007

Sabillon, R., Serra-Ruiz, J., Cavaller, V., & Cano, J. J. (2017). Digital Forensic Analysis of Cybercrimes: Best Practices and Methodologies. *International Journal of Information Security and Privacy*, *11*(2), 25–37. doi:10.4018/IJISP.2017040103

Sadasivam, U. M., & Ganesan, N. (2021). Detecting Fake News Using Deep Learning and NLP. In S. Misra, C. Arumugam, S. Jaganathan, & S. S. (Ed.), *Confluence of AI, Machine, and Deep Learning in Cyber Forensics* (pp. 117-133). IGI Global. https://doi.org/10.4018/978-1-7998-4900-1.ch007

**Related References**

Sample, C., Cowley, J., & Bakdash, J. Z. (2018). Cyber + Culture: Exploring the Relationship. In J. McAlaney, L. Frumkin, & V. Benson (Eds.), *Psychological and Behavioral Examinations in Cyber Security* (pp. 64–79). Hershey, PA: IGI Global. doi:10.4018/978-1-5225-4053-3.ch004

Sarıgöllü, S. C., Aksakal, E., Koca, M. G., Akten, E., & Aslanbay, Y. (2018). Volunteered Surveillance. In J. McAlaney, L. Frumkin, & V. Benson (Eds.), *Psychological and Behavioral Examinations in Cyber Security* (pp. 133–150). Hershey, PA: IGI Global. doi:10.4018/978-1-5225-4053-3.ch008

Shahriar, H., Clincy, V., & Bond, W. (2018). Classification of Web-Service-Based Attacks and Mitigation Techniques. In Y. Maleh (Ed.), *Security and Privacy Management, Techniques, and Protocols* (pp. 360–378). Hershey, PA: IGI Global. doi:10.4018/978-1-5225-5583-4.ch015

Shet, S., Aswath, A. R., Hanumantharaju, M. C., & Gao, X. (2017). Design of Reconfigurable Architectures for Steganography System. In N. Dey, A. Ashour, & S. Acharjee (Eds.), *Applied Video Processing in Surveillance and Monitoring Systems* (pp. 145–168). Hershey, PA: IGI Global. doi:10.4018/978-1-5225-1022-2.ch007

Shrivastava, G., Sharma, K., Khari, M., & Zohora, S. E. (2018). Role of Cyber Security and Cyber Forensics in India. In G. Shrivastava, P. Kumar, B. Gupta, S. Bala, & N. Dey (Eds.), *Handbook of Research on Network Forensics and Analysis Techniques* (pp. 143–161). Hershey, PA: IGI Global. doi:10.4018/978-1-5225-4100-4.ch009

Singh, N., Mittal, T., & Gupta, M. (2018). A Tale of Policies and Breaches: Analytical Approach to Construct Social Media Policy. In M. Gupta, R. Sharman, J. Walp, & P. Mulgund (Eds.), *Information Technology Risk Management and Compliance in Modern Organizations* (pp. 176–212). Hershey, PA: IGI Global. doi:10.4018/978-1-5225-2604-9.ch007

Singh, R., & Jalota, H. (2018). A Study of Good-Enough Security in the Context of Rural Business Process Outsourcing. In J. McAlaney, L. Frumkin, & V. Benson (Eds.), *Psychological and Behavioral Examinations in Cyber Security* (pp. 239–252). Hershey, PA: IGI Global. doi:10.4018/978-1-5225-4053-3.ch014

Sivasubramanian, K. E. (2018). Authorship Pattern and Collaborative Research Productivity of Asian Journal of Dairy and Food Research During the Year 2011 to 2015. In J. Jeyasekar & P. Saravanan (Eds.), *Innovations in Measuring and Evaluating Scientific Information* (pp. 213–222). Hershey, PA: IGI Global. doi:10.4018/978-1-5225-3457-0.ch014

Somasundaram, R., & Thirugnanam, M. (2017). IoT in Healthcare: Breaching Security Issues. In N. Jeyanthi & R. Thandeeswaran (Eds.), *Security Breaches and Threat Prevention in the Internet of Things* (pp. 174–188). Hershey, PA: IGI Global. doi:10.4018/978-1-5225-2296-6.ch008

Sonam, & Khari, M. (2018). Wireless Sensor Networks: A Technical Survey. In G. Shrivastava, P. Kumar, B. Gupta, S. Bala, & N. Dey (Eds.), *Handbook of Research on Network Forensics and Analysis Techniques* (pp. 1-18). Hershey, PA: IGI Global. https://doi.org/ doi:10.4018/978-1-5225-4100-4.ch001

Soni, P. (2018). Implications of HIPAA and Subsequent Regulations on Information Technology. In M. Gupta, R. Sharman, J. Walp, & P. Mulgund (Eds.), *Information Technology Risk Management and Compliance in Modern Organizations* (pp. 71–98). Hershey, PA: IGI Global. doi:10.4018/978-1-5225-2604-9.ch004

Sönmez, F. Ö., & Günel, B. (2018). Security Visualization Extended Review Issues, Classifications, Validation Methods, Trends, Extensions. In Y. Maleh (Ed.), *Security and Privacy Management, Techniques, and Protocols* (pp. 152–197). Hershey, PA: IGI Global. doi:10.4018/978-1-5225-5583-4.ch006

Srivastava, S. R., & Dube, S. (2018). Cyberattacks, Cybercrime and Cyberterrorism. In G. Shrivastava, P. Kumar, B. Gupta, S. Bala, & N. Dey (Eds.), *Handbook of Research on Network Forensics and Analysis Techniques* (pp. 162–183). Hershey, PA: IGI Global. doi:10.4018/978-1-5225-4100-4.ch010

Stacey, E. (2017). Contemporary Terror on the Net. In *Combating Internet-Enabled Terrorism: Emerging Research and Opportunities* (pp. 16–44). Hershey, PA: IGI Global. doi:10.4018/978-1-5225-2190-7.ch002

Sumana, M., Hareesha, K. S., & Kumar, S. (2018). Semantically Secure Classifiers for Privacy Preserving Data Mining. In Y. Maleh (Ed.), *Security and Privacy Management, Techniques, and Protocols* (pp. 66–95). Hershey, PA: IGI Global. doi:10.4018/978-1-5225-5583-4.ch003

Suresh, N., & Gupta, M. (2018). Impact of Technology Innovation: A Study on Cloud Risk Mitigation. In M. Gupta, R. Sharman, J. Walp, & P. Mulgund (Eds.), *Information Technology Risk Management and Compliance in Modern Organizations* (pp. 229–267). Hershey, PA: IGI Global. doi:10.4018/978-1-5225-2604-9.ch009

Tank, D. M. (2017). Security and Privacy Issues, Solutions, and Tools for MCC. In K. Munir (Ed.), *Security Management in Mobile Cloud Computing* (pp. 121–147). Hershey, PA: IGI Global. doi:10.4018/978-1-5225-0602-7.ch006

*Related References*

Thackray, H., & McAlaney, J. (2018). Groups Online: Hacktivism and Social Protest. In J. McAlaney, L. Frumkin, & V. Benson (Eds.), *Psychological and Behavioral Examinations in Cyber Security* (pp. 194–209). Hershey, PA: IGI Global. doi:10.4018/978-1-5225-4053-3.ch011

Thandeeswaran, R., Pawar, R., & Rai, M. (2017). Security Threats in Autonomous Vehicles. In N. Jeyanthi & R. Thandeeswaran (Eds.), *Security Breaches and Threat Prevention in the Internet of Things* (pp. 117–141). Hershey, PA: IGI Global. doi:10.4018/978-1-5225-2296-6.ch006

Thota, C., Manogaran, G., Lopez, D., & Vijayakumar, V. (2017). Big Data Security Framework for Distributed Cloud Data Centers. In M. Moore (Ed.), *Cybersecurity Breaches and Issues Surrounding Online Threat Protection* (pp. 288–310). Hershey, PA: IGI Global. doi:10.4018/978-1-5225-1941-6.ch012

Thukral, S., & Rodriguez, T. D. (2018). Child Sexual Abuse: Intra- and Extra-Familial Risk Factors, Reactions, and Interventions. In R. Gopalan (Ed.), *Social, Psychological, and Forensic Perspectives on Sexual Abuse* (pp. 229–258). Hershey, PA: IGI Global. doi:10.4018/978-1-5225-3958-2.ch017

Tidke, S. (2017). MonogDB: Data Management in NoSQL. In S. Tamane, V. Solanki, & N. Dey (Eds.), *Privacy and Security Policies in Big Data* (pp. 64–91). Hershey, PA: IGI Global. doi:10.4018/978-1-5225-2486-1.ch004

Tierney, M. (2018). #TerroristFinancing: An Examination of Terrorism Financing via the Internet. *International Journal of Cyber Warfare & Terrorism*, 8(1), 1–11. doi:10.4018/IJCWT.2018010101

Topal, R. (2018). A Cyber-Psychological and Behavioral Approach to Online Radicalization. In J. McAlaney, L. Frumkin, & V. Benson (Eds.), *Psychological and Behavioral Examinations in Cyber Security* (pp. 210–221). Hershey, PA: IGI Global. doi:10.4018/978-1-5225-4053-3.ch012

Tripathy, B. K., & Baktha, K. (2018). Clustering Approaches. In *Security, Privacy, and Anonymization in Social Networks: Emerging Research and Opportunities* (pp. 51–85). Hershey, PA: IGI Global. doi:10.4018/978-1-5225-5158-4.ch004

Tripathy, B. K., & Baktha, K. (2018). De-Anonymization Techniques. In *Security, Privacy, and Anonymization in Social Networks: Emerging Research and Opportunities* (pp. 137–147). Hershey, PA: IGI Global. doi:10.4018/978-1-5225-5158-4.ch007

Tripathy, B. K., & Baktha, K. (2018). Fundamentals of Social Networks. In *Security, Privacy, and Anonymization in Social Networks: Emerging Research and Opportunities* (pp. 1–22). Hershey, PA: IGI Global. doi:10.4018/978-1-5225-5158-4.ch001

Tripathy, B. K., & Baktha, K. (2018). Graph Modification Approaches. In *Security, Privacy, and Anonymization in Social Networks: Emerging Research and Opportunities* (pp. 86–115). Hershey, PA: IGI Global. doi:10.4018/978-1-5225-5158-4.ch005

Tripathy, B. K., & Baktha, K. (2018). Social Network Anonymization Techniques. In *Security, Privacy, and Anonymization in Social Networks: Emerging Research and Opportunities* (pp. 36–50). Hershey, PA: IGI Global. doi:10.4018/978-1-5225-5158-4.ch003

Tsimperidis, I., Rostami, S., & Katos, V. (2017). Age Detection Through Keystroke Dynamics from User Authentication Failures. *International Journal of Digital Crime and Forensics*, *9*(1), 1–16. doi:10.4018/IJDCF.2017010101

Wadkar, H. S., Mishra, A., & Dixit, A. M. (2017). Framework to Secure Browser Using Configuration Analysis. *International Journal of Information Security and Privacy*, *11*(2), 49–63. doi:10.4018/IJISP.2017040105

Wahlgren, G., & Kowalski, S. J. (2018). IT Security Risk Management Model for Handling IT-Related Security Incidents: The Need for a New Escalation Approach. In Y. Maleh (Ed.), *Security and Privacy Management, Techniques, and Protocols* (pp. 129–151). Hershey, PA: IGI Global. doi:10.4018/978-1-5225-5583-4.ch005

Wall, H. J., & Kaye, L. K. (2018). Online Decision Making: Online Influence and Implications for Cyber Security. In J. McAlaney, L. Frumkin, & V. Benson (Eds.), *Psychological and Behavioral Examinations in Cyber Security* (pp. 1–25). Hershey, PA: IGI Global. doi:10.4018/978-1-5225-4053-3.ch001

Wu, J. B., Zhang, Y., Luo, C. W., Yuan, L. F., & Shen, X. K. (2021). A Modification-Free Steganography Algorithm Based on Image Classification and CNN. *International Journal of Digital Crime and Forensics*, *13*(3), 47–58. https://doi.org/10.4018/IJDCF.20210501.oa4

Xylogiannopoulos, K. F., Karampelas, P., & Alhajj, R. (2017). Advanced Network Data Analytics for Large-Scale DDoS Attack Detection. *International Journal of Cyber Warfare & Terrorism*, *7*(3), 44–54. doi:10.4018/IJCWT.2017070104

Yan, W. Q., Wu, X., & Liu, F. (2018). Progressive Scrambling for Social Media. *International Journal of Digital Crime and Forensics*, *10*(2), 56–73. doi:10.4018/IJDCF.2018040104

Yassein, M. B., Mardini, W., & Al-Abdi, A. (2018). Security Issues in the Internet of Things: A Review. In S. Aljawarneh & M. Malhotra (Eds.), *Critical Research on Scalability and Security Issues in Virtual Cloud Environments* (pp. 186–200). Hershey, PA: IGI Global. doi:10.4018/978-1-5225-3029-9.ch009

Yassein, M. B., Shatnawi, M., & l-Qasem, N. (2018). A Survey of Probabilistic Broadcast Schemes in Mobile Ad Hoc Networks. In S. Aljawarneh, & M. Malhotra (Eds.), *Critical Research on Scalability and Security Issues in Virtual Cloud Environments* (pp. 269-282). Hershey, PA: IGI Global. https://doi.org/doi:10.4018/978-1-5225-3029-9.ch013

Yue, C., Tianliang, L., Manchun, C., & Jingying, L. (2018). Evaluation of the Attack Effect Based on Improved Grey Clustering Model. *International Journal of Digital Crime and Forensics*, *10*(1), 92–100. doi:10.4018/IJDCF.2018010108

Zhang, P., He, Y., & Chow, K. (2018). Fraud Track on Secure Electronic Check System. *International Journal of Digital Crime and Forensics*, *10*(2), 137–144. doi:10.4018/IJDCF.2018040108

Zhou, L., Yan, W. Q., Shu, Y., & Yu, J. (2018). CVSS: A Cloud-Based Visual Surveillance System. *International Journal of Digital Crime and Forensics*, *10*(1), 79–91. doi:10.4018/IJDCF.2018010107

Zhu, J., Guan, Q., Zhao, X., Cao, Y., & Chen, G. (2017). A Steganalytic Scheme Based on Classifier Selection Using Joint Image Characteristics. *International Journal of Digital Crime and Forensics*, *9*(4), 1–14. doi:10.4018/IJDCF.2017100101

Zoughbi, S. (2017). Major Technology Trends Affecting Government Data in Developing Countries. In S. Zoughbi (Ed.), *Securing Government Information and Data in Developing Countries* (pp. 127–135). Hershey, PA: IGI Global. doi:10.4018/978-1-5225-1703-0.ch008

Zubairu, B. (2018). Security Risks of Biomedical Data Processing in Cloud Computing Environment. In C. Pradhan, H. Das, B. Naik, & N. Dey (Eds.), *Handbook of Research on Information Security in Biomedical Signal Processing* (pp. 177–197). Hershey, PA: IGI Global. doi:10.4018/978-1-5225-5152-2.ch009

# About the Contributors

**Eduard Babulak** is accomplished international scholar, researcher, consultant, educator, professional engineer and polyglot, with more than thirty years of experience. He served as successfully published and his research was cited by scholars all over the world. He speaks 16 languages and his biography was cited in the Cambridge Blue Book, Cambridge Index of Biographies, Stanford Who's Who, and number of issues of Who's Who in the World and America.

\* \* \*

**Muthukumar Arunachalam** received his B.E. degree from Madurai Kamaraj University in 2004, and M.E. degree from Anna University, Chennai, Tamil Nadu in 2006. He received his Ph.D. degree from Kalasalingam University in 2014. He is working as an Associate Professor in Electronics and Communication Engineering department of Kalasalingam University, Tamilnadu, India. His research interest includes image processing with cryptography.

**Parag Chatterjee** received the B.E. degree in Computer Science & Engineering from the Karnatak University, Dharwad, India, in 1998 and received M.Tech. degree from IIEST Shibpur, Kolkata, India, in 2007. Since 2007, he has been with the Department of Computer Science & Engineering, Pailan College of Management & Technology, as Associate professor. His current research interests include Data ware Housing, Data mining and Wireless sensor. He has 11 publication in national and international journals.

**Naif Hussain** is a senior cybersecurity student at University of Jeddah, he is pursuing his bachelor's degree with an academic distinction. At University of Jeddah, Naif was involved in many activities, especially those related to cybersecurity. Naif has presented several workshops and lectures related to the field, in addition to his leadership and involvement in a plethora of cybersecurity related competitions and projects. Naif has also achieved many professional certifications in the field, for instance Security+, eCDFP, and eJPT.

**Lubana Isaoglu** is a Ph.D. student in the computer engineering department at Istanbul University-Cerrahpaşa. Her main interest is working with artificial intelligence, especially neural networks. She has more than 10 years of teaching experience in different organizations, in different countries with different languages: the ministry of education in Kuwait, the higher institute for telecommunications & Navigation-Kuwait University, and Ibn Haldun University in Istanbul. This diversity helped her develop various skills such as simplifying the information, delivering information with ease, and research skills.

**Kapil Kumar** is serving as Associate Professor in Forensic Science. Experienced professor with a demonstrated history of working in the education management industry. Skilled in Research, Forensic Analysis, E-Learning, Criminal Justice, and Teaching. Strong education professional with a doctorate and a Master's Degree focused in Forensic Science, specializing in cybersecurity and digital forensics, questioned documents examination, and Forensic ballistics.

**Derya Yiltas-Kaplan** received the BSc, MSc, and PhD degrees in computer engineering from Istanbul University, Istanbul, Turkey, in 2001, 2003 and 2007, respectively. She studied as a postdoctorate researcher at the North Carolina State University and she received postdoctorate research scholarship from The Scientific and Technological Research Council of Turkey (TUBITAK). She is an Associate Professor in the Department of Computer Engineering at Istanbul University-Cerrahpaşa.

# Index

## A

Adaboost 9, 96
Aghajani 110
AI Tools 50-52, 73
Artificial Intelligence (AI) 1, 3, 8, 10-13, 25-26, 28-30, 32, 35-37, 39, 41-42, 45-46, 50-54, 56-57, 59-68, 74, 76-78, 85-87, 97

## B

Beautiful Soup 148

## C

Computer Vision 166-167, 177, 179
Convolutional Neural Network (CNN) 179
Cryptography 120, 122
Cyber Attacks 15, 110, 133
Cyber Defense 55, 70
Cyber threats 11-12, 30-31, 56, 59, 64, 67, 73-74, 77, 87, 104, 162
Cybersecurity 1-3, 5, 8-15, 25-26, 28-32, 34-37, 44-46, 51-52, 55-61, 65-72, 74-75, 77-78, 87, 90, 92-93, 96-97, 99-103, 109-115, 117, 126, 128, 162-163

## D

Deep Learning (DL) 5, 14, 33-34, 45-46, 59-60, 66, 72-73, 85-86, 162-163, 166-168, 177, 179

Deep Neural Network 6, 170, 179
Detection 1, 5-8, 10-11, 13-15, 25, 29, 34-36, 38-41, 45-46, 51, 57-59, 62, 65-67, 69-70, 73-75, 77-78, 85, 90, 92-94, 96-97, 100, 103-104, 113, 117, 119, 122, 124, 132, 148, 150-154, 158-163, 166-177, 179

## E

Exploits 6, 118, 132-133, 135-138, 140-142

## F

Faster R-CNN 168, 177, 179
Fuzzy Logic 95

## G

Github 62

## H

Hackers 1, 3, 8, 36, 43, 55, 63-64, 66, 68, 71, 76, 109-110, 112-113, 128
Hardware 68, 109, 111, 113, 122-127, 168

## I

Information Security 74, 85-86, 92-93, 95, 97, 99, 110-111, 115, 117
Intrusion Detection System 8, 14

# M

Machine Learning (ML) 5-9, 11, 14, 30, 33, 35-37, 39-43, 45-46, 51, 57, 59-62, 65-67, 85-86, 113, 148-149, 152, 154, 156-163, 168, 179
Malware 3, 8, 10, 12-13, 15, 34-36, 41, 45, 51, 57-59, 67-69, 72, 77-78, 87, 91, 96, 99-100, 103, 111-112, 133, 162

# N

Neural Network 6, 14, 29, 34, 59-60, 89, 95, 170, 179

# O

Object Detection 166-177, 179

# P

Phishing 10, 13-14, 42, 67-69, 90, 100, 102, 111-112, 148-163
Prevention 10, 12, 25, 35, 40, 59, 69, 77, 87, 93, 100, 149

# R

Random Forest 7, 37, 96, 152
Real-Time 26, 37, 39-40, 51, 58, 96, 109, 113, 158, 160, 166-168, 170, 174-175, 177, 179
Risk Prediction 15, 36

# S

Saudi Arabia 50-51, 74-75
Single-Shot Detector (SSD) 179

Software 3, 9, 13, 26, 34, 37, 41-42, 50, 55, 57-58, 68-69, 71, 73, 76, 91, 100, 103, 109-110, 112, 114-119, 122, 124-125, 127, 132-135, 137-139, 141-142, 148, 152, 154, 161, 168
Streamlit 148, 152, 154, 159-161
Support Vector Machines 6, 58, 88, 96

# T

Threat Hunting 41, 77
Threats 8, 10-13, 26, 29-31, 35-37, 42-44, 46, 51-52, 56-60, 62-64, 66-68, 70, 73-77, 85, 87, 90, 92-93, 95, 97, 99-100, 102-104, 110, 112-113, 115, 148, 162
Traffic Monitoring 77, 166-168, 174-175, 177, 179
Traffic Pattern 8
Trojan 91, 111-112, 124-125

# V

Video 9, 166-170, 174-175, 177, 179
Vulnerability Management 42, 77, 132-133

# Y

You Only Look Once (YOLO) 179

# Z

Zero Day vulnerabilities 132

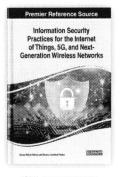
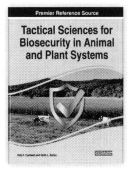

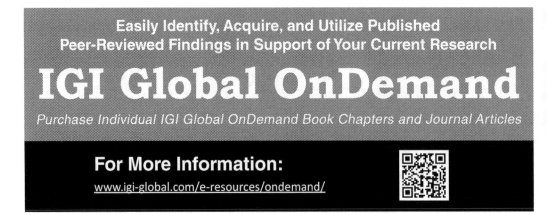

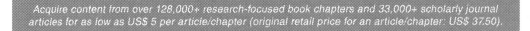

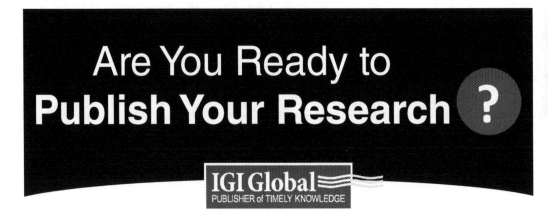

Printed in the United States
by Baker & Taylor Publisher Services